THE TOP 100
MILITARY
SITES IN
AMERICA

Places You Must See—and Perhaps You've Never Heard of!

L. DOUGLAS KEENEY

Guilford, Connecticut

An imprint of The Rowman & Littlefield Publishing Group, Inc.
4501 Forbes Blvd., Ste. 200
Lanham, MD 20706
www.rowman.com

Distributed by NATIONAL BOOK NETWORK

British Library Cataloguing in Publication Information Available

Library of Congress Cataloging-in-Publication Data
Names: Keeney, L. Douglas, author.
Title: The top 100 military sites in America / L. Douglas Keeney.
Other titles: Top one hundred military sites in America
Description: Guilford, Connecticut : Lyons Press, [2018] | Includes index.
Identifiers: LCCN 2018003511 (print) | LCCN 2018007132 (ebook) | ISBN 9781493032297 (Electronic) | ISBN 9781493032280 (pbk. : alk. paper)
Subjects: LCSH: United States—History, Military—Guidebooks. | Military bases—United States—Guidebooks.
Classification: LCC E181 (ebook) | LCC E181 .K37 2018 (print) | DDC 355.00973—dc23
LC record available at https://lccn.loc.gov/2018003511

Printed in the United States of America

Contents

Introduction

A high school field trip to Washington, D.C., invariably includes a trip to the Smithsonian National Air & Space Museum, where the nation's largest collection of aviation-related artifacts is on display. You can see everything from the *Wright Flyer* that began powered flight, to the orange-colored *Bell X-1* rocket plane that propelled Chuck Yeager through the sound barrier, to a supersonic F-4 Phantom fighter jet. The Smithsonian truly has something for everyone and plenty of things to stimulate your imagination.

But instead of your imagination, how about walking in the footsteps of Chuck Yeager and standing where he stood when he looked up to the sky? Or what about that F-4 Phantom fighter jet of Vietnam fame? Instead of walking around a still-and-silent Phantom in a museum, did you know that there are places where you can actually sit in the cockpit of a real F-4 and smell that musty smell and hold that stick and run your fingers over the instrument panel just like pilots did decades ago?

We'll even show you where you can fly one.

We'll show you where in Georgia you can walk into a World War I trench and smell the mud and feel the walls closing in on you just as our doughboys did in France 100 years ago.

We'll show you where in North Carolina you can see the tail rotor from the US Army Blackhawk helicopter that crashed in Mogadishu, the very same chopper that was the subject of the book *Blackhawk Down*.

In New Jersey, we'll tell you how to get on a Navy base and see where the *Hindenburg* crashed to the ground and burned. Did you know you can walk up to that *exact* spot?

We'll tell you where in California you can see the underwater obstacles that were used to train our Underwater Demolitioin Teams (UDT) specialists so they could clear the beaches on D-Day. Or where in New Jersey you can walk around an abandoned Nike missile site used during the Cold War to defend our cities. Or where you can walk through a battleship and then spend the afternoon looking at tanks and the bombers of World War II in Alabama. Or where you can walk to the exact spot where the first atomic bomb was detonated in New Mexico.

Want to fire the big gun on an M4 Sherman tank? How about riding in a PT boat like Jack Kennedy did, or sailing on a Liberty ship as millions of our soldiers did in World War II? Have you ever seen a MiG-29? Or slept on a submarine? Or flown in a F-4 Phantom? You can.

The Top 100 Military Destinations is a journey through the histories, people, artifacts, and places where heroes stood their ground, where technology was advanced in hush-hush hangars, where hardware debuted famously or infamously, and where the guns, helmets, swords, helicopters, tanks, ships, and trucks that saved lives and helped win battles are on display for us to forever remember. On the beaches of Delaware and New Jersey, you will discover a string of imposing World War II fire control towers that still peer out to sea silently looking for Nazi submarines. Among the incredibly large artillery pieces exhibited at the little-known US Army Field Artillery Museum in Fort Sill, Oklahoma, is the M65 cannon that fired a *nuclear* artillery shell (it was nicknamed Atomic Annie). The US Army and the US Air Force both operated land-based *railroad cars* on which were placed massive guns that helped win World War I (in the case of the US Army), or, in the case of the Air Force, kept nuclear-tipped ICBMs on the move so the Russians couldn't target them. Remember those dramatic TV clips of missiles leaping out of the sea? You can touch one—a Polaris Intercontinental Nuclear Missile—at the nearly unknown White Sands Missile Range Museum in White Sands, New Mexico.

And, yes, the 100 Places are overwhelmingly museums, and for good reason. If an object or event was important, someone had to raise money to preserve it, and that meant they created a nonprofit organization for that purpose—and most nonprofits are called museums. But that's a mere technicality; don't be put off by the word. These are not "museums" in the traditional sense. Not if crawling into the turret of a M1 Abrams battle tank is a museum. Or if walking the decks of a battleship is a museum, or if squeezing down a silo 40 feet to see an ICBM is a museum. Not if seeing the real *Enola Gay* or walking through a diorama depicting combat on an island in the Pacific complete with soldiers, guns, flashing lights, the sounds

Today's "museums" are hardly the stuff of your grandmother's generation. Curators encourage you to walk through helicopters and touch tanks and to see, hear, and smell the (re-created) environment of combat. Seen here: The view from the guard tower at the Vietnam Experience at Patriots Point, South Carolina. Photo courtesy of author's collection

of mortars exploding, and even the smell of smoke is a museum. Military museums are destinations that go overboard to bring their stories to life. In a world of 140-word tweets and VR video gaming, museums are now telling stories dynamically, visually, and viscerally—you literally walk into life-sized, high-definition exhibits that immerse you in the sights, sounds, motion, and even smells of battle. In the National Museum of the Marine Corps, you'll walk through a portal unsuspecting of where you are until you realize that you are in fact inside a helicopter and are about to come face-to-face with the enemy in a firefight taking place somewhere in the Pacific. The National Infantry Museum in Georgia has incredibly accurate dioramas with realistic topographies and a confusing swirl of lights that put you in the middle of the chaos of battlefields, be it the Vietnam War or the Persian Gulf. In Texas, you can watch reenactors demonstrate the taking of a Pacific Island, complete with flamethrowers and loud sound effects. In New Jersey, you can listen to the quiet voices of grateful survivors who were evacuated from Manhattan in the aftermath of 9/11 *by boat*. Each of these sites tells the stories of people and places that would otherwise be just another person or place until that moment when they become part of our national story. And, yes, many of the places will tell history *their* way, through *their* eyes, they way *they* experienced it. After all, to understand history we have to see it from every angle possible. What's that mean? It means soldiers sacrificed and war is dirty, and that's part of what you'll see, too.

There are more than 2,000 museums in America drawing 854 million visitors a year to view some of the more than 1 billion artifacts in their holdings. Of those, some 460 museums self-identify as military museums, some well-known, some not, and others well-kept secrets.

The Top 100 List

The Top 100 Destinations were culled from a variety of resources, beginning with my own extensive travels to a great many of these sites as an author, a father, and a grateful American. Some were old favorites to which I have often taken sons and friends; others were new to me. Some came to me from my fellow military historians, some from authors and researchers; still others were recommended by friends on active duty. To get the broadest perspective possible, I asked my 5,000 military-oriented Facebook friends what secret places they loved, and then I scoured regional and local newspapers and magazines, including reviews on social platforms like Trip Advisor. Finally, I visited many of the sites again to reacquaint myself with their offerings, trips that I shall fondly remember.

The destinations are organized by state, with most states having at least one place to visit while others have as many as a half dozen. Yes, there are more than 100 sites listed but the Top 100 are indicated by a small gold wreath and will appear first in each state's listing. What follows are additional destinations that are awfully good and nearly made the Top 100, as well as some that are worthy of a visit under a category we call "While You're in the Neighborhood." Not everyone wants to go halfway across the country to see an SR-71, so we tried to find a road trip with a military destination in every state. In truth, it was easy. There are an amazing number of places where you can reflect on the accomplishments of our soldiers.

To help you navigate these listings, we created four subsets. We list the Top 20 for those who want to narrow it down to the very best of the best; the Top 10 Formerly Secret Sites, for those who are intrigued by that part of our past;

Look at the determined expression on the face of this Marine as he storms a beach on Tarawa. Seen at the National Museum of the Marine Corps. Photo courtesy of National Museum of the Marine Corps

The Top 10 Military Experiences, for those who want a flight in a warbird or want to drive a tank; and The Top 10 Military Base Tours. These destinations are marked just as the others are except each of the Top 20 has a red circle around the wreath. See the appendix for the rankings and a thumbnail of each. A full description can also be found under the appropriate state listings. In all cases we explain why each destination was included in this guide, what to look for when you get there, and what makes it special. All told, between destination, experiences, and bases, we can think of no other guide that is as comprehensive.

A Note about Artifacts

By a terrifically large margin, military aircraft are the dominant artifacts displayed at military destinations, and there are several reasons for that. First of all, airplanes are exceedingly portable. It's hard to move a 60-ton tank, but it's fairly easy to fly an F-14 Tomcat fighter jet into an airfield and put it on display. Second, one has to remember that there were enormous shortages after World War II. Nearly every reusable scrap of steel and aluminum was recycled, which meant that thousands of tanks, Liberty ships, and airplanes were sent home chopped up or in slabs of steel and ingots of aluminum. That's an oversimplification, but the fact is, warbirds are the most prevalent of the large artifacts around which museums have been formed.

So what are these airplanes? The fighter planes of World War II are exceedingly popular and draw visitors, so they are the ones most often displayed. They tend to center around the P-51 Mustang and the P-47 Thunderbolt, two aircraft from the European theater (they were escorts for our B-17s), but we also see the F4U Corsair, the F6F Hellcat, the TBM Avenger torpedo bomber, and the SBD Dauntless dive bomber from the Pacific theater.

Medium and heavy bombers also can be found and frequently include the B-25 Mitchell, the B-26 Marauder, the B-17 Flying Fortress, the B-24 Liberator, and the B-29 Superfortress (rarest of them all). Also to be found in abundance are Vietnam-era fighters such as the F-4 Phantom, the A4 Skyhawk, and the A6 Intruder and the post-Vietnam fighters such as the ever-popular F-14 Tomcat, the F-16 Fighting Falcon, the A-10 Warthog, and the F-18 Hornet. All of these models were produced in large quantities, and many were donated to museums.

"Open cockpit day" means you sit inside the cockpit of a warbird, not just look in. This fighter jet is at the Palm Springs Air Museum. Photo courtesy of Palm Springs Air Museum

Surviving Cold War bombers are harder to find, mainly owing to the intense pace of the Cold War and the terms of SALT treaties, which required that so many of them be cut up and laid out for the Soviets to photograph via their satellites. However, there are a few B-47s, a few FB-111s, several more B-52s, and few (but not many) nuclearized B-29s/B-50s and B-58 Hustlers. Study the model that interests you and find a destination that has one on display.

Tanks and artillery pieces take incredible financial and physical resources to move, so they tend to be found near army bases or in larger collections. Happily, there are options for you. Across the nation we list numerous tanks parks, each with its own combinations of Sherman tanks, Stuart tanks, or the various Patton tanks (there were several models called Pattons).

Ships are the hardest to collect and exceedingly expensive to maintain, so you find even fewer of them. We may have plenty of surviving P-51 Mustangs but only three Liberty ships. That said, there are several aircraft carriers, battleships, a few destroyers, a cruiser, PBRs from Vietnam, and a PT boat.

Which raises a good question: Since some museums own *hundreds* of aircraft or dozens of tanks while others own none, how do you find the exact model that interests you? First, find the air, sea, or land museum nearest you—then drill down on the artifacts they own. The items listed in this guide are the most popular or the rarest ones on display, but certainly not the only ones at a particular destination. For complete listings see the destination's web site. Sometimes items are moved so call ahead if one is important to you.

A word about simulators is in order, too. In the military, simulators are essential training tools for Air Force pilots, Navy seamen, and Army tankers—and they come in a variety of configurations. The simplest ones are static replicas of a cockpit designed to train a rookie aviator in basic switchology, but a top-line sim is a multimillion-dollar tool with a full cockpit mounted on legs with six axis, full-motion hydraulics, and wraparound exterior visual displays The hydraulics pitch, roll, and yaw the "capsule," and the sensations are true to flight.

So why do we make mention of this? Because a true military simulator is not an amusement park ride, nor is it a video game. It's a military tool. When you read that a museum has a simulator, we're talking about a true, $150,000-

A hyper-realistic diorama depicts US Army Delta forces under fire during the Battle of Mogadishu. Photo courtesy of Airborne & Special Operations Museum

plus sim with four to six degrees of hydraulics and at least 120 degrees of exterior visual display. That's no toy. You will get into a capsule and pitch and roll just like your brothers in an F/A-18 or an F-35. Although they usually require an extra ticket, they are more than worth it. Only the most experienced aviators will later say that they can tell the difference between the physical feel of flight in a simulator and real flight. We urge you to experience one.

Finally, some caveats about the listings. With very few exceptions, we omitted Civil War encampments, and national parks. There are a great many guides to these sites and we recommend any of them to you. Also left out are the many "gate guardians," those signature airplanes and tanks that often brace the entrance to a military base, many of which are worthy of your time but only if you live in the area. Equally, some ever-so-tantalizing places that are shrouded in mystery or lore had to be left out mainly because, well, they are still shrouded in mystery and lore. Among them are the Tonopah Test Range (inside of which reside a semi-active squadron of our beloved F-117 Nighthawks); Area 51, secret no longer but off-limits; Plum Island, that mysterious government facility off Long Island where pathogens and diseases are tested; the Sierra Army Depot, which is the largest collection of mothballed tanks but off-limits, too; and Raven Rock, the much talked about but largely secret continuity-of-government site near the nation's capital. I did include the Greenbrier Bunker listed under West Virginia, but not the Peanut Island, Florida, fallout shelter used by JFK, which closed in early 2018.

Finally, we resisted the temptation to include every manner of abandoned Cold War missile silo, every ominous-looking concrete-and-steel World War II coastal battery, and all of those former weapons storage facilities or air defense missile pads (converted to, let's say, a municipal parking lot for city garbage trucks). Each in their own right is interesting—and there are many of them—but let's face it: A slab of concrete or a decrepit building in disrepair is hardly worth a tank of gas. For an in-depth list of coastal batteries and sites where you can see gun emplacements and other ruins, we suggest that you go to this excellent resource: http://www.fortwiki.com/Fort_Wiki.

That said, there are some ICBM silos that are nicely preserved and open to the public, and there are some ever-so-haunting and well-preserved Nike missile sites, including one near San Francisco and one near New York City. There are also a few coastal batteries and fire control stations that *are* worth the drive, including ones in Delaware, Maine, New Jersey, and Florida.

Chronologically, the sites in this guide span the entire history of the United States, beginning with the all-new $150 million Museum of the American Revolution in Philadelphia and ending at destinations where the next generation of weapon technologies and battlefield tactics are being developed. Not yet open but soon to be are the National Museum of the US Army, scheduled to open in 2020 at Fort Belvoir, Virginia, and the National Museum of the Coast Guard, which is under way although no opening date has been set.

In assembling this edition it became obvious that many destinations have added new and rather dramatic exhibits on the Vietnam conflict. Incredible as it may seem, we are actually passing the fiftieth anniversaries of many of the milestone battles in that conflict's history. Among the museums with these exhibits are the Museum of Aviation at Robins Air Force Base, Georgia; Patriots Point in Charleston, South Carolina; the Army Heritage and Education Center at Carlisle Barracks, Pennsylvania; and the National Infantry Museum in Columbus, Georgia. There are others. Call or check websites to see if one is near you.

A customized weapon made for the SEALs seen on display at the National Navy UDT-SEAL Museum. Photo courtesy of National Navy UDT-SEAL Museum

Of course, the larger message here is freedom. "Until the millennium arrives and countries quit trying to enslave others, it will be necessary to accept one's responsibility and be willing to make sacrifices for one's country—as my comrades did," said Marine Corps corporal E. B. Sledge, a veteran of the Pacific theater of World War II. "As the troops used to say, if the country is good enough to live in, it's good enough to fight for. With privilege comes responsibility."[1]

There are plenty of great machines to see at the destinations in this guide—airplanes, helicopters, ships, tanks—but machines are nothing more than hunks of steel until a 29-year-old gets inside one and puts his or her life on the line. From the earliest days of those brazenly defiant drum-and-fife corps to the thumping beat of a dozen Blackhawk helicopters taking flight, we hold dear in our hearts those who gave up their lives to protect our freedoms. It remains today, like it was years ago. *As He died to make men holy, let us die to make men free.*

Encounter now the people who accepted the responsibility.

Encounter now the stories written over the decades and across the continents by citizen-soldiers wearing the uniforms of every branch of our military services.

"Humanity has won its battle," said Marquis de Lafayette, speaking of America's victory over the British during the Revolutionary War. "Liberty now has a country."

THE TOP 100 MILITARY
SITES IN AMERICA

PLACES THAT BRIM WITH HISTORY AND LIFE

Alabama

Alabama is rich in military history. Alabama is home to Air University, the top school for the US Air Force (located on Maxwell Air Force Base in Montgomery). Alabama is home to Fort Rucker, the top training center for US Army helicopter pilots (in Dothan, Alabama). Alabama is home to the Space and Rocket Center in Huntsville, and to the training airfield for the Tuskegee airmen. Oh, and they have a battleship here. It's called the *Alabama* and it's in Mobile, Alabama. Add it up and Alabama is a state that offers more than a few weekends of fantastic military destinations to explore.

USS Alabama *Battleship and Memorial Park, Mobile, Alabama*

Ten battleship museums are located in and around the US (three at Pearl Harbor—the *Arizona,* the *Utah,* and the *Missouri*), but none match the magnificent grounds and the variety of artifacts found here at the *Alabama* Battleship and Memorial Park. Spread across no less than 155 acres is an impressive and well-maintained assortment of military aircraft (a World War II–era B-25 medium bomber and a Cold War–era B-52 heavy bomber, among them), tanks (an M-4 Sherman, an M-60 Patton, and an M-26 Pershing, among them), helicopters (the Coast Guard chopper is easy to spot), the submarine USS *Drum* (you can walk through her hull), plus a land-side museum packed with even more military artifacts large and small.

The USS *Alabama,* of course, is the centerpiece of it all. Although not a single battleship remains in the fleet of the US Navy, who can forget that signature profile etched by the massive, downward-curving hull and the enormous turrets, each with three 16-inch barrels? That's the *Alabama*—35,000 tons, 680 feet long, with engines so powerful she can zip through the water with speedboat-like speeds of 30 knots. Her nine, 16-inch guns are each capable of firing a 2,700-pound shell 23 miles with pinpoint accuracy. Little wonder they were the cornerstone of an attack fleet—and a welcome sight to any tin-can sailor under fire.

The restoration of the *Alabama* was designed not only to maintain the ship's authenticity but also to present facts and stories related to her years at

The US Alabama *Memorial Park is a treasure trove of tanks, fighter jets, helicopters, bombers—even a submarine. Photo courtesy of USS* Alabama *Battleship and Memorial Park*

sea. In the main, the interior compartments look like they did during World War II with period furniture and personal artifacts, but some of the spaces have more to them. There is a "cook" behind the chow line in the mess and "officers" on the softly lit bridge. Her weather decks are in perfect condition, and the ship is as sharp as the day she first set sail. Displays explain her history and the functions of her interior spaces.

After exploring the *Alabama* your next stop is the USS *Drum*. A World War II patrol/attack submarine, the *Drum* is representative of the hundreds of submarines that patrolled the seas during World War II, 52 of which never returned. The *Drum* had a crew of 60 crammed into her narrow 300-foot-by-27-foot-wide hull.

The land-side pavilion is a destination unto itself. Packed with an extensive collection of beautifully restored navy and air force jets and helicopters, inside this large building you'll find all the modern jets—the F-14 Tomcat fighter, the F-15 Eagle fighter, the F-16 Fighting Falcon, and the F/A-18 Hornet, plus the ever-so-spooky CIA's A-12 spy plane (cousin to the SR-71).

In a sense, this is a one-stop shop, the sum and substance of the US military—air, sea, and land—all in one place. Start on the *Alabama* herself and walk her decks. But don't forget the rest of the park—with 155 acres of things to see and do, you could spend a day here (and many do).

Hours: Apr–Sept: 8 a.m. to 6 p.m., Oct–Mar: 8 a.m. to 5 p.m.
Days: Open every day except Christmas Day. Last ticket of the day is sold one hour prior to closing
Website: www.ussalabama.com
Street address/GPS address: 2703 Battleship Pkwy., Mobile, AL 36602

US Army Aviation Museum, Fort Rucker, Alabama

Do you hear the lyrics of "Sweet Home Alabama" ringing in your ears as you arrive at the US Army Aviation Museum in Fort Rucker, Alabama? Maybe not, but you certainly hear the sounds of helicopters lifting off from the nearby air base. Fort Rucker is where army helicopter pilots train, and this excellent destination introduces you to the world of combat aviation, helicopter style.

You'll know you've arrived when you see the helicopters. There is an AH-1 Cobra rakishly mounted on the side of the museum and OH-58 Kiowa circling in the air by the front entrance. Inside, you'll find a display floor filled with the icons of army aviation—more Cobras, more Kiowas, a UH-60 Blackhawk, several UH-1 Hueys, a very classic twin-engine CH-47 Chinook, the CH-21 Shawnee "flying banana," the H-19 Chickasaw, and dozens more. Work your way over to the handsome H-60 Blackhawk. The stylish paint job tells you this wasn't used in combat. In fact, it was assigned to the Military District of Washington, D.C., to transport senior military officials. Almost next to it is *Army One*, an executive airlift version of the H-4 Choctaw.

The centerpieces of this destination are the dioramas, and there are many of them. Using detailed landscapes and realistic mannequins, some of the most iconic moments in army aviation history come vividly to life. There is

The US Army Aviation Museum at Fort Rucker, Alabama. Photo courtesy of WikiCommons

an OH-1 Sioux medevac helicopter from a MASH unit picking up wounded soldiers from a frozen hill in Korea, a heart-stopping diorama of a UH-1 Huey crashed in a Vietnam rice paddy complete with an OH-6A "Loach" circling overhead to check for survivors, and the now-well-known Super 68, one of the Blackhawks from the Battle of Mogadishu. Pay particular attention to the detailed recreation of the 1st of the 9th Cavalry's air assault. It's an image that has become an icon of the Vietnam War and helicopters were an essential part of it. "This is the only game in town when it comes to army aviation," said one veteran helicopter pilot, and we have to agree.

A rotating assortment of helicopters and airplanes selected from an inventory of approximately 160 models are on display, many of them offered as open-cockpits for you to explore. Be sure to call ahead if there is a specific helicopter you want to see, and remember they also feature the fixed-wing aircraft of the army, such as World War I biplanes and planes used as spotters on the battlefield.

Unique artifacts and clothing with insignia are available in the gift shop. Base access is required, so be sure to see the website for the current requirement for credentials.

Hours: Mon–Fri: 9 a.m. to 4 p.m., Sat: 9 a.m. to 3 p.m., Sun: closed
Website: www.armyaviationmuseum.org
Street address/GPS address: Building 6000, Novosel St., Fort Rucker, AL 36362

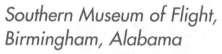

Southern Museum of Flight, Birmingham, Alabama

Nestled in this hilly patch of Alabama is a museum that has evolved from a largely local museum to a military destination of some importance. The Southern Museum of Flight chronicles Alabama's contributions to aviation through its Alabama Aviation Hall of Fame, but it also boasts an assortment of military aircraft that rivals any in the nation. The outdoor airpark and indoor display areas exhibit some 100 military aircraft and helicopters with dioramas depicting them in action and interactive displays telling their histories. Among the favorites are an F-4 Phantom, a B-25 Mitchell bomber, and an F-14 Tomcat. Museum exhibits rotate but include a program on the Tuskegee airmen, the Jets of the Korean War (with an F-86 and a Soviet Mig-15), an exhibit on Vietnam helicopters, and an exhibit on crop dusters.

Start outside with a leisurely walk down the well-maintained line of helicopters, warbirds, and military jets. Even better, why not pack a lunch and spread a tablecloth on one of the many picnic tables that are under the wings of the F-4 Phantom mounted on a pole?

"A hidden gem," writes one reviewer, and we agree. This is an all-in-one place to see excellent dioramas, touch history-laden warbirds, and enjoy a little southern hospitality in the process.

Hours: Tues–Sat: 9:30 a.m. to 4:30 p.m., Sun, Mon: closed
Website: www.southernmuseumofflight.org
Street address/GPS address: 4343 73rd St. N., Birmingham, AL 35206

US Veterans Memorial Museum, Huntsville, Alabama

Unless you're a local, there's almost no chance that you have this destination on your radar, and what a pity. The Veterans Memorial Museum has an excellent collection of tanks and helicopters. It's conveniently located near the US Space and Rocket Center in Huntsville, making this a good way to finish off a day of exploration and discovery.

The US Veterans Memorial Museum focuses on the accomplishments of our men and women in the armed forces. It features specific exhibits on the Revolutionary War, the Mexican-American War, World War I, World War II, Korea, Vietnam, and Iraq with an emphasis on the personal sacrifices our veterans made.

The display of large artifacts is exceptionally diverse. Outside there is an M3 Stuart and an M5 Stuart tank, a Sherman flamethrower, and an M48 Patton battle tank. There is a somewhat-rare PBR patrol boat representative of the Navy's Vietnam-era riverine operations, four helicopters (a Cobra, a Huey, a Kiowa, and a Bell Medevac chopper from Korea), a Humvee, a deuce-and-a-half, and a collection of jeeps that features the oldest-known surviving Jeep Pygmy. Add to that a collection of rifles, uniforms, and a mock–World War II briefing room and you have a day well spent. Tours are available and docents are on premise.

Hours: Wed–Sat: 10 a.m. to 4 p.m.
Website: www.memorialmuseum.org/
Street address/GPS address: 2060A Airport Rd., Huntsville, AL 35801

While You're in the Neighborhood

US Space and Rocket Center, Huntsville, Alabama

Although technically not a military destination, rockets have an obvious connection to the military, which is reason enough to visit the Space and Rocket Center. Here you'll learn everything you want to know about the development of space boosters, launch vehicles, rockets, and missiles and their uses both military and civilian. Of special interest are the displays on engines, propellants, and guidance systems. Be sure to walk the weaving and winding path through the outdoor areas and see the enormous Saturn booster, as well as Space Shuttle Park, Rocket Park, Lunar Crater, and more.

Hours: Daily: 9 a.m. to 5 p.m.
Website: https://www.rocketcenter.com/
Street address/GPS address: 1 Tranquility Base, Huntsville, AL 35805

Tuskegee Airmen National Historic Site, Tuskegee, Alabama

The Tuskegee Airmen National Historic Site is a quiet, contemplative walk back in time. At the heart of this destination is Moton Field, where the first African-American fighter pilots trained for World War II combat. Both Hangars 1 and 2 have been restored, as well as the original control tower. The grass is mowed, the place is perfect. If you stand still you can hear the roar of those Merlin engines and see those young men looping and rolling their red-tailed P-51s through the sky. Now part of the National Park System.

Hours: Mon–Sat: 9 a.m. to 4:30 p.m., Sun: closed
Website: www.nps.gov/tuai/index.htm
Street address/GPS address: 1616 Chappie James Ave., Tuskegee, AL 36083

Alaska

If the Russians ever attacked the US, Alaska would be vital to our national defense. Likewise, Nike surface-to-air missile would fire and air defense fighters would be the first in the air. Little wonder that since the days of World War II a military presence in Alaska has been essential to our nation—but all the more surprising that we find so few military destinations there. That said, there are two that we recommend.

The Best Formerly Secret Military Sites: Nike Missile Site, Summit, Alaska

If we had spotted an attack by Soviet bombers during the Cold War, hundreds of our needle-nosed Nike air defense

At one time, surface to air missile sites ringed our nation's cities ready to pop up out of bunkers, swing skyward, and shoot down an invading Soviet bomber. Once listed as top secret, Nike missile sites are now one of the most interesting military destinations in America. Photo courtesy of Department of Defense

missiles would have risen out of the ground to shoot them down. Happily, tensions abated and the threat dissipated, and the Nike sites were shut down. Happily, too, some civic-minded groups managed to put a few of these on the rolls of historic places so they could be preserved and seen today. One of them is here.

Monthly tours take you out to see Site Summit, a long-ago-abandoned (but restored) Nike missile site, now on the rolls of the National Register of Historic Places. This mountaintop Cold War missile complex was built to protect Anchorage, Alaska, and Elmendorf Air Force Base from a surprise attack. Site Summit is located at the edge of the Artic Valley Ski Area but it is on an active-duty base and access is limited to tours.

Tour Information: You will go on a 28-passenger bus. Check website (www .nikesitesummit.net) for tour dates and registration form. Must be 12 years old or older. Must pre-register at least 30 days in advance. Limited to 28 people.

Lend-Lease Memorial, Fairbanks, Alaska

If you're in the area, take a 30-minute detour to see this Fairbanks, Alaska, memorial built to honor a noble part of our World War II history. Remember Franklin D. Roosevelt's Lend-Lease Act? Best known for the convoys that crossed the Atlantic Ocean and gave Great Britain the lifeline it so desperately needed, Lend-Lease was also a lifeline for Russia. Thousands of fighter planes and other war matériel were funneled through Fairbanks, Alaska, on what was called the Northwest Staging Route for the Alaska Siberian Lend Lease Airway. US pilots, including the Women's Airline Service Pilots (WASPs), ferried airplanes up to Fairbanks, where they were handed over to the Soviets who flew them across the Bering Sea into Siberia and onward to the Russian fronts. This 6,000-mile airbridge was precarious and took the lives of many.

This is a beautiful, spacious urban park with a handsome statue to commemorate the Russian and American airmen and air women who made these sacrifices. The inscription tells the entire story and pays tribute to those years when two nations shared a common cause.

Website: www.alaska.org/detail/lend-lease-monument
Street address/GPS address: 400 Wendell Ave., Fairbanks, AK 99701

Alaska Aviation Museum, Anchorage, Alaska

This has to be one of the most unusual destinations on our list. The Lake Hood Seaplane Base in Anchorage, Alaska, is the largest seaplane base in America, with 70,000 takeoffs and landings a year. Next to it is the Anchorage airport, with jumbo jets headed all over the world. There is surely no better place to take this all in than the Alaska Aviation Museum. It sits right in the middle.

The Alaska Aviation Museum tells the unique and almost otherworldly story of aviation in Alaska. From bush pilots to seaplanes to combat aircraft, it stands apart from anything you'll see in the Lower 48. To start there are more seaplanes here than you'd otherwise see in a lifetime plus some terrific military aircraft on display, including a PBY Catalina seaplane, a Huey chopper, a P-40 Warhawk, and an F-15 fighter jet. But more to the point, the museum sits on a peninsula of land wedged between the international airport and the one-of-a-kind Lake Hood Seaplane Base. In a word, you will be literally surrounded by action.

Grab a seat outside and watch the goings-on. If you're up to it, take the self-guided walking tour of the seaplane base and see the tie-down channels and visit the old control tower. But come here for the view of Lake Hood with its docks and its basins and all the airplanes coming and going. You won't find such an experience—or such a view—anywhere else.

Hours: Daily: 9 a.m. to 5 p.m.
Website: www.alaskaairmuseum.org
Walking Tours: www.alaska.org/guide
Street address/GPS address: 4721 Aircraft Dr., Anchorage, AK 99502

Arkansas

Little Rock Air Force Base, Little Rock, Arkansas, was specifically built for nuclear bombers. Ground was broken in 1953, Strategic Air Command (SAC) bombers moved in in 1956, and the Titan missiles arrived in the 1960s. Arkansas has a storied military history, but nothing matches the role it played in the Cold War. Read on.

Jacksonville Museum of Military History, Jacksonville, Arkansas

Well-loved by those who stumble upon it, the Jacksonville Museum of Military History understandably focuses on the role that Jacksonvillians played in our nation's conflicts. But to dismiss it out of hand as "local" would be a mistake. From our earliest conflicts to today, Arkansas has always played a large role in our nation's defense, and this relatively new museum offers up a long-overdue tribute to that service. At the height of the Cold War, nearby Little Rock Air Force Base was a major bomber base with B-47s ready to launch with just 15 minutes' notice. When the missile age arrived, Little Rock Air Force Base took control of some of our nation's uber-powerful, 9-megaton Titan ICBMs.

Reflecting that history, this handsome museum has a fully interactive Titan II Launch Control Station just like the ones used during the Cold War and numerous other exhibits on the era. The outdoor airpark is small but has a well-known Vietnam-era F-105 fighter jet and a UH-1 Huey helicopter. Other exhibits include Mighty-Mite, the world's smallest jeep.

Small but gracious, this antebellum building is architecturally consistent with the broad spectrum of stories to be found here, starting with the battles of the Civil War and ending with today's war on terror.

Hours: Mon–Fri: 9 a.m. to 5 p.m., Sat: 10 a.m. to 5 p.m., Sun: closed
Website: www.jaxmilitarymuseum.org
Street address/GPS address: 100 Victory Circle, Jackson, AR 72076

Arizona

Arizona's role in our national defense has much to do with both the size of the state and its otherwise inhospitable desert climate. For starters, that climate is ideal for storing airplanes and for that reason you'll find here the largest aviation "boneyard" in world—some 4,400 planes on 2,600 acres placed wing-tip-to-wingtip just outside of Tucson. Second, Arizona spreads out over no less than 113,000 square miles (our sixth largest state), which mattered tremendously when it came time to select sites for our ICBMs. To prevent a Russian nuclear bomb from wiping out a dozen missiles in one blast, silos had to be spread out over thousands of square miles—and Arizona had that kind of land.

That hot climate and those barren stretches of desert were useful in other ways, too. For one, they create a nearly perfect security "moat" behind which one coud conduct secret military experiments. The US Army's Fort Huachuca is here for just that reason. What better place to test ultrasecret military signal technologies and communications gear than in the high desert far from prying eyes?

Pima Air & Space Museum, Tucson, Arizona

Sunshine rains down on this part of Arizona, bringing vividly to life the exquisite colors and shapes of the more than 300 air and space vehicles displayed at the Pima Air & Space Museum in Pima, Arizona. In just one day you can experience the width and breadth of our aerospace history, including a visit to an ICBM missile silo *and* a tour of the nearby US Air Force boneyards. Is all that possible in *one* day? Catch your breath and read on.

Before there was a Pima there was a growing boneyard at Davis-Monthan Air Force Base, where the main activity was chopping up and smelting hundreds if not thousands of airplanes a year. Thankfully, some of the officers on the base recognized that historic aircraft were fast disappearing, so they took a few of them aside and put them up against a fence and developed a sort of drive-by museum. One thing led to another and in a few years, land was bought, a museum was approved by the USAF, and planes started to arrive.

Next came the missiles and the SALT treaties, and once again missile silos were fast being lost to history. A non-affiliated group petitioned the Air Force to let them preserve what is now the Titan Museum. This museum eventually became part of Pima, so now you can visit an incredible collection of fixed-wing aircraft, helicopters, *and* a missile silo.

Let's start with the aircraft. Pima has one of the few surviving examples of the enormous, lumbering B-36 bomber. This behemoth of an airplane was designed in the dark days when we thought Britain would fall to Hitler and the war against Germany would have to be launched from upstate *New York*. Manned by a crew of 10 or more airmen, the bomber could fly to and from Europe on a tank of gas. Well, that never happened, but the B-36 did go on to be a nuclear bomber during the Cold War, which is the story told here.

The lineup of terrific airplanes continues with an equally rare B-58 Hustler supersonic nuclear bomber, *two* B-52s, a B-50, a RB-47, Soviet Migs, and almost every aircraft and helicopter flown by the US Army, Air Force, Navy, Marines, *and* the Coast Guard. It's exhausting and exhilarating at the same time, and it could take days to see it all. After all, Pima has *four* hangars filled with every manner of American, Japanese, Soviet, and German airplane and spacecraft.

So where to start your visit? It's a big museum, so it's best seen with a map in hand. You'll enter through Hangar One, which is the main hangar,

Pima Air and Space invited some of the world's best-known graffiti artists to turn a group of their planes into fascinating works of art. Photo courtesy of Pima Air & Space Museum

with plenty of aircraft old and new. Straight ahead is a model of the *Wright Flyer,* behind which are a dozen early airplanes, such as a Bellanca and a Waco. As you continue you'll come face-to-face with two fan favorites—a pristine F-4 Phantom finished with the markings and colors of the USAF Thunderbirds and an immaculate F-14 Tomcat in its 1979 colors. As you walk around the corner, you'll find the ominous-looking SR-71 Blackbird reconnaissance plane next to the always loved but much maligned (for its looks) A-10 Warthog.

From here it's dealer's choice. You have several more hangars to go, but tops on any list are the B-29 Superfortress in Hangar 4 and the B-24 Liberator in Hangar 3. One thing not to miss—and something you'll find nowhere else—is the spectacular graffiti art of Francisco Rodrigues da Silva, also known as "Nunca," a street artist from Brazil. Along with some 40 other artists, Nunca used the fuselage and wings of some of the old warbirds to create the absolutely joyous art you'll encounter here.

Be sure to bring your walking shoes and dress appropriately. It gets hot here, and this is a big museum (80 acres) with several hangars and an enormous outdoor display area. For a break, try the Flight Grill, and not just for the food. While you relax you'll have a perfectly beautiful, 50-yard-line view of the aircraft on the outdoor ramp.

Hours: Daily: 9 a.m. to 5 p.m. Last admittance: 3 p.m.
Website: www.pimaair.org
Street address/GPS address: 6000 E. Valencia Rd., Tucson, AZ 85706

Davis-Monthan Air Force Base, Tucson, Arizona (aka "The Boneyards")

The scale, the cognitively dissonant images of *thousands* of airplanes lined up wingtip to wingtip in precise rows as far as the eye can see: Can there really be this many airplanes in one place? Yes, there can—in fact, an impressively photogenic 4,400 airplanes, some cocooned in protective white coverings, some chopped up (or being chopped up), but most in neat rows that stretch over the 2,600 acres of dry, barren desert.

This is Davis-Monthan Air Force Base, an active Air Combat Command base with combat-ready A-10 Warthogs on one side and the 309th Aerospace Maintenance and Regeneration Group on the other. Virtually every branch of the services sends surplus planes here to be stripped down for parts, or to be preserved for potential reactivation, or to be chopped up and recycled. Some of the planes seem to be too new to be in a boneyard—modern frontline fighters like the F-15s, F-16s, and F-18s for example—while others seem to be decades overdue, like the B-52s with those sawed-off wings that have been laid on the ground so Soviet satellites can verify that they have been destroyed according to various arms-limitation treaties.

A visit to Tucson has to include a tour of the USAF military "boneyards." Seen here: Mothballed C-130s. Photo courtesy of Department of Defense

Tours leave from the nearby Pima Air & Space Museum. Be prepared to be overwhelmed by the sight. This is a sight you simply won't see anywhere else in the world.

Hours: See Pima Air & Space Museum
Website: www.airplaneboneyards.com/davis-monthan-afb-amarg-airplane -boneyard.htm

The Best Formerly Secret Military Sites: Pinal Airpark, Marana, Arizona

This former CIA airfield in the Sonoran Desert was opened to the public a few years ago, and there's a lot to see. For starters, easily visible from I-10 are more than 100 mothballed and oddly shaped commercial airliners resting in the Pinal Airpark's boneyard. Many of them have missing tails or missing engines or have no names on the sides, and in fact most of them are waiting to be torn down for parts or sent to the smelters. Haunting, to say the least.

But that's not all. The airpark is home to the Silverbell Army Heliport, where hundreds of army helicopter pilots train using the adjacent 3,600-square-mile range. Watch for Blackhawk helicopters taking off and landing, as well as the occasional Army jump planes. Here too is the Special Operations Command Parachute Training and Testing Facility, as of this writing.

The rest of Pinal is as it was for decades. In addition to the mothballed commercial airliners, you'll see some abandoned structures that were base housing for the CIA, as well as some former guard shacks and the remaining warning signs. Remote and barren, yes, but this was once a CIA facility running black ops into Southeast Asia and that's part of what makes it spooky—and special.

Take I-10, exit 232.[1]

Website: www.airplaneboneyards.com/pinal-airpark-airliner-storage-boneyard .htm

Street address/GPS address: 24641 E. Pinal Airpark Rd., Marana, AZ 85653

The Best Formerly Secret Military Sites: Titan Missile Museum, Sahuarita, Arizona

The Titan II ICBM was in service from 1963 to 1987, at which time the Minuteman missiles took over. The Titans were located here in Arizona, and at the height of the Cold War they were on 24-hour alert. Each was armed with a W-53 nuclear warhead known as a bunker buster—so named because of its enormous 9-megaton yield (it was one of the largest warheads in our arsenal).

The Titan Missile Museum is a place frozen in time. Everything here is real (except the bomb) and displayed as it was when it was deactivated in 1982. You'll walk through an exhibit hall with displays that explain the operation of an ICBM missile silo. After that, you'll follow a guide down 35 feet and see a simulated launch from the underground launch control facility. Next, you squeeze down one more level to the missile itself. Chilling, to say the least.

We recommend you take the one-hour guided tour or buy a ticket for the longer but more in-depth Beyond the Blast Doors Tour. This includes a first-hand look at the living quarters and other areas not on the general tour.

Arizona once had 168 ICBM missile sites, but now most of them are gone. This is a gem.

Hours: Sun–Fri: 9:45 a.m. to 4 p.m., Sat: 8:45 a.m. to 5 p.m.
Website: www.titanmissilemuseum.org
Street address/GPS address: 1580 W. Duval Mine Rd., Sahuarita, AZ 85614

Fort Huachuca Historical Museum and the US Army Intelligence Museum, Cochise, Arizona

US Army Fort Huachuca is home to the US Army's Intelligence Center and their Electronic Proving Grounds. The mission here is to develop ways to survey battlefields and enemy positions without the enemy knowing it, or stopping you. The small but interesting US Army Intelligence Museum explains how that's done. There are tableaus depicting the art of gathering and sending MI—Military Intelligence—and numerous drone and other surveillance equipment on display to show how a battlefield is revealed using technology. One exhibit speaks to the importance of space and how International Space Station mission specialists surveil enemy topography. Another breaks down all the codes and ciphers used to transmit MI from one point to another. And be sure to look for the section of the Berlin Wall. It speaks volumes about why we cherish and protect our freedoms.

The nearby Fort Huachuca Historical Museum focuses on the history of the fort and life on an army post during our frontier days. The museum is currently running an excellent exhibit called the Buffalo Soldier, documenting the role of African Americans in the cavalry. Fort Huachuca was home to the Buffalo Soldiers for some 20 years.

If secret operations are your cup of tea, the Intelligence Museum is the destination for you, but no matter which of the two museums you start with, be sure to check their website so you'll have the documents required to get on base. It's a remote place but entirely fascinating, and just being at such an interesting military destination is half the fun.

Hours: Fort Huachuca Historical Museum: Mon–Sat: 9 a.m. to 4 p.m., Sun: closed. US Army Intelligence Museum: Mon–Fri: 9 a.m. to 4 p.m., Sat, Sun: 1 to 4 p.m.
Website: www.huachuca.army.mil
Street address/GPS address: 41401 Grierson Ave., Fort Huachuca, AZ 85613

Yuma Proving Grounds Heritage Center, Yuma, Arizona

The US Army Proving Grounds in Yuma, Arizona, is geographically one of the largest army bases in the world. It has the longest artillery range (40 miles end to end), more than 200 miles of test roads for wheeled and tracked vehicles, and a fully instrumented flight box where combat helicopters can fire weapons and get immediate post-mission performance metrics. Some 500,000 mortar rounds, artillery shells, and missile rounds are fired here each year, and some 36,000 parachute drops take place. Weapons are tested here; soldiers are trained to use them here.[2]

The Heritage Center is a small museum that tells the story of the weapons developed or tested here as well as interesting asides like the geology of the proving grounds. Be sure to see one of the newer exhibits called Liberation of the concentration camps during World War II. It focuses on those army units who were first to see the horror of Hitler's insanity.

The main draw is the outdoor display area called the Wahner E. Brooks Historical Exhibit, so leave plenty of time for that. This is an excellent vehicle park with dozens of tanks, howitzers, and other artillery pieces for you to touch and see. Among them—an M4 Sherman tank, an M60 Patton tank, a Sergeant York antiaircraft gun, howitzers, missile launchers, and a fascinating pair of nuclear surface-to-surface missiles, the Honest John (first army missile to be nuclearized) and the subsequent Little John.

The Heritage Center requires entry onto base, so bring a driver's license.

Hours: Tues–Fri: 10 a.m. to 4 p.m.
Website: www.museumsusa.org/museums/info/21380
Street address/GPS address: 301 C St., Yuma, AZ 85365

While You're in the Neighborhood

Planes of Fame, Valle, Arizona

Here you'll find a small but interesting military museum and a collection of warbirds maintained by volunteers who are well known on the air show circuit. Notable aircraft maintained by them include American, German, Japanese, and Soviet warbirds. Planes are moved between this location and similar locations in California, so check their website or call ahead to determine which model is where. Some warbird rides are available.

Hours: Mon–Sun: 9 a.m. to 5 p.m.
Website: www.planesoffame.org
Street address/GPS address: 755 Mustang Way, Williams-Valle, AZ 86046-5014

California

Sun-drenched southern California is justifiably proud of its place in military history. Start with Edwards Air Force Base in the Mojave, where test pilots took unproven planes into the sky (they were called "first flights"), then consider the ultrasecret airplanes designed at the Burbank, California–based Skunk Works (the U-2, the SR-71, and the F-117). Add to that Area 51, Marine Recruit Depot Pendleton, China Lake Naval Air Weapons Base, the Vandenberg and Pt. Mugu missile ranges north of Los Angeles—plus all those places where advanced aerial combat training takes place like Marine Corps Air Station Miramar—well, you begin to get the picture. Little wonder that more than 40 military- or aviation-themed museums are in this state. With the dogmatism of brevity, here are the best of the best.

Palm Springs Air Museum, Palm Springs, California

The Palm Springs Air Museum is like having a good buddy with a hangar full of warbirds. To understand what we mean, just consider how they run their Open Cockpit Days. At most places, Open Cockpit Day means someone pulls up a ladder and lets you lean in over the rails and look inside. Not so here. Here it means you go up the ladder and hop over the rails and go *inside* the plane. Here it means you sit in the pilot's seat and run your fingers over the instrument panel and hold the stick just like our military pilots did back in the day. In the past they've let you sit in an F-4 Phantom, an F7F Tigercat, a P-47 Thunderbolt, the F-100 Super Sabre, a T-6 Texan, an F4-U Corsair, an F-104 Starfighter, and their P-40 Warhawk. If you do get into a cockpit, let it sink in. Look around, imagine combat back in the day, linger a second. It's an incredibly personal way to experience history, and the staff will encourage you to touch and feel and ask all the questions you want.

You'll start your visit in the center of the museum between the two main wings. From the visitor center you can go left to the Pacific Hangar or go right to the European Hangar. In the European Hangar you'll find exhibits that include a re-created World War II ready room where pilots were briefed before their missions, an exhibit on the gliders of World War II, and an exhibit on the bloody 100th Bomb Group (they sustained some of the heaviest losses in the air war over Europe).

Crossing back to the left side of the visitor center is the Pacific Hangar. Exhibits here include a USO stage with memorabilia related to the comedian and tireless entertainer of our troops, Bob Hope, plus a diorama re-creating the attack on Pearl Harbor and a display on our presidents who have served in the military. Planes you can find here that aren't found everywhere—the PBY

You can play a round of golf—or walk among some of the nation's greatest military aircraft at the Palm Springs Air Museum in Palm Springs, California. Photo courtesy of Palm Springs Air Museum

Catalina "Dumbo" seaplane that was such a relief to airmen who had ditched in the Pacific, the needle-nosed F-104 Starfighter, and the beautiful H-34 helicopter. And be sure to see the scale models of World War II ships and the Vietnam POW bracelets that are in the adjacent Korea/Vietnam Hangar.

The 59 aircraft on display are beautifully restored. In addition to the ones mentioned under Open Cockpit Days, they have Vietnam fighters such as the EA-6B Prowler, the recently retired F-14 Tomcat, and a present-day F/A-18 Hornet.

The docents at this delightful museum are eager for you to experience as much of this as you can, and they are ready to answer your questions. Warbird rides are available here, too. They will take you up in their C-47 or their P-51.

Hours: Daily: 10 a.m. to 5 p.m.
Website: www.palmspringsairmuseum.org
Street address/GPS address: 745 N. Gene Autry Trail, Palm Springs, CA 92262

USS Midway Museum, San Diego, California

A beautifully preserved ship, the USS *Midway* is one of the most-visited military museums in America, and for good reason. Her interior compartments are filled with dioramas explaining life at sea; she has more than 29 military aircraft on display and some 60 exhibits for you to explore.

To start your day, walk up the gangway and enter on the hangar deck. Grab an audio cassette and a map and start to explore. Most of the large exhibits are on this deck along with the trainer aircraft and the displays that talk about the *Midway*'s service at sea. Things to look for—there are several "climb-aboard" cockpits to sit in, an Air Combat 360 flight simulator, and the Battle of Midway Theater, presently showing *Voices of Midway*. Explore this deck and the interior spaces. One of them depicts a seagoing surgical suite complete with doctors and a "patient."

Next, climb up one deck to the flight deck and feast on the airplanes. There are jets and fighter-bombers from World War II to Desert Storm. There is an F6F Hellcat, an F4U Corsair, a SBD Dauntless, and a TBM Avenger

Army parachutists aim for the deck of the USS Midway *during a ceremony in San Diego. This beautifully restored aircraft carrier is the fourth most visited military museum in America. Photo courtesy of Department of Defense*

from World War II. There is a Korea-era F9F Panther fighter, a Vietnam-era Huey gunship, and an A-4 Skyhawk, an F-4 Phantom, an F-14 Tomcat, an A-6 Intruder, and an F/A-18 Hornet, to name but a few. The airplanes are beautifully restored with a story to go with each, so be sure to read the placards and ask questions.

The *Midway* is the largest of the five aircraft carrier museums in America (*Intrepid, Yorktown, Lexington,* and *Hornet* are all World War II–era Essex-class aircraft carriers, which are about 100 feet shorter and 30 feet narrower abeam), and a full tour will take up to three hours. You'll find it's pretty much an open book, top to bottom. You can visit the bridge or the mess and almost everything in between, so the best advice is to come early and explore. This is a popular destination in a city that can be filled with tourists, so lines do form. And if all the climbing between decks wears you down, they do have a café, where you can get off your feet.

Hours: Daily: 10 a.m. to 5 p.m.
Website: www.midway.org
Street address/GPS address: 910 N. Harbor Dr., San Diego, CA 92101

San Diego Air and Space Museum, San Diego, California

The San Diego Air and Space Museum combines exhibits, artifacts, and an impressive display of airplanes and space vehicles to present an excellent overview of California's storied accomplishments in air and space. It's a packed destination, so plan your visit with time for everything. There are several military galleries, excellent flight simulators, and many one-of-a-kinds to explore.

Start your journey at the front entrance. You can't miss the sweeping, curving architecture of the museum and the two impressive gate guardians, the A-12 Blackbird (the CIA's predecessor to the SR-71) and the failed but interesting experiment to develop an amphibious navy fighter jet, called the Sea Dart. Pass between these aircraft and enter the rotunda for some historically significant aircraft soaring over your head and then continue to the Pavilion of Flight. This impressive atrium of glass and steel is the heart and soul of the museum, with reflecting pools over which hang an F-4 Phantom fighter, a PBY Catalina, a Soviet Mig, and a Ford Trimotor.

Explore the aircraft here and then head to the military galleries. The World War II Gallery has German, Japanese, and American warbirds, including the P-51, a B-24 Liberator, and several navy fighter and fighter-bombers, while the Modern Age Gallery has the F/A-18 Hornet in the colors of the Blue Angels and the World War I Gallery has the biplanes. Split your time according to your interest but watch for crowds. There are simulators here and they are popular. If you're up to it, try the Max Flight Sim with the huge 58-inch screens and its blazing-fast processors, or go into the Zable 3D/4D big-screen theater, which has rockin' and rollin' seats to put a fourth dimension into the movies they show. The schedule of features is posted on their website and as you enter, so plan accordingly.

This is a military town and the museum can get crowded. As always, leave time for the gift shop or spend a few minutes resting in the Flight Path Grill and Observation Deck. And why not combine this destination with the USS *Midway* in downtown San Diego? That would be the perfect one-two punch for a weekend of fantastic military destinations.

Hours: Daily: 10 a.m. to 4:30 p.m.
Website: www.sandiegoairandspace.org
Street address/GPS address: 2001 Pan American Plaza, San Diego, CA 92101

Castle Air Museum, Sacramento, California

Castle Air Force Base was once a major Cold War bomber base for Strategic Air Command with nuclear bombers on ground alert 24/7. The Cold War ended and the base was closed in 1995, but the museum lives on, and what a treat it is. "Never knew about it," said one visitor of this excellent destination. "What a wonderful surprise!" said another. We agree.

The main museum is filled with display cases containing Cold War artifacts such as uniforms, signage, helmets, and scale models. There is a Norden bomb sight, a .50 caliber machine gun, and ready rooms brought here from the air base complete with period furniture. This is an excellent place to walk around and remember those tense years and reflect on the tremendous load SAC airmen carried. The SAC legacy permeates everything, and the displays remind us that SAC aircrews flew their missions fully armed least they get caught in the air by a surprise attack. For an interesting bonus, buy a ticket and walk through the DC-9 (VC-9) version of *Air Force One*. It was used by Presidents Reagan and Clinton, as well as various vice presidents and cabinet members.

From inside the museum, head out to the airpark. This place is huge and clearly the main draw. Two things make this particularly special—the first is Open Cockpit Days, and the second is the B-36 Peacemaker. First the B-36. The B-36 bomber was designed when military planners thought Great Britain would fall to Nazi Germany and that the air war to liberate Europe would have to start from air bases in upstate New York. That never happened, but after the war the Cold War kicked off and this was the bomber that had the range SAC needed to strike the Soviet Union. Instead of fighting Hitler, it became a nuclear bomber. To give you an idea of the size of the bomb it carried, there is a mock-up of a Mark 17 atomic bomb sitting right next to it. It was 24 feet long and weighed 10 *tons* and packed a 10 to 15 megaton punch (roughly

1,000 times more powerful than Hiroshima). The B-36 anchors an excellent outdoor display of 70 military aircraft, including a World War II–era B-17 and B-24s plus a B-20, the B-47, which was our first jet bomber, and a B-52, a KC-135 tanker, an SR-71, a C-47, and an F-14 and F-16, plus numerous cargo, fighter, and attack aircraft.

Hours: Daily: 9 a.m. to 4 p.m.
Website: www.castleairmuseum.org
Street address/GPS address: 5050 Santa Fe Dr., Atwater, CA 95301

Air Force Flight Test Center Museum, Edwards Air Force Base, California
Blackbird Airpark, Palmdale, California
Joe Davies Heritage Airpark, Plant 42, Palmdale, California

One feels no limits standing in the middle of the Mojave Desert. The horizon stretches out as far as the eye can see, the dry lake beds are pancake flat and endless; the sky is a deep blue that goes far out into space. *A person can do anything* seems to be the message—and judging from this history-making destination, we'd have to agree. We're speaking of course of Edwards Air Force Base and the Flight Test Center and Chuck Yeager's milestone flight through the sound barrier and the more than 150 aircraft that made their maiden flights here. We're speaking of the Flight Test Center Museum and nearby Blackbird Airpark and Joe Davies Airpark, which is adjacent to Blackbird Airpark. Vibrant, interconnected, and geographically all in the same neighborhood, this is one of the most unusual military destinations in the nation, and certainly one of the most important ones in aviation history.

Let's start with Edwards. Edwards Air Force Base is home to the US Air Force Test Pilot School, the Air Force Test Center, and the Flight Test Center Museum, which tells the story of flight testing at Edwards. Located on base, the Flight Test museum is a modest museum with several interesting displays, including a wall of scale-model airplanes depicting all of the planes that made their first flight here. Other exhibits tell the stories of the many avia-

tion milestones and records set here, most illustrated with artifacts and photographs. Aircraft on display include one of the few remaining B-58 Hustler
supersonic nuclear bombers, the only two-seat-version of the A-10 Warthog,
an SR-71 Blackbird, various experimental "X" planes, and the YF-22, which
was tested here and led to the F-22 Raptor.

Twenty minutes away is Blackbird Airpark in nearby Palmdale, California, operated by the same nonprofit that operates the Flight Test museum.
Here you'll find *two* SR-71s nose to nose, or, rather, one SR-71 and one A-12,
the single-seat version of the SR-71 flown by the CIA (this is the only place
where you can see the two side by side). You'll also find a U-2 spy plane here,
a black-project D-21 supersonic drone (*blackbirds*, right?), plus various parts of
an SR-71 displayed inside a small museum also located here.

Joe Davies Heritage Airpark is next to Blackbird Airpark. It's run by the
city of Palmdale and named after one of the region's military luminaries. The
Joe Davies Airpark has 21 additional aircraft and scale models on display,
including a B-52, a Boeing 747 that carried the space shuttle on its back, an
A-7 Corsair, an A-4 Skyhawk, four "Century"-series jets, the F-100 Super
Sabre, the F-101 Voodoo, the F-104 Starfighter, the F-105 Thunderchief,
and some NASA test planes.

The Flight Test Center Museum is located inside Edwards Air Force Base,
so to get there you have to take the tour that runs on the third Friday of the
month. If that's sold out, they'll take groups of 15 or more on private tours
Tuesday through Friday (excepting Fridays when they're giving the regular tour).
On the way to the museum, you'll get a "windshield" view of the base, including a trip along the flight line. Be sure to look for the statue of Chuck Yeager.

If you can't get on any of the tours, don't despair. Drive up to Edward's
North Gate and see the B-52 mothership that carried so any X planes aloft.
Then drive over to the West Gate and see Century Circle. Century Cir-
cle isn't named for any particular century but rather for a series of fighter
jets that were 100-series aircraft. Lined up in a circle around the original
Edwards Air Force Base control tower are an F-100, an F-101, an F-102, an
F-104, an F-105, and an F-106.

Were the museum more accessible to the public, this would rank in our
Top 20. Be that as it may, this is an excellent driving destination that puts you
at the heart of cutting-edge military flight, and no matter how you spend your

day, be sure to stop and reflect on where you are. You are literally under the same sky through which Chuck Yeager broke the sound barrier and countless other test pilots put their lives on the line to move the envelope out. Enjoy your proximity to history.

Flight Test Museum Tour Information: General public tours conducted on the third Friday of the month from 9:30 a.m. to 1 p.m. Check website (www .edwards.af.mil/tours) for dates. Large group tours will take place on Tues, Wed, Thurs, and Fri except on the third Fri of the month. Reservations required. Start and end times flexible.

Joe Davies Airpark Hours: Guided tours available by appointment
Park hours: Fri, Sat, Sun: 11 a.m. to 4 p.m.
Website: www.cityofpalmdale.org/airpark
Street address/GPS address: 2001 E. Avenue P, Palmdale, CA 93550

Pacific Battleship Center, USS Iowa, San Pedro, California

The richness of this destination stems from the unusual story of a president and a meeting in Tehran at the height of World War II. As risky as it now seems, in 1943 President Franklin D. Roosevelt left Washington, D.C., and in utter secrecy steamed across the Atlantic Ocean to attend a pivotal meeting with Churchill and Stalin in Tehran. Incredibly, they avoided German U-boats and Luftwaffe fighters and docked in Algeria some eight days later. FDR completed the final leg to Tehran by airplane. His ship was the USS *Iowa*.

The Iowa-class battleships were our nation's largest—and last—class of battleships, each as long as three football fields and as tall as an 11-story building. After safely delivering the president to Algeria, the *Iowa* served in the Pacific and later went on to serve in the Korean War. She was decommissioned in 1994 and moved to Los Angeles in 2012.

When you visit the *Iowa*, be sure to walk in the gap between the forward turrets and the superstructure. While they were underway FDR was pushed back and forth through this passage to view his convoy's destroyer escorts. On his trip to Tehran, FDR had with him the who's-who of the US command staff—General of the Army George C. Marshall, General of the Air Force Henry H. "Hap" Arnold, Commander in Chief of the Navy Admiral Ernest J. King, and Chairman of the Joint Chiefs Admiral William D. Leahy. All of these walked the very same decks you'll be on as the *Iowa* steamed through the Atlantic radio silent and blacked out. The *Iowa* is the only navy ship with a bathtub: FDR like to bathe his paralyzed legs.

This beautifully restored battleship is run by a very active group of volunteers who see to it that it doesn't become a dusty old relic of the sea. Be sure to ask a docent about the wayward torpedo that almost sunk her! There are movie nights, lectures, dances, and, of course, tours. Located 40 minutes from the glitter of Beverly Hills, there is plentiful parking and a gift shop on board.

See their website for the latest tours—they do change.

Hours: Daily: 10 a.m. to 4 p.m.
Website: www.pacificbattleship.com
Street address/GPS address: 250 S. Harbor Blvd., Berth 87, San Pedro, CA 90731

Pacific Coast Air Museum, Santa Rosa, California

Aviation history. Boy Scout merit badges. Family friendly. Those words perfectly describe the Pacific Coast Air Museum in Santa, Rosa, California. Nestled in the ever-so-relaxed atmosphere of California's wine country, this delightful destination focuses on the evolution of flight from the discovery of the principles of basic aerodynamics, to today's supersonic jets. A grassroots organization run by passionate volunteers (many of whom are military veterans) keeps the grounds beautifully maintained, and the museum is loaded with military jets, including the actual F-15 Eagle that was the first to arrive over New York City on 9/11. Aptly named, it is called *First Responder* and is showcased in an exhibit by that name.

Although there are plenty of aircraft outside the museum, start your visit inside and explore the cutaways of engines, the collection of flying helmets that goes back to World War I, and the flight simulator. After that, take in the scale-model of the aircraft carrier *Intrepid*, the diorama of a Korean War landscape, and the layout of the original Santa Rosa Army Airfield. Finally, explore it all. The museum has a collection of 35 planes both civilian and military, with some perennial favorites among them including an F-14 Tomcat, an F-16 Fighting Falcon, an A-6 Intruder, and an A-7 Corsair, both of Gulf War fame. There is also a not-often-seen HU-16 Albatross, the first dedicated Search-and-Rescue seaplane built after World War II, and a plane they particularly love is the A-26 Invader. It is aptly named *City of Santa Rosa.*

By all means, try to come on Open Cockpit Days. It's a great opportunity to lean in and take a look at a jet and in some cases sit in the pilot's seat. For their Vietnam weekend they opened up their F-4C Phantom, their F-105 Thunderchief, the A-4, the A-6, and their UH-1 Huey.

This is a family destination. The exhibits are both informational and entertaining, and there are plenty of docents to answer questions. This compact 5-acre campus, located on the grounds of the Sonoma County Airport, is easy to get to and is a solid half-day of military fun.

Hours: Wed–Sun: 10 a.m. to 4 p.m., Mon, Tues: closed
Website: www.pacificcoastairmuseum.org
Street address/GPS address: 1 Air Museum Way, Santa Rosa, CA 95403

USS Hornet *Sea, Air & Space Museum, Alameda, California*

At first you think, what's with this ship? As you come aboard you wonder—where are the airplanes, the dioramas? Fear not: This is a place where authenticity trumps everything.

So, what will you find here? The *Hornet* has a small but well-curated collection of 15 warbirds and helicopters, most from the Vietnam era or later (like an A-4 Skyhawk, an F-8 Crusader, an F-4 Phantom, and an SH-3H Sea King helicopter, for example), plus an F-14 Tomcat. Her interior spaces have various displays, but what stands out is the number of compartments restored to their seagoing days. What does that mean? There's a debate between those who like to stuff a ship's interior compartments with displays and exhibits and those who want them kept in their natural state, tidy but old. The *Hornet* is of the later

Don't despair as you weave your way through an abandoned navy base: You're not lost. The Hornet *waits on the other side. Photo courtesy of author's collection*

camp. Including the various docent-led tours, there are some 40 interior compartments all left as they were when she was at sea (albeit restored and cleaned). Those include the Captain's Cabin, the Admirals Cabin, the CIC, the Pilots Ready Room, the berthing area for the marine detachment, medical spaces, the sick bay, the Officer's Wardroom, the Petty Officer's mess, and on and on.

Treat this as a chance to see a true warrior with plenty of salt water in her veins. You'll find her on the far side of the old Alameda Naval Air Station past a lot of lonely looking, abandoned buildings. And be of brave heart. If you think you're lost—press on. You're headed in the right direction. She's out there on the East Bay waiting for your visit.

Hours: Daily: 10 a.m. to 5 p.m.
Website: https://www.uss-hornet.org/
Street address/GPS address: 707 W. Hornet Ave., Pier 3, Alameda, CA 94501

US Navy Seabee Museum, Port Hueneme, California

If bulldozers are your thing, and exotic, impossible construction sites fascinate you, this is the destination for you. The Seabees are the US Navy equivalent of the Army Engineers. They are combat-qualified sailors who work alongside their fellow seamen to build piers, runways, hospitals, temporary bases, and whatever else the navy needs. One example: During World War II they built 111 airstrips on six continents and had battalions operating on almost every Pacific island during the campaign to defeat Japan.[3]

All that and more is detailed inside this museum with thematic exhibits that include life-sized reconstructions and scale models of some of their more difficult projects. There are bulldozers and trucks and countless tools and small weapons on display. Exhibits trace the Seabees history from the first Quonset huts to the roles they've played in various humanitarian missions around the world. Dioramas incorporate heavy equipment (some of it battle scarred) with mannequins and landscapes to transport you back in time. Be sure to see the exhibits on their use of underwater diving equipment.

Somewhat unexpected, and on display here, is what the Seabees call "trench art," that is, small things sailors made by hand from scrap metal or spent shell casings. There is a bracelet made from Australian coins, model airplanes made from .50 caliber bullets, and ashtrays and small plaques made from the metal taken from crashed Japanese planes. These small objects are surprisingly moving and put a personal touch to the Seabees story. "A Seabee is a soldier, in a Navy uniform, with Marine training, doing the work of a civilian, getting W.P.A. wages," says one period poster on display, and that about says it all.

There is an excellent gift shop with numerous one-of-a-kind souvenirs to memorialize your visit.

Hours: Mon–Sat: 10 a.m. to 5 p.m., Sun: closed
Website: www.history.navy.mil/content/history/museums/seabee.html
Street address/GPS address: 3201 N. Ventura Rd., Port Hueneme, CA 93041

The Best Formerly Secret Military Sites: Nike Air Defense Missile Site SF-88L, Sausalito, California

By our book, this is one of the best Nike missile sites in the nation. The elevators work on the launch pad, the missiles are in excellent condition, and, across the board, things are generally in better shape here than anywhere else. Nike Site SF-88L is listed in the National Register of Historic

A restored Nike missile site today at Sausalito, California. Photo courtesy of National Park Service

Places and is part of Fort Barry, which is located in the Golden Gate National Recreation Area near San Francisco. Site SF-88L has the original tracking station, the actual missile launchers, and some restored Nike missiles on the rails (yes, you can touch them!). Drive out to the Recreation Area and walk around the abandoned radomes, the control buildings, and the magazines. The docents are veterans of the Cold War, and they will take you on a tour that includes a walk around the actual missiles. If you have time, be sure to add the one-hour walking tour of the old Fort Barry army post while you're here.

Hours: Thurs–Sat: 12:30 to 3:30 p.m.
Website: www.nps.gov/goga/nike-missile-site.htm
Street address: Golden Gate National Recreation Area, US 101, San Francisco, CA 94109

The Best Formerly Secret Military Sites: Military Ghost Ships. The Suisun Bay Reserve Fleet, Suisan Bay, California

At one time more than 100 ships were anchored in these brackish backwaters of San Francisco Bay, but after recalling some to active service and scrapping others, just a half-dozen ships remain (although more will soon be anchored here). To see the ships up close, contact Bay View Charters (www.bayviewcharters.com) to schedule a place on the Magic of Suisun Bay Navy Reserve Fleet Tour. It takes about 20 minutes to get to the anchorage, and then you'll sail around the ships so you can take pictures. If you don't take the charter, try driving Highway-680 near Benicia for the best view.

The Best Military Base Tours: Fort Irwin, Fort Irwin, California (near Barstow)

Fort Irwin is a special treat. Before our soldiers deploy overseas, they're sent to Fort Irwin for some final preparations, foremost among them, "the Box." The Box is a Middle Eastern village into

Simulated combat missions are run in "The Box" at Fort Irwin, California—and you get to observe. Tours are also given, and visitors are allowed. Photo courtesy of Department of Defense

which our soldiers are sent without any idea of what lies ahead. They roger up as if on a mission and enter this simulated village. Like a real-life mission, they have to be ready for the unexpected. Will there be insurgents mixed in with the shoppers in this fictional Middle East village? Will they be ambushed instantly, or will it be an uneventful market day in the square? The soldiers have no idea, so the Box is tense and unforgiving.

So, what does this have to do with you? You get to watch. Box tours are available to the public through the Fort Irwin Public Affairs Office. They are designed to help us all understand what our soldiers face when they go overseas, that there's nothing "routine" about a routine deployment. You will be taken to the observation deck overlooking the Box and observe military maneuvers, often including simulated combat fire. The tour lasts about six hours, including a stop on base for lunch (bring money) and a visit to the small museum there.

Box tours are announced on Fort Irwin's website or through their Public Affairs Office. The tours start at the Painted Rocks (look it up; it's a fascinating pile of rocks with military insignia painted on them). Wear clothing appropriate to the weather that day.

Hours: Mon–Fri: 6 a.m. to 6 p.m.
Website: http://www.irwin.army.mil/pages/VisitorsTab/BoxTour.html
Street address/GPS address: 983 Inner Loop Rd., Fort Irwin, CA 92310

The Best Military Base Tours: Vandenberg Air Force Base, Lompoc, California

Vandenberg Air Force Base is a space port. Oh, it's other things, too—all bases are multitaskers—but what makes this base unique are the launch pads. Tours are offered on the third Tuesday of each month starting at 1 p.m. The base van will meet you at the gate (the visitor center) and take you to the Vandenberg Space & Missile Heritage Center at Space Launch Complex 10. There you'll see boosters and learn more about the different types of launches that have been (and are being) conducted here.

You must request a place on the tour at least 10 days in advance.

Website: http://www.vandenberg.af.mil/Public-Tours/
Street address/GPS address: 47 Nebraska Ave., Vandenberg AFB, CA 93437

The Best Military Base Tours: Travis Air Force Base, Travis AFB, California (Located between San Francisco and Sacramento)

Travis Air Force Base is part of our Air Mobility Command (AMC) and home to KC-10 tankers, C-5A cargo planes, and C-17 cargo planes. The on-base Heritage Center runs a shuttle bus Tuesday through Friday that will pick you up at the gate (the visitor center) and take you inside. The driver will deliver you to the museum, where there is a wonderful outdoor display of 30 or so restored modern jets, old warbirds, and cargo planes.

Inside the museum are numerous smallish exhibits on World War II, Korea, and Vietnam as well as some inspiring stories on AMC's selfless, humanitarian missions. They hope to have a C-5A on display by early 2018, but look around while you're there. Depending on the day, you may see one of these magnificent cargo planes in flight. Either way, half the fun is going on base and viewing these heavy lifters in their native habitats.

Website: http://www.travis.af.mil/Contact-Us/Questions/Base-Tours/
Street address/GPS address: 690 Airman Dr., Travis AFB, CA 94535

The Best Military Base Tours: Edwards Air Force Base, Edwards AFB, California

Edwards Air Force Base is home to the elite USAF Test Pilot School, and it is where the Air Force breaks in all sorts of new planes. Edwards doesn't offer a base tour per se, but there is a close second. The only way to get to the Flight Test Museum, which is inside the gates, is to go on the museum tour, which means you go there by bus. On the way in, the driver will give you a windshield tour of the flight line, and, because this is Edwards, that can be pretty interesting.

The museum tours are offered monthly on the third Friday, but they fill up fast. If you can't get on it, your best bet is to organize a group of your own and coordinate it through the Edwards Air Force Base public affairs offices. They allow private group tours on Tuesday, Wednesday, Thursday, and Friday, except for those Fridays when they are running the public tour.

If all else fails, the two gates into Edwards have fascinating displays of static aircraft. For more on this, see the Flight Test Museum listing in this section.

Website: http://www.edwards.af.mil/Tours/
Street address/GPS address: 1 South Rosamond Blvd., Edwards AFB, CA 93524

The World War II–era Liberty ship the SS Jeremiah O'Brien *makes San Francisco's Pier 45 a terrific weekend destination. Not only is she in perfect condition, in 1994 they sailed her back to Normandy for the fiftieth anniversary of D-Day. Next to her is berthed the submarine USS* Pampanito. *Photo courtesy of WikiCommons*

The 10 Best Military Experiences: National Liberty Ship Memorial, Pier 45, San Francisco, California

SS Jeremiah O'Brien

USS Pampanito

Nowhere Else: Feel the engines come to life as you sail on a real World War II Liberty Ship. Squeeze through the 27-foot-wide hull on a World War II electric-diesel submarine.

SS Jermiah O'Brien. To transport war matériel to Europe and the Pacific, some 2,700 Liberty ships were built during World War II. Some of them were sunk, others were battle damaged, but many were simply scrapped after the war for the steel in their hulls. Today, three Liberty ships remain, but none as good as this one. The SS *Jeremiah O'Brien* is a big, lumbering, 440-foot ship, "as ugly as they come," quipped President Franklin D. Roosevelt back in the day. But what a hero. The *Jeremiah O'Brien* was one of the 6,939 ships that made up the D-Day armada for the invasion of France. She survived that bloody day and her restoration has been top-notch, so much so that in 1994 they cast off her lines and slipped her under the Golden Gate Bridge and sailed her all the way back to France for the fiftieth-anniversary D-Day celebrations. She is now docked year-round at Pier 45 in San Francisco.

This is a tremendous opportunity to walk on an icon of World War II and explore her decks and compartments. Buy a ticket and take a self-guided tour, or go on one of her regularly scheduled bay cruises and feel those engines vibrate under your feet. Docents will tell you her history and how Liberty ships served in both theaters of war (extra docents are available Wednesday through Saturday).

Hours: Daily: 9 a.m. to 4 p.m.
Website: https://www.ssjeremiahobrien.org/
Street address/GPS address: Pershing Pier 45, Fisherman's Wharf, San Francisco, CA 94133

USS Pampanito. Moored just feet away from the *Jeremiah O'Brien* is the USS *Pampanito*, a Balao-class submarine. Although by today's standards her 27-foot-wide hull is small, she fought like a heavyweight in the Pacific. She poured torpedoes into the side of Japanese ships, took hits from depth charges, and went to Pearl Harbor for repairs only to go back and fight again. In total she sank six ships and damaged four others.

The *Pampanito* has been restored to her actual 1945 colors and fittings, and there are audio segments for you to listen to as you tour the ship. Tours run daily. Or sleep on a sub! She hosts overnights, too.

Hours: Daily: 9 a.m. to 5 p.m.
Website: https://maritime.org/hours.htm
Street address/GPS address: Pershing Pier 45, Fisherman's Wharf, San Francisco, CA 94133

The 10 Best Military Experiences: California Overland Desert Excursions, Borrego Springs, California

The Anza-Borrego is a barren desert plain that butts up against the Santa Rosa Mountains and extends out to the Sonoran Desert. It's hot and dry and dusty and as inhospitable as it gets—which made it the perfect place to train soldiers for desert warfare. Amateur historians say this area was used to prepare for Operation Torch, the November 1942 invasion of North Africa, and they're right. Tanks maneuvered out here as did army and marine corps companies 1000-men strong. Large concentric circles still can be seen on the desert floor, targets that were used by World War II navy pilots to practice air-to-ground strafing and bombing.

California Overland Desert Expeditions will take you out to the training areas in an army surplus M35A2 "deuce and a half." You'll feel the grit of dust and sand in your teeth and might see a shard of metal or a fragment of a shell on the ground from back in the day. Either way, a bumpy ride in an army truck is half the fun, and this excellent organization does it right. Check temperatures for appropriate clothing.

Website: www.californiaoverland.com
Street address/GPS address: 1233 Palm Canyon Dr., Borrego Springs, CA 92004

The Flying Leathernecks Aviation Museum, MCAS Miramar, California (San Diego)

Naval Air Station Miramar, once home to the navy's Top Gun air combat school (now relocated to NAS Fallon, Nevada), is now called MCAS Miramar, as in *Marine Corps* Air Base Miramar. Located inside the gates of the air station (but with its own entry, so you don't need base access) is the Flying Leatherneck Aviation Museum. This is a small museum with big ambitions (be sure to donate to their building fund), but don't let that put you off. Start inside the temporary building and see the exhibit on the Navajo Code Talkers, as well as the overall story of Marine Corps aviation.

Dedicated to the history of the air arm of the US Marine Corps, the Flying Leathernecks sport a very impressive and a very complete outdoor airpark consisting of 40 USMC warbirds, helicopters, and modern jets. Among them—the venerable F-4U Corsair of World War II and Korea fame, the frontline F/A-18 Hornet, plus Avengers, Intruders, Harriers, Skyhawks, Hueys, Crusaders—you name it—all displayed in their Marine Corps markings and well maintained.

For now, this is largely an outdoor museum so be sure to arrive on Open Cockpit Days. There's nothing like sitting in a cockpit of a jet to feel what it was like to be a Marine Corps aviator.

Hours: Tues–Sun: 9 a.m. to 3:30 p.m., Mon: closed
Website: www.flyingleathernecks.org
Street address/GPS address: 4203 Anderson Ave., San Diego, CA 92145

March Field Air Museum, Riverside, California

We learned about this gem from our fighter pilot friends, and we're glad we did. Located on a distant corner of March Air Reserve Base, the March Field Air Museum has an outstanding outdoor display of aircraft that includes more than 70 bombers and fighters. Remarkable for its breadth of aircraft, the map you receive as you enter claims that you can see 100 years of military aviation here, and we'd have to agree. The bombers alone cover 80 years, starting with a beautiful B-17 and a B-29, and continuing up through today's B-52s and FB-111s.

The main hangar has a red-and-white checkerboard roof, so it's easy to spot. Inside it you'll find various exhibits and artifacts on our conflicts plus the history of March Field, including the first Predator drone to be sent to a museum after serving active duty. And be sure to walk around the half-acre re-creation of a Vietnam forward-operations base complete with helicopters and sandbags. It's now the fiftieth anniversary of so many events from our Vietnam War years.

Interestingly, because of how the planes are arrayed, you immediately see how airplanes have grown in size. Next to a 265,000 pound, 159-foot-long B-52, the B-17 Flying Fortress seems more like a Flying Cottage. Ditto for a fragile-looking 2,000-pound World War I biplane just a few dozen feet from a 19-ton F-15 Eagle.

Hours: Tues–Sun: 10 a.m. to 5 p.m., Sun: closed
Website: www.marchfield.org
Street address/GPS address: 22550 Van Buren Blvd., March Air Reserve Base, CA 92518

While You're in the Neighborhood

Point Mugu Missile Park, Port Hueneme, California

Mysterious light trails streaking the night skies of Los Angeles were common enough in the 1950s, 1960s, and 1970s, but explanations were rarely forthcoming. Just 50 miles north of Los Angeles is the navy's number one base for the development and testing of missiles, and off-course missiles and mysterious lights go hand in glove with flight testing. Naval Air Warfare Center Point Mugu runs the US Navy's Pacific Test Range.

Leaving mysterious lights aside, just outside the gates to Point Magu is your destination—the Point Mugu Missile Park. Here, a porcupine-like patch of concrete bristles with the many missiles and rockets used by the Navy, including air-to-air missiles, surface-to-air missiles, surface-to-surface missiles, and even knockoffs of the German V-1s. There is a Regulus Missile, a pioneering sea-to-surface missile that was launched by submarines, the AIM Sidewinder carried by fighter jets, the submarine-launched Polaris ICBM, the radar-guided Phoenix air-to-air missile, the HARM anti-radar missiles—and so much more.

The missile park is a little-known gem about 90 minutes from the mid-Wilshire area of Los Angeles. In addition to missiles you will find a handsome F-14 Tomcat and two beautiful F-4 Phantom fighter jets, one of which is painted in the hi-viz colors of a target drone.

Hours: Open 24 hours
Website: www.air-and-space.com/Pt%20Mugu%20Missile%20Park.htm
Street address/GPS address: 10A Naval Air Rd., Port Hueneme, CA 93041

This Polaris missile is one of the dozens of missiles you'll see at the Point Mugu Missile Park north of Los Angeles. Photo courtesy of WikiCommons

US Naval Museum of Armament and Technology, China Lake, California

Naval Air Weapons Station China Lake is, in fact, the land-based counterpart to the Pacific test range at Point Mugu. Like Point Mugu, China Lake is responsible for developing, testing, adapting, improving, and training sailors in the use of air-delivered weapons. That means rockets, guided missiles, free-fall bombs, nuclear weapons and all the related fuses, sensors, and guidance technologies associated with them.

The US Naval Museum of Armament and Technology is here to tell that 75-year story and does so with dioramas and artifacts that include dozens of inert missiles and rockets on their weapons carts. What they developed here comes down to a lot of clever nicknames that mean nothing to the average civilians but to a lot of Vietnam veterans or Naval aviators, these were their tools. It was here that they developed or adapted the Zuni rocket, millions of which have been used in combat, the Snakeye retarded bomb, the Walleye guided glide bomb, and the Phoenix, Tomahawk, Harpoon, Maverick, and Aim-9 Sidewinder missiles.

The Armament Museum is located inside the gates of China Lake, so you have to bring identification and clear a basic security check to get in. When you do, you'll be greeted by an A-6 Intruder, an F-18 Hornet, and a Polaris missile standing tall. Once past those impressive gate guardians, you enter the modernistic museum itself and begin to explore and learn. Perhaps a bit heavy on military terminology and abbreviations, you'll be immersed in a story about adapting and pioneering technologies to support the combat mission of the US Navy. Around you, inert shapes seem to be everywhere with placards, exhibits, and tableaus explaining the unique attributes of each. In addition to the missiles, rockets, and free-fall bombs mentioned before, there are antisubmarine weapons on display, FLIR and night-targeting sensors with explanations on their use, and numerous cutaways explaining propulsion and explosive technologies.

There's a small gift shop for souvenirs of your visit. China Lake was established in 1943. Call ahead for current ID requirements.

Hours: Mon–Sat: 10 a.m. to 4 p.m., Sun: closed
Website: www.chinalakemuseum.org
Street address/GPS address: 1 Pearl Harbor Way, China Lake, CA 93556

Mare Island Shoreline Heritage Preserve, Vallejo, California

This old military ammunitions depot affords you some of the best views anywhere of the East Bay Hills. Take the Mare Island Causeway to Nimitz Way. Park and take the walking path up to the top. On the way you'll see some curious ruins, including the old navy cemetery, the abandoned groundskeeper's cottage, and other artifacts.

As you head back to Vallejo, be sure to notice LSC-102 moored on the waterfront. Landing Support Craft were agile, fast-moving gunships designed to come in close and provide firepower in support of a beach landing. LCS-102 fought in the Battle of Okinawa. Tours are offered.

Across the Napa River is the small but attractive Vallejo Naval and Historical Museum, which you can easily combine to make a good day of it

Hours: Park: Fri–Sun: 10 a.m. to sunset. LCS-102 Tours: Tues, Thurs, Sat: 9:30 a.m. to 3:30 p.m.
Website: www.mareislandpreserve.org
Street address/GPS address: 1595 Railroad Ave., Mare Island, Vallejo, CA 94592

General George Patton Memorial Museum, Chiriaco Summit, California

This is a small museum honoring US Army general George Patton and his leadership in building the first national desert warfare training center (it encompassed 18,000 square miles of California, Arizona, and Nevada, including the scruffy patch of desert you'll be standing on). At present, the main feature here is the tank park. They have an M4 Sherman tank, an M48 Patton and an M60 Patton tank, a M26 Pershing tank, a DUKW duck amphibious landing craft, and other vehicles.

If you're a Patton fan, this is where his ascendancy began. Patton was the founder and the first commanding general of the Desert Training Center, where more than one million men trained. Patton then went on to command soldiers in North Africa before moving to the European theater for the drive to Berlin.

The museum is small but has big ambitions, so check their website for the latest new exhibits or new armor in their tank park.

Hours: Daily: 9:30 a.m. to 4:30 p.m.
Website: www.generalpattonmuseum.com
Street address/GPS address: 62510 Chiriaco Rd., Chiriaco Summit, CA 92201

Colorado

Known for Cheyenne Mountain and NORAD, the national airspace control center, Colorado has a military history that spans generations and includes the most secret and most important air-defense site in North America.

Peterson Air & Space Museum, Colorado Springs, Colorado

The mountains are breathtaking, a weekend at the famous Broadmoor Hotel tempting—but so too is the Peterson Air & Space Museum. This beautifully landscaped 8-acre site is brimming with history and thousands of military artifacts from our various air defense and military space commands.

First the grounds. Many destinations will welcome you with spectacular architecture and soaring facades. Here, landscaping is what sets this museum apart. The organizers created an all-new airpark in a series of half-circles that surround a Medal of Honor Park, all of which is tastefully landscaped and beautifully designed. You enter the airpark through the old Colorado Springs Airport passenger terminal (beautifully restored), which is the main entranceway to the museum. Inside you'll see exhibits about the old airport period plus ones on the the World War II years at Peterson Air Force Base (hence the museum's name).

When you exit out the back, you're in the airpark. Walk clockwise around the circle and explore the airplanes (and some missiles) on each of the main "pads." Your eye can't help but be drawn to the beautiful EC-121 airborne early warning radar aircraft directly opposite the main building. Depending on when you were born, you might recognize the

In this aerial view, an EC-121 Warning Star airplane is seen facing the aerial interceptors it would launch if the Soviets mounted a surprise attack on our country. Photo courtesy of Peterson Air & Space Museum

airframe. In civilian life this was known as the Super C Constellation or, simply, the Connie.

There are jets and planes everywhere and more in the Old City Hangar, which is one of the hangars that braces the circular path. Here you will see exhibits on air defense, US Air Force space and missile operations, and Colorado's role in NORAD—our North American Aerospace Defense command. Here you'll also find an exhibit on the Cheyenne Mountain Operations Center, an example of an early fighter-interceptor, and a training simulator for Air Force ICBM launch crews. Note that several Canadian aircraft are here, too. NORAD is a joint US-Canada endeavor.

Most of all, walk, think, and reflect. These grounds are as beautiful as in any military destination in America.

Hours: Tues–Sat: 9 a.m. to 4 p.m.; closed Sun, Mon, and federal holidays
Website: www.petemuseum.org
Street address/GPS address: 150 E. Ent Ave., Colorado Springs, CO 80914

A B-52 Cold War bomber in the reflective white undercarriage. The white paint was designed to reflect back the heat from a nuclear bomb's blast. Photo courtesy of Wings Over the Rockies Museum

Wings Over the Rockies Air & Space Museum, Denver, Colorado

This medium-size museum is located just outside of Denver, which means you'll visit a terrific military site while enjoying the clean, crisp air of Colorado.

Largely a local museum dedicated to the role of Coloradoans in the military, Wings Over the Rockies nonetheless has an excellent selection of important aircraft, including the always popular F-14 Tomcat, the rare and rocketlike F-104 Starfighter, a B-52, which guards the entrance, and a B-1B Lancer.

The museum started in a hangar from the old Lowry Air Force Base and has since grown to more than 50 aircraft and hundreds of artifacts and displays. Dioramas are used extensively, and there are temporary exhibits to explore (check their website for the current ones). Be sure to see the four-seat EA-6B Prowler, an airborne controller used by the Navy, and the F-104 Starfighter. The latter is one of the few F-104s that saw combat (over Vietnam with the Thai Air Force).

One note: This museum can get crowded at times—they have the always popular hyper-realistic MaxFlight simulator, which allows you to choose which aircraft you're flying while you dogfight an adversary, and the Extreme Simulator, a two-person setup that allows you to dogfight against a friend in real time. Plan your time and watch for lines. Parking is plentiful.

Hours: Mon–Sat: 10 a.m. to 5 p.m., Sun: 12 to 5 p.m.
Website: www.wingsmuseum.org
Street address/GPS address: 7711 E. Academy Blvd., Denver, CO 80230

Connecticut

When we think of Connecticut we think of Yale and the dignified, well-educated graduates in their stately mansions in Greenwich. Or perhaps the Minutemen soldiers who cried out the alarms during our early years. But think again. What California is to aviation, Connecticut is to the supersecret, stealthy world of undersea warfare. Here we find one of our nation's most important submarine bases with two great destinations to explore.

The Submarine Force Library and Museum, Groton, Connecticut

There's nothing quite like the sight of a submarine silently moving up a river. The hull is an ominous black, the water mysteriously ripples in its wake, it moves serpent-like, half above the water, and half below. See it when you're not thinking, and you'll do a double take—and that's part of the fun of visiting the Submarine Force Museum in Groton, Connecticut. Located adjacent to Naval Submarine Base New London, the Sub Force Museum explores and documents the history of our nation's silent service. Inside the main building, you'll find displays and videos that show how submarines evolved from the tiny cramped vessels of old to today's almost spacious Los Angeles-, Ohio-, and Seawolf-class subs. There are three operating periscopes to try plus two mockups of a real submarine attack center, one depicting a World War II–era submarine, the other a more recent Sturgeon-class submarine.

The Nautilus *is tied off in front of the Naval Submarine Force Museum, which is located next to the Naval Submarine Base New London.* Nautilus *is one of just a handful of submarines open to the public. Photo courtesy of Department of Defense*

The centerpiece here is the USS *Nautilus*. As our nation's first nuclear-powered submarine, the *Nautilus* ushered in an era when a submarine could traverse enormous stretches of the ocean, pass under the polar ice cap, and slip through the oceans with unheard-of stealth. Moreover, *Nautilus* was nuclear deterrence perfected. Nuclear subs such as *Nautilus* were eventually fitted with SLBMs, meaning that from the depths they could launch a crippling retaliatory strike that would all but decapitate the Soviet Union. Using their stealth to hide from the Soviets, they made the thought of a first strike against the US almost unthinkable. *Nautilus* was the first step toward that capability.

Start inside the museum and walk through the main hall. Be sure to see the wall with the scale models of our submarines, the attack centers, and the weapons our submarines carried, including deck guns, mines, and torpedoes. There is also a 50-foot scale model of the World War II–era Gato-class submarine. The cutaway lets you visualize the interior spaces on one of the workhorses of that war.

Next, take the tour of *Nautilus* and her interior compartments. You will receive an audio wand to explain things as you walk through her torpedo room, the wardroom, the Attack Center, the Control Room, and the crew's mess. Next, visit the other submarines here, including the Japanese World War II mini-subs and our own X-1 Navy mini-sub, which proved to be inadequate in the role of harbor defense.

Note the adjacent Naval Submarine Base New London. More than 9,500 sailors and support people are based here. They have 11 submarine piers and some 15 nuclear submarines home ported here, plus all of the support facilities that go with that.[4] And as you drive along the Thames, watch for one coming or going. There's nothing like it.

Hours: Wed–Mon: 9 a.m. to 5 p.m., Tues: closed
Website: www.ussnautilus.org
Street address/GPS address: 1 Crystal Lake Rd., Groton, CT 06340

Delaware

One look at a map and you'll remember that Delaware is a coastal state with frontage on both the Atlantic Ocean and the Delaware River, which feeds into Philadelphia. This makes it an ideal place to erect coastal defenses, as well as a jumping-off point for cargo and soldiers headed to Europe. Our destinations here reflect those two strategic considerations.

Air Mobility Command Museum, Dover, Delaware

When we airlift relief supplies to earthquake victims or hurricane-ravaged islands, Air Mobility Command provides the cargo planes. Equally, when the president sends soldiers to Iraq or Afghanistan, Air Mobility Command gets the call. These stories, and the aircraft they use, are told at the Air Mobility Command Museum in Dover, Delaware.

Start your visit by exploring the enormous outdoor airpark. Here you'll find no less than 30 types of cargo planes and air refuelers, including the largest-in-the-nation C-5 Galaxy cargo plane, the older C-141 Starlifter cargo plane, the C-97 Stratotanker aerial-refueling tanker, and the once hush-hush

The only place in the world where you can see a C-5A Galaxy is at the Air Mobility Command Museum in Delaware. The command's initials are painted on the cargo plane's tail. Photo courtesy of Department of Defense

C-133 Cargomaster (it was specifically designed to load an ICBM and move it to a secret silo without revealing anything to the Soviets). Also on the ramp are a KC-135 Stratotanker, a C-54 Skymaster, a C-124 Globemaster, and (even) a B-17 Flying Fortress.

   If walking among these giants hasn't exhausted you, go inside the main hangar for the beautifully presented dioramas and tableaus with stories and histories, one of which is the history of the Berlin Airlift, that 24/7 round-robin air-cargo delivery service that supplied the citizens of Berlin with food and coal during the Soviet blockade. Also on display are histories of airlifts during the Korean War and in Vietnam, plus other exhibits on meritorious pilots and aircrews.

   An otherwise quiet museum lacking the immersive display found elsewhere, the Air Mobility Command Museum nonetheless makes good use of its planes. On open cockpit days you are welcome to walk through cargo holds or visit the cockpits of some of the airlifters. What makes it extra interesting is the period cargo they have tied down in the back. You might see a 1950s fire truck or a pallet of M-1 rifles.

By far, the star of the show is the C-5 Galaxy. With a wingspan of 223 feet and a length of 247 feet, one plane alone is almost as long and as wide as a football field. It can airlift tanks and helicopters—or hundreds of soldiers—and fly them almost anywhere in the world. The C-5 is the largest plane flown by the US military, and this museum has the only one on display anywhere in the world.

One final note: Before you leave, be sure to go up into the control tower to listen to live radio chatter between air traffic controllers and pilots. This is the old tower, so you'll also be transported back in time while you enjoy the tremendous view of the display ramp.

Hours: Tues–Sun: 9 a.m. to 4 p.m., Mon: closed
Website: www.amcmuseum.org
Street address/GPS address: 1301 Heritage Rd., Dover AFB, DE 19902

The Best Formerly Secret Military Sites: Abandoned Fire Control Towers, Rehoboth Beach, Delaware/Delaware Seashore State Park, Delaware/Cape Henlopen, Delaware

World War II on Main Street USA is perhaps best remembered for bond drives, scrap metal collections, Victory Gardens, and the much-hated rationing cards for food, gas, and even shoes. But there were also very real fears back then, most of them centering on the prospect of yet another surprise attack by either the Japanese or the Germans. Remember the blackout curtains that were mandatory on the eastern seaboard? That's part of it.

To guard against a second Pearl Harbor unpleasant eventuality, our nation built a chain of coastal fire control towers that were linked to inland gun batteries that would swing into action if a hostile ship appeared on the horizon. Manned by volunteers in long coats wearing World War I–era tin-pan helmets, these coastal lookouts would feed coordinates to the batteries who would open fire on any German submarine or ship approaching our shores.

Abandoned World War II fire control towers and gun batteries dot the beaches on the East Coast. Here we see Fire Control Tower 23 in New Jersey. Photo courtesy of WikiCommons

There were once scores of these fire control towers—and hundreds of guns—but only a few remain today. Here's the best of what's left, concrete-and-steel artifacts of World War II, impervious to the ravages of weather and storms, stark reminders of another era, still standing where they were built to protect us from a German invasion.

A pair of fire control towers (#5 and #6) still stand tall side by side, still staring silently out to sea. Often photographed together, #5 and #6 are along DE 1 at Whiskey Beach just north of Rehoboth. Next drive to the Delaware Seashore State Park and see Tower #3. Preservation efforts have been under way to restore it and open a museum. Tower #7 is in Cape Henlopen State Park in Dewey, Delaware, and has been restored so you can get to the top and see the view out to sea just as the lookouts saw it in the 1940s.[5]

Built in 1943, all of these towers were part of the defensive perimeter around Delaware Bay tied back to the big guns at Fort Miles, Delaware (worth a visit, too, and soon to be reopened as the Museum of Coastal Artillery).

Street address/GPS address: Tower #3: Delaware Seashore State Park, 39415 Inlet Rd., Rehoboth Beach, DE 19971

Towers #5 and #6: Whiskey Beach, 1306 Coastal Hwy., Dewey Beach, DE 19971

Tower #7: Cape Henlopen State Park, 15099 Cape Henlopen Dr., Lewes, DE 19958

While You're in the Neighborhood

Delaware Aviation Museum, Georgetown, Delaware

The Delaware Aviation Museum operates a fully restored, silver B-25 Mitchell medium bomber called *Panchito*. They offer rides on the air show circuit or when it's at its home base. Flights depart from Coastal Airport inland from Rehoboth Beach. There's a limit of seven persons per flight.

Call: (443) 458-8926 to reserve your seat and flight time

Website: www.delawareaviationmuseum.org

Street address/GPS address: 21781 Aviation Ave., Georgetown, DE 19947

District of Columbia

We sometimes forget that Washington, D.C., was once a vital old port city with naval bases and army forts to protect it from foreign invaders. Reflecting that history, Washington, D.C., today is home to one of our nation's most visited museums, to many of our national war memorials, and, of course, to Arlington National Cemetery. Long story short: You could easily spend a week here exploring, learning, and seeing. We'll help you get around.

Smithsonian National Air & Space Museum, Washington, D.C.

You might not think of the Smithsonian as a top military destination, but that would be a mistake. Yes, the Smithsonian is filled with civilian artifacts, but to forego it would be to forego a chance to stand before history. What gives this venerable institution an edge over all other military destinations is the sheer number of military artifacts on display, and the historical significance of each. Almost without exception, the airplanes and space vehicles here are the exact ones that set a particular record or wrote a particular chapter in our history books. For instance, while many museums have a B-29, the B-29 here is the *Enola Gay*, the exact B-29 that dropped the bomb on Hiroshima. While other museums have scale models of the orange *Bell X-1* that rocketed through the sound barrier, this is the real one. True also for the *Wright Flyer*, the *Apollo 11* capsule, and the X-15. That's the Smithsonian—if it flew, and if it was important, it is here.

The best way to see it all is to select the plane that interests you most, and head for it. For instance, to see Chuck Yeager's *Bell X-1*, go down the hall to your right and look up. It's hanging from the ceiling. So too is the X-15. That's the rocketlike X plane that set the world speed record for an airplane (4,519 mph) and the world altitude record (100,000 feet). Interestingly, this X-15 was flown by Neil Armstrong, among other test pilots. Both planes are easy to find.

Farther down the hall (but still on the main floor) is a Messerschmitt Me 262 Swallow jet fighter, a P80 jet fighter, and a navy FH-1 Phantom jet fighter. The Me 262 jet was introduced by the Nazis toward the end of World War II and easily flew rings around our own P-51s and P-47s, but they arrived too

The Udvar-Hazy Annex helps accommodate the overflow of military and space vehicles from the Smithsonian's main museum building on the Mall. Photo courtesy of Department of Defense

late to do much good and few saw combat. Our first jet, the P-80, also arrived late, and it was never flown during the war. The FH-1 Phantom, on the other hand, was the first jet to take off and land on an aircraft carrier. Together, these three aircraft represent the dawn of the jet age and each is a "first" for military flight—the first German jet, the first American jet, and the first jet to take off from an aircraft carrier. That's the Smithsonian.

Actually, the Smithsonian is two museums in one. So many objects have come their way that they ran out of room on the Mall and opened the Stephen F. Udvar-Hazy Center at Dulles Airport to hold the overflow. The Udvar-Hazy Center has two enormous hangars filled with military aircraft. The P-38 Lightning on display was flown once by Richard Bong himself, America's number one ace in World War II, and the Focke-Wulf Fw-190 was flown by the German Luftwaffe in combat against our bombers. There is a beautifully restored B-26 Marauder medium bomber named *Flak-Bait*. This plane flew more missions over Europe than any other American aircraft.

Other notables here? Our favorite X-plane is the N-1M flying wing, which was designed by Jack Northrop and is the aeronautical predecessor to today's

B-2 stealth bomber. There is an F-100 Super Sabre, the first fighter jet to attain supersonic speed in level flight and the exact one that flew combat patrols during the Cuban Missile Crisis, and an F-4 Phantom, the exact one that set the low altitude speed record (902 mph at 125 feet). And by all means be sure to see the exceedingly rare World War II–era Northrop P-61 Black Widow twin-engine fighter. You won't find this intimidating aircraft in many other museums, and yet this model shot down more than 100 enemy aircraft.

Beyond the mere importance of the aircraft they own, the richness of these destinations stems from the thousands of hours put in by countless volunteers to painstakingly restore these artifacts to their appropriate period colors and fittings. But if there is any weakness in the Smithsonian's military collection, it is the sheer breadth of it all. There are more than 60,000 artifacts on display, and it can be a bit overwhelming. The focus on objects can understandably leave one wanting to know more, but space and time limit what can be seen.

One final note: Parking around the Mall is limited and D.C. traffic can be terrible, particularly in the summer months. To avoid all that, get up early and start your morning on the Mall and leave for Udvar-Hazy after lunch. You'll have enough time to see everything you want without the frustrations of downtown D.C. traffic.

Hours: Daily: 10 a.m. to 5:30 p.m.
Website: www.airandspace.si.edu
Street address/GPS address: 600 Independence Ave. SW, Washington, DC 20056

Arlington National Cemetery and Memorial, Washington, D.C.

There is perhaps no place as sacred as a cemetery and none more so than Arlington National Cemetery and Memorial. It is here that we honor the sacrifices of our citizen-soldiers and accord our dignitaries their burial. Among the later, you can visit the gravesite of President John F. Kennedy, the memorials for the crews of space shuttles *Challenger* and *Columbia*, the US Marine Corps War Memorial, and the Pentagon Group Burial Marker, honoring the 184 who died in the Pentagon attack on September 11.

Of course, it is the Tomb of the Unknown Soldier that truly sets Arlington apart. American men and women are buried around the globe—perhaps more so than any other country, said JFK during a speech at the Tomb of the Unknowns—but it is here at Arlington that you will find the memorial to the thousands who died and whose names we will never know. This is called "the double sacrifice of the Unknowns." They are the soldiers, sailors, marines, and airmen who lost their lives, but who also lost their identities.

Don't overlook the Welcome Center with its histories, art, and the moving, life-size mannequin of a bugler playing taps. You should download the ANC Explorer app while you're there and use it for your self-guided tour.

Bus tours of Arlington are available through a tour operator accessed through Arlington's website. The tour stops at the Tomb of the Unknown usually in time to witness the very powerful, very solemn Changing of the Guard (hourly during daylight).

Website: www.arlingtoncemetery.mil
Street address/GPS address: 1 Memorial Ave., Fort Myer, VA 22211

The National Museum of the US Navy, Washington, D.C.

Did you know that our sailors come out on deck and man the rails as their ship passes the *Arizona* Memorial? Traditions. History. Respect for the past. These things are part of what makes the Navy tick, and they are reflected in the breadth and comprehensiveness of the exhibits on display at the National Museum of the US Navy. This is the only Navy museum that tells the entire story of the US Navy, that is, the history of its surface fleet, the air arm, its special operations, its undersea warfare division—all of it, and all of it under one roof. There are guns, airplanes, model ships, uniforms, weapons, and countless artifacts displayed in a hands-on environment. The exhibits cover all of the Navy's wars, starting with the Revolutionary War and ending with the present war on terror.

Start with Willard Park and take a look at the cannons and guns there. What makes this unusual is that most of these guns were captured from our enemies. The Civil War–era 100 pounders were taken from the CSS *Atlanta* by the USS *Monitor*. There is also one of the eight railroad guns built for our army during World War I. Next, go inside the main hall where you'll find a German

"Enigma" machine, equipment from Richard Byrd's polar expeditions, videos on the World War II convoys and the landings on D-Day, a simulated submarine combat center, and an extensive collection of photographs and paintings.

The museum is located in the Washington Navy Yard, which is the Navy's oldest shore establishment (1799). The classic architecture dates from the late 1800s.

Hours: Daily: 10 a.m. to 2 p.m.
GPS Address: Research Rd., Homestead, FL 33034
Website: www.history.navy.mil/nmusn
Street address/GPS address: 736 Sicard Street SE, Washington, DC 20374

Florida

Florida is a vital coastal state and the first line of defense against a foreign invasion that originates offshore. Little wonder that it is dotted with military bases, many of which had fighter pilots in interceptor jets sitting in their cockpits 24/7 on "strip alert" (particularly during the Cuban Missile Crisis). Tensions have abated over the years but the bases are still here, as are military destinations that make this more than just a sun-and-fun trip to the Sunshine State.

National Naval Aviation Museum, Pensacola, Florida

An F-14 soaring skyward tells you've arrived at the National Naval Aviation Museum at NAS Pensacola. In a nutshell, this is the history of naval aviation in all its afterburning glory, beginning with those first tentative pilots pioneering flight on aircraft carriers all the way up to rocket boosters blasting Navy astronauts into space. Thirty-seven acres and 350,000 square feet of exhibit space display more than 150 aircraft and thousands of artifacts. There is a Coast Guard exhibit, a *Marine One* display (the president's helicopter), a Korean War display, a Vietnam POW exhibit, cockpits to sit in, atomic bombs to be amazed by (and yes, the Navy carried A-bombs, too), cutaways to view, aircraft carrier exhibits, and on and on. Plus those airplanes—150 of them, including a formation of Blue Angels in the lobby-atrium. To spend less than a full day here would be a mistake.

An F-14 Tomcat stands vigil outside the National Museum of Naval Aviation. In addition to a spectacular collection, the Blue Angels practice here, and the museum has outdoor seating so you can watch. Photo courtesy of Department of Defense

Some notes. Starting at the main entrance, spend some time with the dozen or so scale models of our aircraft carriers. Through these large models (complete with planes on their decks) you can see in an instant the history and evolution of naval aircraft carrier design and operations. This prepares you for the aircraft and technologies in the two main wings, and in Hangar One. Walk inside and browse the numerous exhibits, each organized by specific topics (i.e., carrier operations, how arresting cables work, etc.) and conflicts There are top-notch flight simulators here and a fascinating cutaway of a PBY Catalina flying boat. Other things to see—there's a PB2Y Coronado patrol/bomber, cockpits of the F/A-18s flown by the Blue Angels, an SBD Dauntless dive bomber, and dozens of other pre-war and World War II–era planes.

Hangar Bay One is next, and it's filled with Vietnam-era and Cold War–era aircraft. Look for the F-4 Phantom, an A-6 Intruder, a P2-V Neptune, and the *Marine One* helicopter, an exhibit on naval aviation in the Persian Gulf, and much, much more. Of interest—many of the modern jets were "delivered" to the museum by a specific pilot who landed it here and taxied it up to the museum. Read the placards you see in front of each aircraft.

If you can arrange your schedule just so, try to visit the museum on Tuesday or Wednesday morning (the actual days may vary). That sound you'll hear will be the afterburners of the Blue Angels as the run through a 55-minute practice of their performance. There are 1,000 seats outside for those who want to watch (NAS Pensacola is home to the Blues; the pilots will later come over to sign autographs).

If you miss the run-through, go see the 4-D Blue Angels Experience in Hangar Bay One. If not, try the flight simulators and "take off" from a carrier deck or fly in formations like the Blue Angels do. Of course, there is the Giant Screen Theater, which usually has three movies rotating throughout the day (it seats 325 people). The Cubi Bar Café serves food and drinks in an authentic officers club setting from the Philippines, and the museum gift shop is stocked with one-of-a-kinds. And if you see it here, buy it here; you won't find these things in your local big-box store.

Hours: Daily: 9 a.m. to 5 p.m.; closed Thanksgiving, Christmas Eve, Christmas Day, New Year's Day
Website: www.navalaviationmuseum.org
Street address/GPS address: 1750 Radford Blvd., NAS Pensacola, FL 32508

The National Navy UDT-SEAL Museum, Ft. Pierce, Florida

During World War II, the Navy built a 20,000-acre amphibious training base at nearby Fort Pierce Inlet where thousands of frogmen and combat demolition specialists trained. Among their missions was to clear the beaches on D-Day. When the war ended, the training base was closed but lest the story of what it accomplished be forgotten, a small group of former SEALS and UDT men got together and started this special place.

Today, The National Navy UDT-SEAL Museum is all about the US Navy's special forces and the incredible missions they've been given dating back to the first World War II frogman. If you remember the movie *Captain Phillips*, you'll remember that terrorists boarded the cargo ship *Maersk Ala-*

The lifeboat from the Maersk Alabama *depicted in the movie* Captain Phillips *and from which SEAL snipers rescued a sailor held hostage by Somalian pirates. Such artifacts help museums bring history vividly to life. Seen at the UDT-SEAL Museum. Photo courtesy of National UDT-SEAL Museum*

bama and took the captain hostage in one of the ship's lifeboats. The Navy SEALs extracted him using high-power rifles. That lifeboat is right here. What else? You'll find a wall of sniper rifles and other special weapons used by the SEALs, including combat knives, plus Vietnam-era machine guns, a ready-for-combat Blackhawk helicopter with doors open for you, and mannequins rogered up with NVGs. There is a Fast Attack Vehicle on display from Iraq, a PBR patrol boat from Vietnam, an underwater Seal Delivery Vehicle (SDV), and a scale model of the Bin Laden compound.

The point is, everything here was actually used in planning, in combat, or on a mission—and there are no replicas. Even those Hedgehogs and other underwater obstacles used in 1944 to train the UDT specialists for D-Day. Not only are they real, but they can be found in the grassy area behind the museum. Walk among them and let your mind go back to *that* fateful day.

The museum is located on Hutchinson Island just across the causeway from Fort Pierce. To make sure you don't miss it, there is a rakish Seawolf combat helicopter on a pedestal out front plus a spaceship command module (used to train divers to recover our astronauts in the ocean) and a statue of a special forces operator with a gun in one hand and a fallen comrade over his shoulder.

Driving directions are on the website and they are sure to make you smile. Leave it to our SEALs to give you all the information you need to get there— even if you *parachute* in!

Hours: Tues–Sat: 10 a.m. to 4 p.m., Sun: 12 to 4 p.m., Mon: closed
Website: www.navysealmuseum.org
Street address/GPS address: 3300 N. Highway A1A, Fort Pierce, FL 34949

The Best Formerly Secret Military Sites: Nike Site HM-69, Homestead-Miami, Florida (South Florida Natural Resources Center in Everglades National Park)

Said to be one of the best-preserved Nike sites in the Southeast, HM-69 is open to the public although it's a bit of a drive and ranger-guided tours are required but are readily available. What we like about this is that the site remains as it was at the height of the Cuban Missile Crisis, including an inert Nike Hercules missile on a portable launcher. It lacks some of the spit and polish of the Sausalito site, but you won't regret the visit.

Website: https://www.nps.gov/ever/learn/historyculture/hm69.htm
Hours: Daily: 10 a.m. to 2 p.m.
GPS Address: Research Rd., Homestead, FL 33034

The Best Formerly Secret Military Sites: Battery 234, Gulf Islands National Seashore, Fort Pickens, Florida

You may not remember it, but the Gulf of Mexico and the Caribbean Sea were once plied by German ships and submarines. That's why Fort Pickens and Battery 234 are of interest. The fort's two 6-inch guns were each capable of firing a 105-pound armor-piercing shell 15 miles. The guns are in perfect condition and easy to find; the entire area is maintained by the National Park Service and makes for a day of discovery in the panhandle of Florida.

Be sure to leave some time for a tour of Fort Pickens (1834–1947). Pickens was one of many forts built to protect Pensacola and is now a national park. There are rangers here to give you a tour and you'll find a visitor center and a small museum. Self-guided tour maps can be downloaded from the website.

Website: https://www.nps.gov/guis/learn/historyculture/upload/032516_ Fort-PickensSelfGuiding.pdf
Street address/GPS address: 1801 Gulf Breeze Pkwy., Gulf Breeze, FL 32563

The Best Military Base Tours: MacDill Air Force Base, Tampa, Florida

MacDill Air Force Base is a busy, important air base. It's home to Central Command, which controls our forces in the Middle East (CENTCOM), and Special Operations Command (which directs all of our special forces), and it's a major USAF air-refueling base to boot. To explain all this to you, MacDill runs a well-organized tour on the first and third Friday of the month. Stops typically include the air traffic control tower, the security forces' working dogs area, the explosive ordnance disposal units (EOD), and the flight line where you will see a tanker and perhaps meet the pilots or a boom operator. The exact itineraries change according to the duty requirements of that day, but the tour is always fascinating. Contact the base Public Affairs Office. At least 25 people must sign up (and no more than 40) or they won't run.

Contact: 6th Air Mobility Wing Tours: (813) 828-3460
Street address/GPS address: 3108 N. Boundary Blvd., Tampa, FL 33621

Air Force Armament Museum, Eglin Air Force Base, Florida

This little-known destination is packed with all sorts of Gatling guns, bombs, rockets, and missiles that were carried by USAF aircraft. The gigantic MOAB bomb—the Mother of All Bombs—is here, too. It was recently dropped on a rabbit warren of ISIS underground tunnels in Afghanistan and blasted a hole in the ground the size of a city block. Want to see a GBU laser-guided bomb like the ones that flew through the windows of Saddam Hussein's command centers? How about a radar-guided, advanced medium-range air-to-air AMRAAM launch-and-leave missile like the ones carried by our forces today? Go no farther.

Inside the main building are exhibits organized by major conflicts. The Vietnam War area, for instance, has the Sparrow missile and the M61 20mm Vulcan cannon front and center (among many others). There is a Korean War area, one for the Gulf War, an Air Power exhibit, which is essentially a World War II exhibit, a Gun Vault with dozens of guns, a Missiles & Bombs display, and one on the AC-130 Spectre gunship and its Gatling gun.

The outdoor airpark is a gem. An SR-71 greets you as you drive up and around it are 29 military aircraft, including a B-52, the AC-130, a relatively rare B-47 bomber, an F-111, an A-10 Warthog, an F-15C Eagle (with the next-door-neighbor's Eglin Air Force Base tail flash), and an F-16, to name a few.

No base access is required. Plan on two hours to see it all.

Hours: Mon–Sat: 9:30 a.m. to 4:30 p.m., Sun: closed
Website: www.afarmamentmuseum.com
Street address/GPS address: 100 Museum Dr., Eglin Air Force Base, FL 32542

Camp Blanding Museum and Memorial Park, Starke, Florida

In general, we exclude war memorials from this list, but the Camp Blanding Memorial Park is far too wonderful to ignore. Back in the day, hundreds of thousands of soldiers trained here for World War II. Blanding was a beehive of activity, and the grounds were so vast that it wasn't merely a base—it was called a military *reservation*.

Today, those years are remembered with acres and acres of beautiful, well-manicured grounds on which are displayed a World War II M4 Sherman tank, an M3 Half Track, towed and self-propelled artillery pieces, jets (an A-7 Corsair and an A-6 Intruder among them), a Kiowa helicopter and a Huey Medevac chopper, a C-47 with the invasion strips of D-Day, and other tracked and wheeled vehicles, including 1940s trucks and ambulances as well as vehicles captured in Iraq.

The museum is inside one of the camp's restored buildings and has several well-crafted tableaus and displays, many of which show what life was like in a typical army camp in the 1940s. The centerpiece is a refurbished World War II–era barracks complete with dioramas depicting the sort of training a soldier went through before deployment, and so much more. There is an extensive collection of guns including enemy guns, scale models of tanks and Armored Personnel Carriers, and period photography, to name just some of the things you'll see.

Local, yes, but the stories here are timeless and they apply to any soldier who trained anywhere in the US. Well worth a side trip. There is a small gift shop in the main building.

Hours: Daily: 12 to 4 p.m.
Website: www.campblanding-museum.org
Street address/GPS address: 5629 SR16W., Starke, FL 32091

The 10 Best Military Experiences: Stallion 51, Kissimmee, Florida

The FAA says you have to sit back with your hands in your lap unless the pilot up front is an FAA Certified Flight Instructor (CFI). If your pilot has those extra qualifications, happy day for you. Under strict guidance, you can actually grab the controls and fly the plane. That's the essence of Stallion 51. Well known on the air show circuit, this highly qualified group of warbirders maintains two P-51 Mustangs and a T-6 Texan, all with full-cockpit second seats and dual flight controls. You will meet with an experienced, professional pilot, and, because he or she holds that extra certification, you will be able to take the stick and experience the thrill of flying one of the greatest warbirds of World War II.

Two P-51s are available, both two-seaters with full cockpits in the back (other dual-cockpit P-51s cram you into half cockpits), and both with the unmistakable sound of a Merlin engine up front. You will be thoroughly briefed on the dos and don'ts and learn basic flight procedures as well as emergency procedures. This will essentially be a flying lesson but this is no Cessna-152! There is also a T-6 Texan with dual flight control for a somewhat tamer experience.

Hours: Mon–Fri: 8 a.m. to 5 p.m., Sat, Sun: closed
Website: www.stallion51.com
Street address/GPS address: 3951 Merlin Dr., Kissimmee, FL 34741

Georgia

Several of our favorite destinations are located in Georgia—and all within an hour or two of each other. Start at the National Infantry Museum at Fort Benning, Georgia, for an immersive experience called the Last 100 Yards. Then drive across town to the incredibly well-done National Civil War Naval Museum (the lighting on the building is spectacular at night!). After that, get back in your car and head toward Macon, Georgia, and Robins Air Force Base, where you'll find a sprawling museum with some of the most detailed dioramas and panoramas on our list.

Finally, if Great Britain is your cup of tea (as it was for the tens of thousands of airmen who were stationed in England), try the National Museum of the Mighty Eighth Air Force outside of Savannah, Georgia. This is where those "damn Yankees!" who flew our B-17s and P-51s are remembered.

Finally, for the adventurous, there's also a lost nuclear bomb somewhere in Wassaw Sound, which is between Savannah and Tybee Island. Rent a boat and try your luck.

National Infantry Museum, Columbus, Georgia

A stately (and perhaps staid) exterior masks one of the most alive, vibrant, and interesting military destinations in America. Using beautifully designed and utterly realistic dioramas, the curators of this superb museum have re-created some of the most famous battle scenes in American history complete with the sights, sounds, *and confusion* of war. These life-size exhibits are called the Last 100 Yards, and they take you directly into the chaos of battles that include Yorktown, Antietam, Soissons, Normandy, Corregidor, Korea's Soam-Ni, Vietnam's Landing LZ X-Ray, and the Persian Gulf. Look closely as you walk through them. Artifacts large and small have been carefully arranged to convey the battlescapes, and the detail is absolutely

The role of our foot soldiers is celebrated at the National Infantry Museum, a handsome destination in Georgia. Photo courtesy of National Infantry Museum

exquisite. You'll walk through a hole blasted in a wall in a French village near Soissons as the battle rages around you to take the town back from the Germans. Later, you'll be with our soldiers as they face the cliffs on D-Day, or you'll find yourself in Korea charging a pillbox with bayonets out during Millett's bloody Bayonet Attack. That's the Last 100 Yards—it puts you in the middle of it with foliage, rocks, damaged terrain, special lighting, and background audio to convey urgency and drama, good, bad, or ugly.

Look at the tension in the faces of the soldiers advancing with the TOW missile in the Sole Superpower Gallery. Those expressions of angst, resignation, and pain you see in the faces of the men in the Vietnam POW display are real. To achieve the intensity and degree of realism they wanted, the museum cast these mannequins using live soldiers. In addition to the Last 100 Yards, there are *10* more themed galleries, all done with this same attention to detail. That's how you bring history to life.

One of the unexpected treats here is just outside the museum. A World War II army camp was saved from demolition and reassembled here on what is called World War II Company Street. Walk down the row of barracks.

Soldiers claw their way to the top during D-Day. From the Last 100 Yards at the National Infantry Museum. Notice the detail and the lighting. Photo courtesy of National Infantry Museum; John Helms, photographer

Go inside and see the wood desks and period furniture in the orderly room, and the narrow bunks in the barracks. Close your eyes and imagine tens of thousands of soldiers priming for combat and ready to take on Hitler or even it up with Japan. It takes little effort to imagine the past in a setup as authentic as this.

This newly opened $100 million masterpiece of a museum is located just outside the gates of Fort Benning, which is home to 120,000 soldiers, civilians and their families, the US Army Armor School, and the US Army Infantry School. That makes Benning one of our nation's most important Army bases and the museum plays an instructional role so don't be surprised if you find yourself standing next to a soldier from the base—they're brought here to learn the history of the infantry, and the realism helps get it across. Crowds do form so plan on an early arrival. There's plenty to do here, and a day will go by quickly. A giant-screen theater has a schedule of movies that play all day (some in 3-D), and there is a down-home restaurant where the food is plentiful and you can get off your feet.

Hours: Tues–Sat: 9 a.m. to 5 p.m., Sun: 11 a.m. to 5 p.m., Mon: closed
Website: www.nationalinfantrymuseum.org
Street address/GPS address: 1775 Legacy Way, Columbus, GA 31903

Museum of Aviation, Robins Air Force Base, Georgia (near Macon, Georgia)

Unexpected. Thorough. Overwhelmingly complete. Visitors who discover Robins Air Force Base and the adjacent Museum of Aviation scratch their heads and wonder how something this good could have been here so long without them knowing about it. Well, they're not alone.

The Museum of Aviation consists of four large hangars with indoor and outdoor displays spread across 51 acres with more than 85 airplanes, cockpits, missiles,and helicopters. It was one of the first museums to incorporate dioramas in its exhibits, and over the years they've only gotten better at it. Some examples: The museum's F-15 Eagle is positioned in front of a "hangar" as if it's on the ramp moments before taxiing out to the runway. (A plexiglass panel lets you see inside its instrument bay.) The C-47 is painted with D-Day invasion stripes and seen over a landscape of European countryside. The post–World War II B-29 is

The top-notch Museum of Aviation spreads across 51 acres and has more than 80 military aircraft on display. Photo courtesy of Department of Defense

displayed next to a rare Mark 6 atomic bomb. Then there is the most immersive exhibit of them all, the all-new Vietnam hangar. Set against the landscape of Southeast Asia are no less than 16 Vietnam War–era airplanes, including an 0-2 Skymaster, an OV-10 Bronco, and the ever-so-sexy F-100 Super Sabre. As they say, this place is complete.

Start at the front desk and pick up a guide so you don't get lost (admission is free). To see everything this fabulous place has to offer, you'll need to work your way through "paths" that can feel like a maze. The scale model of Claire Chennault's command headquarters in the China Burma India Gallery is along a route with shoulder-high "walls" painted in various shades of red that weave and wind through stories and histories. The P-40 Warhawk is surrounded by a large-scale poster, small tableaus, dioramas, and mannequins. It's easy to get turned around. So, grab a guide, start in the Eagle Building, and explore both floors, and then go over to Hangar One for the Southeast Asia exhibit and on to the Century of Flight Hangar for the SR-71 and the beautifully painted US Air Force Thunderbirds display with their iconic F-16A Fighting Falcon front and center.

This top-notch destination sports an important collection of aircraft and artifacts that in turn has attracted the crowds, making it one of the most visited military museums in America. Part of that has to do with the one-of-a-kinds they display, and part of that has to do with the *depth* of aircraft they show. For example, there are 16 aircraft in the Southeast Asia exhibit and 18 fighters in the grouping of fighter planes in the fighter display. They have two variants of the iconic P-51 Mustang, plus the F-86, the F-104, the F-105, and everything in between, ending with today's frontline F-16s and F-15s. Among the one-of-a-kinds—and very much related to today's headlines—is an MRAP, a Mine Resistant Ambush Protected vehicle. The one you see here was hit by IED in Afghanistan and nearly destroyed. But the vehicle worked as advertised: The airmen inside not only survived but were cleared for duty the next day. By the way, the SR-71 they have on display is the one that set the world speed record for an airplane. It was clocked at 2,193 mph.

As when you are visiting any museum this size, be sure to wear comfortable shoes. If you need a break go over to Jet Fuel Java for a coffee or a sandwich, or browse the well-stocked gift shop for something unique to take home. As a rule, what you see in a museum gift shop like this won't be found anywhere else. If you like it, buy it.

Hours: Daily: 9 a.m. to 5 p.m.
Website: www.museumofaviation.org
Street address/GPS address: 1942 Heritage Blvd., Warner Robins, GA 31098

National Civil War Naval Museum, Columbus, Georgia

A curator might be offended if we compared the detail and completeness of some of the dioramas here to that of Madame Tussauds Wax Museum, but we say that as a compliment. The realism here is incredible. The depiction of the port of Plymouth, North Carolina, will take you back in time until, with no effort on your part, you're dockside with the CSS *Albemarle*. Add to that the docents in their period uniforms and you have living history done ever so well.

The main attraction here is the USS *Monitor* and how it forever changed the way that warships were built. The Battle of Hampton Roads (March 9, 1862) pitted the ironclad *Monitor* against the Confederate ironclad CSS *Virginia* in the first naval battle between two iron ships. The outcome was a draw—neither could sink the other—but it was the turning point in naval warship design. The armor plating was so effective that ships now had to have it, and the rotating gun turret on the *Monitor* was so useful that it too became de rigor. Out of the battle came a new "monitor" class of ships that would influence ship design forever. From this day forward all Navy ships

The stunningly beautiful entrance to the Civil War Naval Museum in Georgia. Photo courtesy of National Civil War Naval Museum

would have iron hulls and a main gun rotating inside what is called a bar-bette (barbettes are easily visible on battleships).

This handsome museum is solely focused on the navies and the naval bat-tles of the Civil War. Plan to spend some time here. In addition to exceptionally well-done visual displays and panoramas, on display here is the CSS *Jackson*, the only surviving Confederate gunship of the Civil War, plus the wreckage of the CSS *Chattahoochee*, a replica of the USS *Hartford*, and of course the replica of the *Monitor* and the *Albemarle* (with exterior and interior views). Be sure to see the incredible collection of Civil War flags and the complete timeline of war events, all with this unique focus on the battling Civil War *navies*.

Hours: Mon–Sat: 10 a.m. to 4:30 p.m., Sun: 12:30 to 4:30 p.m.
Website: www.portcolumbus.org
Street address/GPS address: 1002 Victory Dr., Columbus, GA 31901

National Museum of the Mighty Eighth Air Force, Pooler, Georgia (Savannah)

The Eighth Air Force is probably the best known of the army air forces of World War II. The Eighth had the B-17s, the Eighth had *Memphis Belle*; the Eighth had Chuck Yeager, the P-51 Mustangs, and the "name" officers of the air war: Jimmy Doolittle, Carl Spaatz, and Curtis LeMay.

The National Museum of the Mighty Eighth Air Force is a repository for the people, histories, and airplanes of the Eighth Air Force. It is beautifully appointed with dioramas and exhibits inside and out, including bombers and fighters up to the Cold War and through the present day (the Eighth didn't stand down after World War II; it is active to this day). Enter through the main rotunda and go inside. There is a Ploesti diorama, a nose section of a B-24, and the visual sensation called the Mission Experience. Step inside and

A bust of the much-loved Jimmy Doolittle stands guard at the entrance to the Mighty Eighth Museum near Savannah, Georgia. Doolittle commanded the Eighth during World War II. Photo courtesy of Department of Defense

be transported back to an air base in England as you watch several short films explaining what it was like to fly a bomber over Nazi Germany.

The planes here are not numerous, but they include a B-17, a Cold War B-47 Stratojet, an F-4C Phantom, and a MiG-17A. But for those who served in the Eighth, this museum has become nothing less than sacred ground. On any given day you can sit in the parking lot and watch a 90-year-old veteran walk in with a box containing his logbook and his old uniform. Some even arrive with a grandson in tow.

The Eighth is a numbered air force of today's Global Strike Command in Barksdale, Louisiana, but it all began here at the Savannah Army Air Base in nearby Savannah, Georgia (later to be a SAC base called Hunter Air Force Base and now called Hunter Army Airfield). Reflecting that legacy, the museum stands just a few miles down the road from the place of its birth.

Hours: Daily: 9 a.m. to 5 p.m.
Website: www.mightyeighth.org
Street address/GPS address: 175 Bourne Ave., Pooler, GA 31322

The 10 Best Military Experiences: Army Aviation Heritage Foundation, Hampton, Georgia (South Atlanta Regional Airport)

There's a feeling of raw, urgent power when you fly in a UH-1 Huey. That big rotor slaps the air with brute force, the *thump! thump!* is overwhelming, and the experience is unlike any other—and this is *the* place to experience it. The private, nonprofit Army Aviation Heritage Foundation has no less than four UH-1 Hueys, four AH-1 Cobras, and one OH-58 Kiowa (plus an O-1 Bird Dog scout plane, if you're so inclined). All of the helicopters are flown by highly experienced pilots, many of them former military. Six of their choppers (3 Hueys and 3 Cobras) are based in Hampton, Georgia. They also have a Huey and an OH-58 Kiowa at their air base in St. Louis, Missouri, and a Cobra in Meza, Arizona.

A Vietnam-era Huey thunders into the air. The Army Aviation Heritage Foundation offers flight experiences in Hueys and Cobra helicopters. Photo courtesy of Army Aviation Heritage Foundation

Here's how it works. When you arrive, you'll meet your pilot, who will walk you around your helicopter and tell you the history of combat helicopters and their mission. You'll be briefed on the helicopter's flight envelope, what your flight will entail, the dos and don'ts of being a passenger, and the various safety protocols. After that, you're up in the air—and what an experience that will be. "Just like in Nam," said one reviewer. "Fantastic!" wrote another.

From the utterly cinematic Hueys (like the ones in *Apocalypse Now*), to the bristling-with-guns Cobra gunships, this is the number one stop for those who want to experience the unique feel of army combat helicopters. Spend an afternoon here and you will see the world like you've never seen it before. More importantly, you will have an unforgettable connection to a generation of pilots who flew these warbirds to defend our freedoms.

Be sure to check their website for an up-to-date listing of helicopters and locations—they are fluid. This group is extremely active and they are growing.

Hours: Tues–Thurs and Sat: 8 a.m. to 5 p.m., Fri: 9 a.m. to 5 p.m., Sun, Mon: closed
Website: www.armyav.org
Street address/GPS address: 506 Speedway Blvd., Hampton, GA 30228

While You're in the Neighborhood

National Armor and Cavalry Museum, Columbus, Georgia

Currently residing as a gallery inside the National Infantry Museum at Fort Benning are the tanks and armored vehicles that will soon be part of the all-new National Armor and Cavalry Museum. Scheduled to open in 2020, the museum does, however, have an impressive outdoor display area with tanks that is available for your inspection. Called Patton's Park, this open-air walking trail takes you past nine major tanks and armored vehicles, including an M4 Sherman tank, an M26 Pershing tank, an M48 Patton tank, an M60 Patton tank, an M1 Abrams tank, an M3 Bradley Fighting Vehicle, an M113 Armored Personal Carrier, an M114 Armored Fighting Vehicle, and an M551 "Light" Sheridan Tank.

Hours: See National Infantry Museum for indoor exhibits; Patton's Park: 24/7
Website: https://www.armorcavalryheritagefoundation.org/
Street address/GPS address: Fort Benning Road at the National Soldiers Center, Columbus, GA 31903

Heritage Park Veterans Museum, McDonough, Georgia

Once again, our military friends alerted us to this destination, and we're glad they did. McDonough's Heritage Park pays tribute to the soldiers of this local county (home to two Medal of Honor recipients) but also to those who served in Vietnam. When you step out of your car, you'll be greeted by silence, which will evolve into a moment of respect and, perhaps, your own tribute to the men and women who fought and served in our military. That is the essence of this soulful destination: Respect for our soldiers. When you arrive you'll see a red barn (which is a small museum) and a UH-1 Huey Medevac chopper out front next to a lone flagpole flying an American flag just above a POW/MIA flag. Privately funded, this place feels like home.

Hours: Wed–Sat: 10 a.m. to 3 p.m., Sun–Tues: closed
Website: www.heritageparkveteransmuseum.com
Street address/GPS address: 99 Lake Dow Rd., Mcdonough, GA 30252

Thermonuclear Bomb (lost) in Wassaw Sound (Savannah, Georgia)

It's makes news every 10 years or so and it's worth a boat ride to see if you might find it, but there is a live, full-sized thermonuclear bomb burrowed into the mud and silt under the waters of Wassaw Sound. No, that's not a typo—the Department of Defense confirmed it under oath before Congress in 1958 (although they dispute the facts today; we hope they're right). If you go out on Wassaw Sound (boat rentals available) look up and imagine a B-47 circling in for a landing with one engine dangling by a thread. They suffered a midair collision and feared they could break apart at any moment when they sighted the runway at Hunter Air Base and decided to attempt an emergency landing. The crew felt it was safer to eject the bomb than to risk it rifling through the fuselage if they crashed, so they ejected it—and it was never found.

Okay, so maybe you won't find the bomb. But while you're here, be sure to drive by Hunter Army Airfield and see the lengthy runway that once landed nuclear bombers. At one time this was a Strategic Air Command bomber base, which is why the crippled B-47 made an emergency landing here.

Hawaii

There are four important destinations in Hawaii, but we have consolidated them into one and listed them under Pearl Harbor as a top pick.

Pearl Harbor

Hawaii is a natural military center of gravity, particularly when you realize that there are *four* important Pearl Harbor sites all within a few miles of one another. Start at the *Arizona* Memorial (the Valor in the National Monument) and then visit the Battleship *Missouri* Memorial, the *Bowfin* Submarine Museum, and the Pacific Aviation Museum. Each destination has a special message, a special meaning—and taken together they *are* the full story of Pearl Harbor.

Sailors on the USS John C. Stennis *render honors as they pass the USS Arizona Memorial. Photo courtesy of the Department of Defense*

World War II Valor in the Pacific National Monument, Pearl Harbor, Hawaii

The story is well known. The surprise attack took place on December 7, 1941. That day, 2,403 died and 18 vessels were sunk or damaged. The *Oklahoma* suffered the second-highest fatality count with 429 dead; the USS *Arizona* sank with 1,177 souls on board. The Valor in the Pacific Memorial is *the* destination at Pearl Harbor and how best to remember that "day which will live in infamy."

The Valor in the Pacific Memorial is managed by the National Park Service. They limit the flow of people out to the *Arizona* through a ticketing process that is complicated but is completely detailed on their web site (see below). You will start your visit at the at the visitor center, where you will absolutely want to view the 23-minute documentary on the attack as well as look at various interactive exhibits on the prelude to war. You may rent headsets in almost any language; the Navy runs the shuttle craft out to the site. Expect to spend 2½ hours here.

Hours: Daily: 7 a.m. to 5 p.m.
Website: www.nps.gov/valr/index.htm
Street address/GPS address: 1 Arizona Memorial Place, Honolulu, HI 96818

Battleship Missouri Memorial, Pearl Harbor, Hawaii

"Today the guns are silent. A great tragedy has ended. A great victory has been won. The skies no longer rain with death—the seas bear only commerce—men everywhere walk upright in the sunlight," said Gen. Douglas MacArthur.

That speech was broadcast to the world from the surrender deck of the battleship USS *Missouri* after the surrender of Japan. It would forever make the *Missouri* one of the most celebrated ships in the navy, but by no means did it end her seafaring career. From World War II she went on to serve in Korea in the 1950s and then in Operation Desert Storm in 1991. She was decommissioned in 1992 and returned to Pearl Harbor in 1999 to be berthed as a museum ship.

The *Missouri* has been restored to her World War II battle colors and her interior spaces have exhibits that show a ship at sea, but don't expect a lot of glitz and flash. Maintaining her period authenticity has been a guiding principle. Audio sets are available for self-guided tours, but there are several optional guided tours. The surrender deck is included in all tours.

Hours: Daily: 8 a.m. to 4 p.m.
Website: www.ussmissouri.org
Street address/GPS address: 63 Cowpens St., Honolulu, HI 96818

USS Bowfin *Submarine Museum & Park, Pearl Harbor, Hawaii*

Launched exactly one year to the day after Pearl Harbor, the *Bowfin* was called "The Pearl Harbor Avenger." She completed nine major combat patrols in the Pacific and is credited with 16 large Japanese vessels sunk plus 22 others. The surrender of Japan occurred as she embarked on her tenth patrol.

The *Bowfin* stands as a tribute to the submarines and submariners lost in service to our nation during World War II. Her exhibits include battle flags, ship's bells, models, an example of a Regulus cruise missile, a Poseidon SLBM missile (which carried multiple 40-kiloton warheads), and one of the infamous manned Japanese suicide torpedoes. You can enter the submarine and tour the museum on your own or elect the optional VIP tour conducted by former submarine commanders ($600 for a group of up to six). You can also buy tickets

that combine the *Bowfin* with the other Pearl Harbor museums. See https://
visitpearlharbor.org/pearl-harbor-tours/.

Hours: Daily: 7 a.m. to 5 p.m.
Website: www.bowfin.org
Street address/GPS address: 11 Arizona Memorial Dr., Honolulu, HI 96818

Pacific Aviation Museum, Pearl Harbor, Hawaii

The final piece of any Pearl Harbor remembrance would be a stop at Ford Field.
Here you will discover the exceptionally well-done Pacific Aviation Museum
and learn the full story of the Japanese air attack not only on the ships but on
Ford Field, too. Start in the old Hangar 37 and see the 12-minute movie on
the attack. Then walk the exhibits starting with an actual Japanese Zero fighter
presented in a diorama depicting the Japanese aircraft carrier *Hiryu* with sur-
rounding audio effects. Hangar 37 has several World War II–era planes. There
is the B-25 Mitchell like the one Doolittle used to strike back against Japan; a
P-40 Warhawk, one of the warhorses of the CBI (China-Burma-India) theater;
a Navy SBD Dauntless dive bomber used against the Japanese fleet; and an F4F
Wildcat fighter, which bridged us over in the early days of the war.

*The Japanese prepare to launch their planes. A diorama seen at the Pacific Aviation
Museum, one of four destinations to include on your Pearl Harbor visit. Photo
courtesy of Department of Defense*

Continue on to Hangar 79 and see the bullet-riddled glass on both ends (yes, those are from the attack). This hangar is literally overflowing with a well-preserved assortment of military aircraft restored to their period colors and markings. Here the museum diverts from the Pearl Harbor story to present the rest of military aviation. Among the planes you'll see are a B-17 bomber, all of the Century-series fighters (the F-100, F-102, F-104, F-105), many of our Korean- and Vietnam-era helicopters (the Kiowa, Choctaw, Cobra, Seahawk, and Sea Knight, among them), plus the modern fighter jets (the F-14, the F-15, and an F-111 Aardvark fighter-bomber of the Gulf War).

Docent-guided tours are available, or you can do a self-guided tour with audio headsets. To round out your visit, try your hand in a flight simulator, stop for a snack in the cafe, or visit the gift shop. Various vendors offer ticket packages that combine this destination with the *Bowfin*, *Missouri*, etc.

Hours: Daily: 8 a.m. to 5 p.m.
Website: www.pacificaviationmuseum.org
Street address/GPS address: Historic Ford Island, 319 Lexington Blvd., Honolulu, HI 96818

All-in-One Tickets

You can visit one or all of these destinations, although each requires a ticket (they are independently operated). However, discounted all-in-one tickets are available through a number of tour operators. We suggest the Pearl Harbor Visitors Bureau website, where numerous combinations of these four destinations can be purchased at significant discounts. They also offer optional intra-island air travel to Oahu, if needed, and air-conditioned buses. See https://visitpearl harbor.org/pearl-harbor-tours/.

Military Ghost Ships. Middle Loch, Pearl Harbor, Hawaii

For variety, try spotting some of our ghost ships. They can be seen resting at anchor in the Middle Loch, including a few marine troop carriers. Get out your GPS and enter "Waipio Point Road" or the "Inactive Fleet Pier." The ghost ships are across the road from the Ted Makalena Golf Course. Eleven ships were there as of this writing.

Military ghost ships can be spotted at anchor in Philadelphia, in San Francisco (Suisun Bay), in Bremerton (Washington), on the James River (Virginia), and at Pearl Harbor. Track them down for a fun weekend of exploring. Photo courtesy of WikiCommons

Illinois

While many of the destinations listed here focus on military aviation or the naval side of the fence, from one end of Illinois to the other, you encounter an exceptional assortment of *army* destinations. Who would have guessed that Illinois would be loaded with tanks, armored personal carriers, rifles, and other artifacts of the infantry? Here are some exceptional opportunities to see artillery, guns, tanks, Vietnam-era patrol boats, and World War II tanks.

First Division Museum at Cantigny Park, Wheaton, Illinois

On May 28, 1918, the US First Division leaped out of their trenches and bravely raced forward behind a rolling barrage of artillery fire into the village of Cantigny, France, and liberated it from the Germans. One of the commanders that day was Chicagoan (and *Chicago Tribune* publisher) Col. Robert McCormick. For the next two days, McCormick's men repulsed German counterattacks and held their position, thus ending America's World War I baptism by fire with a decisive victory. McCormick made sure that victory would not be forgotten.

Upon returning to the US, Colonel McCormick renamed his 500-acre family estate Cantigny Park and endowed a foundation to honor the First Division. Now, decades later, the First Division Museum at Cantigny Park has evolved into one of the finest military destinations in America.

First, the tank park. This is possibly one of the best tank parks in the nation if not one of the most complete. Under a canopy of trees (evocative of the Ardennes) are nested an amazing assortment of beautifully preserved tanks and military vehicles. Among them—the M24 Chaffee tank, an M1 Abrams main battle tank, an M41 Walker Bulldog tank, an M46 Patton tank (in tiger paint!), an M47 Patton, an M48 Patton, an M60 Patton, an M5 Stuart, and an M26 Pershing. In addition there are trucks, jeeps, half-tracks, assault vehicles (an M551 Sheridan), and artillery pieces. This is a see-and-touch park, so don't hesitate to climb into the seat of a howitzer or scramble onto a tank as our soldiers did.

Next comes the museum itself. Newly reopened after a multimillion dollar face-lift, the museum fills a magnificent yet understated building with beautifully detailed exhibits that entertain, inform, instruct, and challenge you to think about our nation's wars. These in-depth, sensory experiences transport you back in time to the trenches of World War I or out to the front lines of today's war on terror. The designers made extensive use of the latest technologies to provide immersive interactive exhibits with touch screens, special lighting, large-scale dioramas filled with mannequins and foliage, and walls that are realistic murals or graphic panoramas. Visually, the displays are at once chilling, realistic, haunting, and beautiful—and yet somber reminders of the nature of war.

An all-new gallery called Duty First is an excellent overview of our post–Vietnam era conflicts and the role the First Division has had in them. Like all of the exhibits, the museum presents a broader perspective of the conflict within which is the story of the First. This holds true for the main gallery, First in War, a 100-year history of the First.

The US Army's First Division was called the Big Red 1, and whether you remember it as Lee Marvin's finest movie or from your military history, it is our nation's oldest continuously active military division, tracing itself back to World War I. No place better serves to preserve its history and artifacts than here in Wheaton, Illinois.

Hours: Check website
Website: www.fdmuseum.org
Street address/GPS address: 1s151 Winfield Rd., Wheaton, IL 60189

Russell Military Museum, Zion, Illinois

If military hardware is your thing, this is your nirvana. Located between Chicago and Milwaukee, the family-run Russell Military Museum is so unusual, so interesting, and so down-home that we had to make it one of our must-sees.

First some background. The Russell Museum actually began as a roadside attraction featuring a collection of the armored vehicles acquired by owner Mark Sonday and his family. Over the years the collection grew in size and popularity, but unexpected condemnation proceedings forced them to move it to a new location (a new interstate highway was coming through). Landing in the small town of Russell, Illinois (hence the name), the new museum reopened in 2007.[6]

A World War II Sherman tank has been repainted and will now be transported to a museum. Photo courtesy of Department of Defense

First of all, don't expect a lot of glitz here. Gone are the fancy dioramas and elaborate video walls of some other destinations. Instead, this is a "feel, touch, and smell" experience, and that's what makes it special. Some 200 tanks, armored personnel carriers, military helicopters, airplanes—and even jets—are crammed in here, giving the place a bit of an "army surplus" feel to it. There are tracked vehicles (including a Sherman tank), "wheeled" vehicles (like Humvees and jeeps), plus various military guns, howitzers, and other weapons, but none of it sits behind ropes. You're encouraged to touch the planes and vehicles and even get in the Huey.

In the back of the museum there is something akin to an aircraft bone-yard, albeit without the mothballing. You'll see an eclectic mix of helicopters (including a Huey, a Cobra, and a Soviet Hind), jet fighters (no less than an F-15 Eagle, an A-7 Corsair, a somewhat-rare F-84 Thunderjet, and many more), boats (including a Higgins boat and a Vietnam PBR), and even missiles (there's an Honest John and a Corporal, both once nuclear tipped). Eras repre-sented in the collection include World War II, Korea, Vietnam, the Gulf War, and the war on terror.

Again, there's nothing quite like this place, which means it's a military destination you have to see. And call ahead if you have a large group. They'll probably offer to order you some pizzas. Someone from the family is usually on premise.

Hours: See website for hours
Website: www.russellmilitarymuseum.com
Street address/GPS address: 43363 N. US Highway 41, Russell, IL 60075

Rock Island Arsenal Museum, Rock Island, Illinois

Although this handsome museum is on an active-duty base and requires identification and a security check to get in, it has a collection of small arms that surely makes it worth your visit. A little history explains it all. During World War II, the little-known Rock Island Arsenal was an enormous manu-facturing facility for the US military. Some 84,945 machine guns were built here, plus 715,000 machine-gun barrels and 5,000,000 metallic belt links to feed machine guns their bullets (replacing cloth ones). In addition, the arse-nal overhauled or modified tens of thousands of rifles, carbines, and pistols and manufactured hundreds of thousands of parts for other weapons systems. At its peak in July 1943, 18,675 people worked here, almost one-third of them Rosie the Riveters.[7]

The museum is located in a handsome limestone building that houses the small-arms collection. Displayed in cases, cabinets, and on the walls are more than 1,200 pistols, rifles, machine guns, swords, and artillery pieces used by the US military, by our special forces, and by the militaries of a half dozen other countries. The rifles and pistols go back to the earliest days of our nation and continue up to and include the guns carried by our soldiers today. Important models include a collection of rifles used in the Battle of Little Bighorn (including an iconic Winchester rifle), a Springfield rifle, a gold-plated M60 machine gun (read why when you get there), plus the iconic M1 Garand carbine (Serial #2) and the Browning submachine gun, both of World War II.

The nearby outdoor Memorial Field is the second part of your visit with 31 large artifacts on display, including an M50 Antitank gun, an M4 Sherman tank (hit by a German shell at the Battle of the Bulge—still visible), an M22 Locust Light Tank, an M65 Atomic Annie, the US Army's nuclear cannon, plus various artillery pieces, rockets, antiaircraft guns, and other large guns.

And yes this is an island—also called Arsenal Island—a 946-acre federal military reservation. It is in the Mississippi River between East Moline, Illinois, and Davenport, Iowa. Check the website for identification requirements and make sure your insurance and tags are up to date.

Hours: Tues–Sat: 12 to 4 p.m.
Website: http://www.arsenalhistoricalsociety.org/museum/index.html
Street address/GPS address: 3500 North Ave., Rock Island, IL 61299. Memorial Field Artillery Park: Rodman Avenue and East Street, Rock Island, IL

While You're in the Neighborhood

The Pritzker Military Museum & Library, Chicago, Illinois

Handsome reading rooms and an extensive collection of books and documents on the role of the citizen-soldier in a democracy is the theme of this downtown

Chicago museum. Check the website for current exhibits, but as of this writing they have a World War II exhibit titled Lest We Forget. The Pritzker is located on Michigan Avenue in Chicago.

Hours: See website for hours
Website: www.pritzkermilitary.org
Street address/GPS address: 104 S. Michigan Ave., Ste. 400, Chicago, IL 60603

Indiana

National Military History Center, Auburn, Indiana

While this is mainly an automotive and motorcycle museum, it has an amazing and ever so tempting assortment of military artifacts ranging from a restored PT boat to some German tracked vehicles from World War II. This unusual combination comes about because two collections are housed under one enormous roof evenly split between the Military History Center and the Automotive & Carriage Museum. Let's focus on the military side of the fence.

The National Military History Center is essentially a collection of World War II and Vietnam artifacts with exhibits and dioramas depicting and explaining combat scenes. One full-size diorama shows a German combat unit manning a World War II–era 88mm antiaircraft gun in accurate World War II uniforms. Another full-size diorama depicts the meeting of the Americans and the Russians on the Elbe. A third full-size diorama uses a real PT boat with a sailor ferociously firing at an inbound Japanese plane.

Explore this impressive destination. You'll find mannequins in various military uniforms, scale models of battlefields, handguns, and machine guns, a Vietnam gun truck (nose art names it *Rolling Thunder*), a landing craft, Patton's command car, and more. Plan on a good two hours here—this is a place where it can be said that there's more here than immediately meets the eye. The center is located off I-69 just north of Fort Wayne, Indiana.

Hours: Mon–Sun: 9 a.m. to 5 p.m.
Website: http://www.nationalmilitaryhistorycenter.org/
Street address/GPS address: 5634 Co Rd. 11A, Auburn, IN 46706

Kansas

It's hard to resist the draw of a museum that focuses on the frontier days of our young nation. Particularly in Kansas with those wide-open spaces that pulled our nation west like metal to a magnet.

Frontier Army Museum, Leavenworth, Kansas

During our nation's frontier years (1817–1917) one traveled across country by covered wagon, the army rode horses, and Fort Leavenworth was a beachon of hope out there on the frontier. Because this was often the end of the road for a traveler, wagons accumulated at the fort and a collection grew, as did a museum. By 1939, the Old Rolling Wheels Museum came into being with one of the nation's most extensive collections of nineteenth-century military artifacts and covered wagons. The Frontier Army Mustum still has that impressive, one-of-a-kind collection for you to see today, but it has much more, hence the new name.

The Frontier Museum tells the story of our westward expansion and uses several dioramas that depict cavalry soldiers, supply wagons, and those old, 12-pound wheeled howitzers. There is an exhibit on the Lewis and Clark

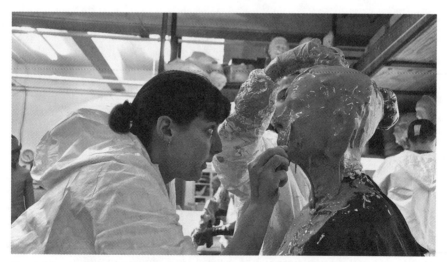

Special latex material is applied to a soldier's face to create a face cast. Face casts are placed on mannequins to impart emotion and realism to a diorama. Photo courtesy of Department of Defense

Expedition and a tableau on Gen. John J. "Blackjack" Pershing's expedition to bring Pancho Villa to justice. Other displays depict a typical wagon train with a line of beautifully restored wagons, and followed by an utterly handsome hallway filled with impressive visual displays, each telling part of the story of a young nation on the move.

This newly remodeled museums offers cellphone audio tours and a small gift shop. The museum is accessed through the Grant Gate. Bring identification.

Hours: Tues–Fri: 9 a.m. to 4 p.m., Sat and Sun: closed
Website: http://www.armyupress.army.mil/Educational-Services/Frontier
-Army-Museum
Street address/GPS address: 100 Reynolds Ave., Fort Leavenworth, KS 66027

Kentucky

Because Fort Knox was once the place where tank crews trained, Fort Knox was the natural place to open a museum on armored vehicles and, by extension, Gen. George Patton. Well, the Armor School has long since moved on (and there are no more tours into the legendary gold vaults), but the museum is still here, although its focus has shifted from armor to leadership.

General George Patton Museum and Center of Leadership, Fort Knox, Kentucky

Harry Hopkins, one of President Franklin D. Roosevelt's advisors, reflected on the victory of World War II. He could understand how American factories had scaled up production to manufacture tens of thousands of airplanes, tanks, and billions of bullets, but he had one question he could not answer. "How did it happen," he asked his biographer, "that the United States, an unwarlike and unprepared country if ever there was one, was suddenly able to produce so large and so brilliant a group of military leaders competent to deal with situations that had never before existed in the world?"

How indeed? What is leadership and how do you identify it, bring it out, nurture it? What lessons can one learn about leadership though the disciplines of an army? To answer those questions, the Patton Center places heavy emphasis on the leadership of General Patton himself (and many of his most notable quotes are emblazoned on the walls), but the museum doesn't stop there. Throughout, a multitude of lessons learned on the battlefield inform that answer. As you walk through the exhibits and digest what you see, you begin to see how military disciplines and the principles of command help define that elusive quality of leadership. Truisms emerge, absolutes are proffered, methods suggested. Best of all, the messages here cross over from the military to the general public and help us understand how they apply to our own lives. Which is exactly the conversation this museum hopes to stimulate.

Open: April 1–December 31
Hours: Tues–Fri: 10 a.m. to 4:30 p.m., Sun, Mon: closed
Website: www.generalpatton.org
Street address/GPS address: 4554 Fayette Ave., Fort Knox, KY 40121

Louisiana

Louisiana is home to a boat builder who relieved the bottleneck in landing craft that caused so much consternation in Washington, to a Global Power air base that began with a few thousand acres of cotton fields, and to a national museum that started with a curious professor and a few oral histories. Does that make you curious? Read on and get ready to travel.

National World War II Museum, New Orleans, Louisiana

They say a good story grabs you by the gut and pulls you forward through space and time. That certainly applies here. From its humble beginnings as a collection of oral histories taken from World War II veterans, through the many years of tireless work by the determined scholar and author Stephen Ambrose, to the National World War II Museum of today, storytelling is of the highest order.

This 6-acre campus in the center of New Orleans consists of five separate buildings, each crammed with artifacts arrayed to communicate a theme, a story, a battle. Every theater of World War II is covered and nothing is left out good or bad, including the voices of those who were vehemently opposed to the war. Dioramas are too numerous to adequately cover. Suffice it to say they

The spectacular campus of the National Museum of World War II in New Orleans. Photo courtesy of National Museum of World War II

are detailed and artistically rendered with theatrical effects added to convey a beachhead, a cliff, a hill, a forest, or a pillbox, including foliage, sounds, and lighting (or lack thereof) to add to the realism.

The Louisiana Memorial Pavilion is a good starting point. Here you'll find an excellent overview of World War II starting with life on the home front and the conversion of our industry to a war footing (the Arsenal of Democracy exhibit), starting with Pearl Harbor, and on to D-Day. Each topic is explained using detailed exhibits, large-scale graphics, and objects big and small. Artifacts include 1940 newspapers and period clothing, and they are all real.

Next visit the Campaigns of Courage Pavilion. The Road to Tokyo: The Pacific Theater Galleries uses large-scale dioramas to stage battle landscapes filled with artifacts, mannequins, foliage, lighting, and audio effects appropriate to the combat depicted. In the main, these are walk-through exhibits presented in chronological order starting with the attack on Pearl Harbor and continuing through Coral Sea, Midway, Guadalcanal and every island fought in the Pacific until the surrender on the USS *Missouri*. There is a large diorama depicting the bridge on the aircraft carrier USS *Enterprise* as it launches its planes, and a jungle landscape on Guadalcanal where you literally walk through foliage,

A battle-torn flag in the Guadalcanal tableau at the World War II Museum. Photo courtesy of National Museum of World War II

sandbags, and mosquito-breeding ponds of stagnant water, a gallery on Tarawa, another gallery on the CBI theater (with a P-40 Warhawk fighter soaring overhead), and a gallery on Iwo Jima and Okinawa. There is a gallery on the Philippines and one on the B-29 bombing campaign against Japan culminating with the A-bomb and the surrender of Japan. Each gallery combines photographs and graphics with interactive storytelling that includes the facts and figures that make history come to life.

Next is the Road to Berlin: The European Theater Galleries. Again, we find numerous galleries, exhibits, tableaus, and dioramas that are every bit as thorough and as immersive as the Pacific galleries. What stands out first and foremost, though, is the red-and-black flag with the swastika in the center. This is Nazi Germany, and the war in Europe is told with big, bold graphics. Once again, as you walk you will progress chronologically through the war, starting with a briefing room somewhere in the Mediterranean emblematic of the planning that took place in the months before the invasion of North Africa, then to the North African campaign itself, followed by the invasion of Sicily, off mainland Italy, the dramatic story of the bloody air war against Germany, followed by the carnage of D-Day itself. From D-Day, the war progresses inland toward

Germany, where we encounter a heartbreaking diorama depicting the frigid cold of the Battle of the Bulge, then across Germany and on to Berlin. Every stop is personalized with soldier stories and personal artifacts. Every gallery is filled with large and small artifacts, maps, photos, foliage, and landscaping that easily transports you back in time.

The Freedom Pavilion is your next stop, and it's another visual feast. The lobby is crisscrossed by the legendary warbirds of World War II in flight—the P-51 Mustang, the B-17 Flying Fortress heavy bomber, the B-24 Liberator heavy bomber, the B-25 Mitchell medium bomber, the F4-U Corsair Navy fighter, and the TBM Avenger torpedo bomber, to name a few. This side of the campus will immerse you in the physical world of sailors, airmen, and soldiers through ships, planes, howitzers, and more.

The Kushner Restoration Pavilion is where restoration projects are almost always under way—and where you press your face to the glass and watch. An ongoing mission of the museum is to grow its collections so be sure to leave time for a stop here. And be sure to watch the movie in the Solomon Theater. This is the one narrated by Tom Hanks. As we said, this destination is storytelling of the highest order. Lines form early so plan ahead.

This is a large museum, so pace yourself. You could easily spend two days here, and many do. For a rest, try the American Sector Restaurant & Bar, or the Jeri Sims Soda Shop. Although this is largely a self-guided destination, there is a Behind the Lines tour, which takes you into the "vault" to see artifacts not on display. It costs $299 per person and lasts five hours.

Hours: Daily: 9 a.m. to 5 p.m.
Website: www.nationalww2museum.org
Street address/GPS address: 945 Magazine St., New Orleans, LA 70130

The 10 Best Military Experiences: PT-305, Lake Pontchartrain, Louisiana

Here you can roar across Lake Pontchartrain in a restored World War II PT boat just like the one JFK commanded in the Pacific. PT-305 was in sorry repair when it was found, and it took years to restore it—but what a restoration. PT-305 is now in perfect condition and is the only operating PT boat in the world, or says the World War II Museum in New Orleans, which led its restoration (it took almost 10 years) and sells tickets to see it. You can take the deck tour—it lasts about 45 minutes and is exhaustive in detail—or you can pay extra for the thrill of a lifetime and do the full 90-minute experience, which puts you on the boat for a hair-on-fire trip on Lake Pontchartrain. Either way you will experience a part of our naval history while you learn the ins and outs of PT boats in World War II.

No more than 17 guests can board at one time and, because she only goes out on Saturdays you have to plan ahead to reserve your spot. The boat house is located in South Shore Harbor off I-10.

Hours: See website
Website: http://www.pt305.org/
Street address/GPS address: 6701 Stars and Stripe Blvd., New Orleans, LA 70126

Barksdale Global Power Museum, Barksdale, Louisiana

In 1991, one of the first combat sorties of Operation Desert Storm started and ended in Louisiana. It's true. Seven B-52s flew nonstop from Barksdale Air Force Base in Louisiana to Iraq, where they launched cruise missiles against key Iraqi targets and returned 35 hours later. If that's not the definition of "global air power," what is?

Second fact. Did you know that Cold War B-52s flying Chrome Dome routes that circled the arctic were often in the air for 20 hours? That, too, is global air power.

With air-refueling tankers and high-technology avionics on our bombers, our Air Force is able to project power to any point on the globe and return home in time for a hot shower and dinner. That's part of the story told through displays and aircraft at the Global Power Museum, located just down the road from Barksdale Air Force Base. This small museum houses a history of the air base, starting with a group of community leaders who responded to a War Department solicitation for a site to build a new airfield to train aviators. Seeing an opportunity for federal funds, they put together 20,000 acres of cotton fields and won the day. The museum tells that story with an abundance of artifacts from those early years, including a rebuilt World War II–era preflight briefing room. The briefing room is filled with period furniture, and they show videos depicting the conflicts supported by Barksdale, World War II to present day.

An FB-111 Aardvark, a B-52, and a KC-135 tanker can be seen in the distance under the nose of a B-24 Liberator. Seen at Barksdale Global Power Museum. Photo courtesy of Department of Defense

While the museum building is small, the outdoor airpark is anything but. Here on display is the heavy metal of air power. You can see and touch World War II–era B-17 and B-24 bombers, a C-47, a B-29, a B-47, two B-52s, an FB-111, a KC-135 aerial tanker, and an SR-71 Blackbird reconnaissance plane. Add in a P-51 and a Mig-21, plus a few historic aircraft, and you have a fabulous afternoon of walking among some of the greatest airplanes of our US Air Force.

Hours: Daily: 9:30 a.m. to 4 p.m.
Website: www.barksdaleglobalpowermuseum.com
Street address/GPS address: 88 Shreveport Rd., Barksdale AFB, LA 71110

While You're in the Neighborhood

USS Orleck Naval Museum, Lake Charles, Louisiana

This World War II–era destroyer never saw combat during the war, but it saw duty during the atomic tests in the Pacific and then served in Korea and Vietnam. A little worn around the edges, this ship is nonetheless a chance to see a true destroyer; to walk her decks, explore unpretentious interior spaces, visit a bridge and get a feel for duty at sea on a destroyer. Inside is a display of scale models of aircraft and ships and a "museum" dedicated to a sister ship, the USS *Radford*.

Hours: Mon–Fri: 10 a.m. to 3 p.m., Sat: 10 a.m. to 4 p.m., Sun: closed
Website: www.orleck.org
Street address/GPS address: 604 N. Enterprise Blvd., Lake Charles, LA 70601

The 10 Best Military Experiences: USS Kidd Veterans Museum, Baton Rouge, Louisiana

Here is an opportunity to board a US Navy World War II–era "tin can" destroyer and see what life was like for sailors on these rugged ships. A battle-weary veteran of the Pacific War, the USS *Kidd* saw action in Tarawa, the Marshall Islands, and Okinawa before she was hit by a kamikaze. After repairs she continued to serve until she was decommissioned and moored here. Restored to her World War II colors and configuration, she opened for tours in 1983. Her guns can still fire and her interior compartments are top-notch.

Hours: Mon–Fri: 9:30 a.m. to 3:30 p.m., Sat, Sun: 10 a.m. to 4 p.m.
Website: http://www.usskidd.com
Street address/GPS address: 305 S. River Rd., Baton Rouge, LA 70802

Maine

The Best Formerly Secret Military Sites: Fort Foster, Kittery Point, Maine

This coastal town in Maine stands at the mouth of Portsmouth Harbor and the shipyards at Portsmouth, Maine (often called Portsmouth, New Hampshire, in a border dispute that to this day is an amusing sidebar to modern geography). Fort Foster was built to protect the harbor and was active between 1901 and 1946. Head out to Fort Foster Park and discover gun emplacements, a fire control tower, *and* a mine observation tower, the later to arm and manage mines (if needed) to block enemy passage into Portsmouth. Now part of Kittery Point's municipal parks system, the gun batteries, the fire control tower, the mine control tower, and the old fort are easy to find and well worth an afternoon exploring.

Hours: Daily: 10 a.m. to 8 p.m.
Website: www.fortfoster.weebly.com
Street address/GPS address: 51 Pocahontas Rd., Kittery Point, ME 03905

Maryland

Forget the crab cakes and the boardwalk taffy. Maryland will keep you busy with military destinations starting with Annapolis, where our newest naval officers are minted, and ending at a flight test center in southern Maryland where tomorrow's naval aircraft are broken in. And don't forget the Civil War. There is a nearly forgotten story told here by an almost-unknown museum in Frederick, Maryland.

US Naval Academy Museum, Annapolis, Maryland

The US Naval Academy is a destination in and of itself. The campus is filled with statuary; there are historic cannons and battle histories told in every nook and cranny. Just being on campus is nearly enough, but there is also a small but handsome museum here, too. The US Naval Academy Museum tells the story of our Navy through the largest collection of model ships in North America as well as one of the largest collections of navy-themed paintings anywhere in the world. If a sense of place, a sense of tradition and history is what you're after, start your Maryland journey here.

Hours: Mon–Sat: 9 a.m. to 5 p.m., Sun: 11 a.m. to 5 p.m.
Website: www.www.usna.edu/Museum/index.php
Street address/GPS address: 118 Maryland Ave., Annapolis, MD 21402

Patuxent River Naval Air Museum, Patuxent River, Maryland

Like its counterpart at Edwards Air Force Base in California, Maryland's Naval Air Station Patuxent River is where

Navy airplanes are flight-tested before they gain entry to the fleet. Are they fully airworthy? Will they survive operations are sea? Those answers entail flight testing, weapons separation testing, and, of course, the violently hard takeoffs and landings from the deck of an aircraft carrier (they have a carrier catapult and land-based carrier arresting gear here). New planes—or any plane that is modified to, let's say, carry a new weapon—are handed over to Patuxent River test pilots, who put them through the paces here until the Navy sees fit to OK them for the fleet.

Located in southern Maryland two hours out of Washington D.C., the Patuxent River Naval Air Museum is a beautiful new facility with a curvaceous roofline and plenty of interior space for a riches of exhibits. Start with the artifacts inside the museum and learn all about flight testing and carrier evaluations. There are cockpits to sit in, simulators to fly, a collection of ejection seats, displays on the rigors of carrier evaluations, and a scale model of the headline-grabbing X-47 Pegasus unmanned jet, plus one of the X-35C concept planes, predecessor to the F-35C Lightning Joint Strike Fighter now at Patuxent River for testing.

The outdoor display area is called the Flight Line, and it has 22 ever-so-familiar naval aircraft, all turned into test aircraft and painted with those distinctive orange wingtips and tails. Well-known planes include the F-4 Phantom, the F-15 Tomcat, and the F/A-18 Hornet, but also on display are an E-2 Hawkeye, an S-3 Viking, an S-2 Tracker, an F9F Cougar, an F-4 Skyray, and an A5 Vigilante, among others

Located just outside the gates of the air station, the Pax River Museum lets you get up close to this special breed of aviator and the history of naval flight testing. Spend some time here. Take a moment to contemplate the audacious idea of compressing a 7,500-foot land-based concrete runway into a carrier deck the size of a postage stamp. Souvenirs are available in the gift shop.

Hours: Tues–Sat: 10 a.m. to 5 p.m., Sun: 12 to 5 p.m., Mon: closed

Website: www.paxmuseum.com

Street address/GPS address: 22156 Three Notch Rd., Lexington Park, MD 20653

While You're in the Neighborhood

National Museum of Civil War Medicine, Frederick, Maryland

This place is disturbing on some levels and deeply moving on others. What was it like to walk onto a battlefield filled with hundreds if not thousands of men who were wounded and dying? Gettysburg? Appomattox? Antietam? How were they cared for? This small but handsome museum is one of three connected sites that tells the fascinating story of medical care in the late 1800s. Start at Antietam to see the Pry House Field Hospital Museum. Union officers were treated here, and there is a scene re-created upstairs depicting Maj. Gen. Israel Richardson's struggle to survive his battlefield injuries. Richardson was visited here by President Lincoln and was well attended by doctors, but he died months later of pneumonia.

Next, visit the Clara Barton Missing Soldiers Office. Well known around the nation for attending to the battlefield injured, after the war ended Barton began receiving letters from families looking for loved ones. Barton rented this boardinghouse and went to work and over the next several years she located thousands of soldiers, thus helping countless families be reunited with their loved ones or, sadly, find the closure they needed. Fully restored, this building tells that story.

Finally, there is the National Museum of Civil War Medicine itself. Here you will see how the Civil War injured were cared for, but brace yourself. There are full-scale tableaus and dioramas depicting doctors and nurses caring for the gravely injured, many of which will cause you to gasp while others are simply heartbreaking. Start on the second floor and work your way down.

Hours: See website
Website: www.civilwarmed.org
Street address/GPS address: 48 E. Patrick St., Frederick, MD 21701

Massachusetts

Massachusetts' great seagoing history and its contributions to our national defense are chronicled at these five destinations.

USS Constitution *Museum,* Charlestown, Massachusetts

Our naval history goes back to 1794, when warships were first authorized by Congress. Foremost among them was the beautiful three-masted frigate named *Constitution*. Named by President George Washington in honor of our constitution (but nicknamed *Old Ironsides* because of the cannon balls that miraculously bounced off her hull during the War of 1812), the *Constitution* has been newly overhauled and recently returned to the water. Walk her decks, feel the polished wood under your feet, and take in the exhibits that are located in her land-side building. Be sure to see All Hands on Deck, a fascinating portrait of a sailor's life circa 1812, and Old Ironsides in War and Peace.

An excellent gift shop is just to the left as you enter the Constitution Museum. Note the architecture of this building. The museum is housed in Charlestown Navy Yard Building 22, the old engine room. Building 22 was designed by Alexander Parris, the same architect who designed Boston's Quincy Market.

Hours: Daily: 10 a.m. to 5 p.m.
Website: www.ussconstitutionmuseum.org
Street address/GPS address: Charlestown Navy Yard, Building 22, Charleston, MA 02129

Battleship Cove America's Fleet Museum, Fall River, Massachusetts

Battleship Cove in Fall River, Massachusetts, is the nation's largest floating exhibit of US Navy warships. There is the battleship USS *Massachusetts* (more on that in a minute), the submarine USS *Lionfish*, the destroyer USS *Joseph P. Kennedy Jr.*, and a Russian corvette, as well as two PT boats. They are all displayed in their period colors with their period fittings, and the interior spaces are as they were when they were at sea.

Start your visit by seeing the nautical exhibits in the land-side Maritime Museum. Here you'll learn the seafaring history of Massachusetts and her contributions to our nation's defense. Be sure to save some time for the undeniably fascinating collection of scale-model ships, the most popular of which is a 28-foot model of the *Titanic*.

Next, board the battleship *Massachusetts*. Walk her weather decks. Then explore her interior compartments. Most of them are fully restored, and many have mannequins to help you visualize crew functions. Be sure to look at the big guns. You can actually go inside the gun deck of Turret #3 or the barbette of Turret #2.[8] (Plus, amazingly you can also go *inside* one of the 5-inch guns.)

After that, take a walk through the submarine *Lionfish*. This is an excellent example of Balao-class World War II–era patrol/attack submarines. One hundred and twenty were built and nine were lost during the war. The *Lionfish* was never modified after the war and is historic for that reason. She is seen exactly as she was built in 1943.

Be sure to see the PT boat area and then the destroyer *Joseph P. Kennedy Jr.* The "Joey P" was built in nearby Quincy and served during the Korean War. She was also part of the flotillas of ships that enforced President Kennedy's blockade of Cuba during the Cuban Missile Crisis. She was decommissioned in 1973.

From the very first, the mission of this vibrant destination was to bring all aspects of military seamanship to life, to let you *touch* the steel of a battleship's armor, *walk* the confined spaces of a submarine, *feel* what it was like to be a sailor of a destroyer. Yes, the bunks are narrow, the wardroom is almost claustrophobic—but that's the way of it. Pause and reflect and let yourself be transported back in time. The museum is located just south of Boston.

Hours: See website
Website: www.battleshipcove.org
Street address/GPS address: 5 Water St., Fall River, MA 02721

The Best Formerly Secret Military Sites: Nahant Fire Control Towers, Nahant, Massachusetts

A pair of fire control towers are located in the beachfront town of Nahant, Massachusetts. These darkly ominous twin towers continue their silent vigil watching the oceans for an invading German force. Now privately owned, they are off Swallow Cave Road.

Website: www.coastdefense.com/nahant.htm

While You're in the Neighborhood

US Naval Shipbuilding Museum, Quincy, Massachusetts

USS Salem. The centerpiece of the US Naval Shipbuilding Museum is the cruiser USS *Salem*. The USS *Salem* is the only US Navy Heavy Cruiser afloat, and for that reason alone it deserves a trip. She is 717 feet long and literally bristles with guns, the largest of which are her 8-inchers. Rough around the edges though she may be, there is nothing else like her. Her configuration is much like a battleship with two gun turrets forward and one aft. Unlike a battleship, she fired a cased projectile, meaning she did not use the shell-and-bag arrangement.

Her interior compartments are filled with artifacts and exhibits, leaving many visitors to recommend a good two hours to see it all. The *Salem* served from 1945 to 1959 and was moved here in 1994.

Hours: Sat, Sun: 10 a.m. to 4 p.m.
Website: www.uss-salem.org
Street address/GPS address: 551 South St., Quincy, MA 02169

Michigan

As we go inland we find neither the coastal defenses nor the naval bases to visit. Rather here we find thematic destinations—forts that explain the frontier days of America, preserved missile silos that recall the Cold War years, or a place with the odd name of Willow Run that speaks to the great Arsenal of Democracy. Read on.

Air Zoo, Portage, Michigan

What's it like to skim the tops of cumulus clouds as you fly across a line of thunderheads? Have you ever seen a B-17 coming in for a landing, the crosswinds buffeting her wings?

From the moment you walk into this celebration of flight, your senses will be pleasantly overwhelmed by the large-scale panoramas and videos that will greet you—things like the 28,800-square-foot hand-painted mural depicting the history of flight, or the 36,000 square feet of art on the floor that let you "walk" across a World War I airfield and then a World War

This is the only surviving example of a SR-71B trainer—and you can find it only at the Air Zoo in Portage, Michigan. Photo courtesy of Air Zoo

II airfield and then the flight deck of an aircraft carrier. How imaginative is that! So back to the original question: What is it like to skim the clouds? Well, it's like the entrance to Michigan's oddly name museum, Air Zoo. To enter the main exhibit halls, you have to weave your way through a tunnel of clouds set against a bright blue sky.

But the joy! Once inside, you'll be surrounded by beautifully painted warbirds, space capsules (including a model of the space shuttle flight deck), and exquisite dioramas staged with mannequins in period uniforms. To make sense of the riches, start in the Main Campus building and walk around this exceptionally beautiful 50-aircraft collection. Here you'll find dozens of restored warbirds, including a lineup of the Grumman "cats"—that is, the World War II FM-2 Wildcat, the World War II F6F Hellcat, and the navy's twin-afterburning F-14 Tomcat fighter jet (plus the lesser-known Grumman G-73 Mallard seaplane). Next, see the dark-as-night SR-71 Blackbird reconnaissance plane, or the lineup of four classic warbirds from Douglas Aircraft, the World War II Douglas SBD Dauntless dive bomber, the nimble Vietnam-era A-4 Skyhawk (affectionately called a "Scooter" by some), the AD-4 Sky Raider (affectionately called the "Spad" by others), and the iconic C-47 Skytrain, also known as the civilian DC-3 transport. Next, go to the East Campus building. There is an F-4 Phantom and an F4-U Corsair and a pair of Soviet MiGs grouped together—a Mig-15 Faggot and a Mig-21 Fishbed.

Finally, stop and consider the National Guadalcanal Memorial Exhibit. The battle for Guadalcanal went on for months and took the blood and sweat of our marines, our soldiers, our airmen, and our sailors. It was a land battle, an air battle, and a sea battle all in an inhospitable environment where poisonous snakes, disease, and starvation took lives that bullets spared. This deeply moving, highly immersive display winds through dioramas, a full-sized bunker, artifacts, and personal stories, which include the stories of 20 brave young men who were awarded Medals of Honor.

This a large, happy place with plenty to do for the kids, including a half dozen amusement park rides and some flight simulators. There is also a 4D theater, the Fly Buy gift shop, the Kitty Hawk Café, and an observation deck. Taken together, it is by far the premier destination in Michigan for the military minded and their families, and one of our favorites.

And the name? Well, when airplanes in your museum are called Bearcats, Tomcats, Hellcats, Tigers, and Cougars, you have, err, a zoo.

Hours: Mon–Sat: 9 a.m. to 5 p.m., Sun: 12 to 5 p.m.
Website: www.airzoo.org
Biplane rides: Available mid-May through Sept Mon—Sat 10 a.m. to 5 p.m., Sun: 12 to 5 p.m.
Street address/GPS address: 6151 Portage Rd., Portage, MI 49002

Selfridge Military Air Museum, Selfridge ANGB, Michigan

This destination focuses largely on Michigan's airmen and women with a fantastic airpark that is national in scope. You begin your visit here by going through the main building back to the airpark, but do notice a few items on the way. There are several display cases containing well-built scale-model replicas of airplanes from the *Wright Flyer* to the present day. Plus, there's an F-15 cockpit and an A-7 cockpit, both open to sit in, and an excellent way to see the basic switchology of a jet fighter.

After seeing the displays, exit the museum for the airpark. You'll pass between a C-130 and the P-3 Orion as you go outside. Take the winding walkway. You'll see modern fighter jets like the F-14 Tomcat, the A-10 Warthog, and the F-16 Fighting Falcon, but also the sexy F-86 Sabre and the sleek F-100 Super Sabre next to a F-101 Voodoo fighter, an F-106 Delta Dart, an F-102, and an F-106. Many of the aircraft here are loaded with the weapons they carried in combat, and that's not seen in many other displays. Some 30 aircraft and helicopters are along the walking path.

Plan on a good hour here and be sure to bring proper identification. The museum is located on an active-duty base.

Hours: Sat, Sun: 12 to 4:30 p.m.
Website: www.selfridgeairmuseum.org
Street address/GPS address: 27333 C St., Bldg. 1011, Selfridge ANG Base, MI 48045

Yankee Air Museum, Belleville, Michigan

There is an interesting story here, and it makes sense to hear it. Belleville, Illinois, was once home to the enormous, 5-million-square-foot Willow Run manufacturing plant. Willow Run was one of those miracles of production of World War II. Willow Run was built from scratch yet produced a B-24 Liberator bomber at the rate of one every *hour*. In total, 40,000 workers worked here—nearly a third of them women—and they built some 8,600 bombers. Part of that old plant will soon become the new and bigger Yankee Air Museum which will then be renamed The National Museum of Aviation & Technology.

But for now, this is a small museum with relatively few displays or exhibits but with a fine collection of warbirds, making it an easy weekend outing just outside of Detroit. Adjacent to the airport at Willow Run, the Yankee Air Museum has a fully restored F-4 Phantom and a Huey helicopter as part of its Vietnam exhibit, a B-24 cockpit and manufacturing display as part of its Rosie the Riveter exhibit, the cockpit of a KC-135 tanker with flight controls you can maneuver, and an O-2 Skymaster. There are a dozen more planes in restoration or soon to be on display, including a B-52, so call ahead.

Warbird rides are available in a variety of aircraft flown by experienced pilots. Aircraft available for flight experiences include the B-17, B-25, C-47, and a Waco biplane.

Hours: Tues–Sat: 10 a.m. to 4 p.m., Sun: 11 a.m. to 4 p.m.
Website: www.yankeeairmuseum.org
Street address/GPS address: 47884 D St., Belleville, MI 48111-1126

K.I. Sawyer Heritage Air Museum, Marquette, Michigan

Located on a former SAC base, the Sawyer airpark has a nice outdoor display of Cold War aircraft that includes a B-52 bomber (this one saw duty in Vietnam), an FB-111 fighter-bomber like the one that flew the Libyan raid, a somewhat-rare F-101 Voodoo air defense interceptor, and others. There is a small museum next door with assorted display cases and plaques, but come here for the outdoor displays or just shop the gift shop with its selection of items with military insignia. Other aircraft—the F-106 Delta Dart (notice the delta wing) and the T-33 Shooting Star on a pedestal. In its day the T-33 was the stepchild of the P-80, which was the first all-jet-powered combat aircraft.

Hours: Wed–Sun: 1 to 5 p.m.
Website: https://www.kishamuseum.org/index.php
Street address/GPS address: 402 Third St., K.I. Sawyer, MI 49841

Minnesota

Like Michigan, our destinations in Minnesota are more general in nature— a combination of regional histories and displays but with artifacts that are national in scope. What makes Minnesota unique, though, are the tanks. Read on.

Minnesota Military Museum, Camp Ripley, Little Falls, Minnesota

A pair of tall columns stands on either side of the entrance to Camp Ripley hinting at the many treats inside. This

Many of our destinations have outdoor tank parks with howitzers, self-propelled guns, and tanks like this. Photo courtesy of Fort Sill

army-oriented museum is focused on the role of Minnesotans in our nation's armed conflicts. There is an impressive collection of tanks, military vehicles, artillery pieces, and helicopters in an outdoor display area that is 100 percent GI Joe. By last count some 60 pieces were exhibited on the grounds, including a formidable line of tanks (Pattons, Shermans, Abrams, and so on), a cluster of Huey helicopters, and howitzers and self-propelled guns, all positioned with informative placards facing you as you walk.

Start your visit in the old barracks area. The museum saved some of Camp Ripley's old barracks and creatively reopened them as a wonderful indoor display area for some of the artifacts in this 80,000-piece collection. There are uniforms, exhibits of jeeps, an exhibit on the Airborne, and others on our nation's conflicts to the present day, plus some one-of-a-kinds, including an impressive collection of German Lugers. The exhibits make extensive use of detailed, realistic dioramas with mannequins. Be sure to see the exhibit called Voices from the Vietnam War.

This is a very hands-on place—kids and adults alike can climb the tanks and walk about the various pieces without a docent frowning at them. And notice the beautifully maintained grounds, the shade trees, and the various memorials. You wind you way through towed and self-propelled howitzers and such tanks as the M4 Sherman as well as statues and memorials on a well-maintained walkway. Utterly perfect.

Camp Ripley Training Center is used by the Minnesota National Guard, so don't be surprised to see a soldier next to you as you walk around. This is an excellent place for them to learn the history of our mechanized forces.

You will have to show a driver's license at the gate.

Hours: See website
Website: www.mnmilitarymuseum.org
Street address/GPS address: 15000 Highway 115, Little Falls, MN 56345

The 10 Best Military Experiences: Drive A Tank, Kasota, Minnesota

An extensive collection of tanks and armored vehicles is available at Drive A Tank, including an M4 Sherman, a British Chieftain main battle tank, and a 58-ton British Mark 5 Centurion with a 105mm gun. Drive or be driven: They have a 1-mile-long wooded course that takes you through a "battlefield" complete with rough terrain, elevations, and a mud pit. For an extra fee they'll put a car in front of your tank and let you crush it. They even let you plow through a small house!

Drive A Tank is open to the public Friday through Sunday (they host corporate events during the week). For those who want to shoot machine guns, they will take you to the indoor gun range. Hotel rooms are available in nearby Mankato, Minnesota.

Hours: Check website for reservation instructions
Website: www.driveatank.com
Street address/GPS address: 550 W. Cherry St., Kasota, MN 56050

Mississippi

Although little known to most, Mississippi was home to one of our nation's largest World War II training bases. Our first stop will take you back in time to an army base filled with young soldiers itching to take on Hitler or avenge Pearl Harbor.

Mississippi Armed Forces Museum, Camp Shelby, Mississippi

At the height of World War II, Camp Shelby was one of our nation's largest army training bases, with 1,800 buildings and bunks for no less than 85,000 soldiers. It was also a major POW camp for German soldiers captured in North Africa and Europe, so its history runs deep.

Today, Camp Shelby's enormous footprint (134,000 acres) allows it to host joint training exercises for combat units from across the nation. Major ground maneuvers are easily accommodated with M1 Abrams tanks and air assets shooting at will.

The Mississippi Armed Forces Museum is both a regional museum honoring Mississippians and a national museum with tableaus that cover all of our major conflicts up to and including the war on terror. The excellent dioramas inside the main building are detailed down to dramatic lighting and staging—World War II soldiers with period handguns, the wounded in Vietnam being carried to Medevac choppers, a realistic fallout shelter as an entrance to a Cold War exhibit, and a World War I bunker, all designed to be walked through.

The outdoor park is on a whole other level and packed with armor. There are rows of tanks, helicopters, and artillery pieces lined up like soldiers at parade rest. Turn one way and there are a dozen tanks, turn another and you see flamethrowers and self-propelled antiaircraft guns or a line of combat helicopters. If it's armor that you want, it's armor that you get. The short list includes an M5 Stuart tank, an M41 Walker Bulldog tank, an M1 Abrams, a rare M2A2 tank, plus an M48 Patton and an M60 Patton, an M42 Sherman flamethrower, an M56 Scorpion, an M26 Pershing—the list goes on and on with even more howitzers and self-propelled guns, and Hueys and Cobras all beautifully maintained.

Plan time here and enjoy the close encounter with the heavy stuff of our army. It's an excellent destination with plenty to see and much to learn.

Hours: Tues–Sat: 9 a.m. to 4 p.m., Sun, Mon: closed
Website: https://www.armedforcesmuseum.us/visit
Street address/GPS address: 1001 Lee Ave. W., Building 850, Hattiesburg, MS 39407

Tank parks and artillery parks include missiles and rockets, too. Seen here: Fort Sill Field Artillery Park. Photo courtesy of WikiCommons

African American Military History Museum, Hattiesburg, Mississippi

Originally a USO club designated for African American soldiers (during a time when the army was segregated), the African American Military History Museum chronicles the role of African Americans in the US military beginning with the Revolutionary War. Little known fact: Some 500 African-American nurses took care of our soldiers during World War II. This handsome building houses beautifully designed exhibits that tell the story of African-American soldiers up to and including present-day conflicts.

Hours: Wed–Fri: 10 a.m. to 4 p.m., Sat: 12 to 4 p.m. (10 a.m. to 12 p.m. appointment only)
Website: www.hattiesburguso.com
Street address/GPS address: 305 E. 6th St., Hattiesburg, MS 39401

Missouri

Two important but hugely different destinations lead you to Missouri. The first is the elegant and deeply moving National World War I Museum in Kansas City. The second is a cluster of museums at Fort Leonard Wood anchored by the Engineers Museum. One is an in-depth look into how a war changed the world, and the others tell us how we continue to prepare for the next one.

National World War I Museum and Liberty Memorial, Kansas City, Missouri

World War I and the memory of the soldiers who fought there are honored here in Kansas City. Anchored by the 217-foot-tall Liberty Memorial Tower and flanked by the Exhibit Hall and the Memory Hall, you enter this incredibly beautiful destination by walking across a glass pedway that arcs over 9,000 red poppies, each representing 1,000 deaths during the war. A powerful start to a powerful museum.

The National World War I Museum is a comprehensive telling of the origins, battles, and consequences of World War I. The exhibits and dioramas are presented chronologically and are both factual and interpretative in nature. There are airplanes, guns, bombs, mortars, bayonets, and uniforms, all of which are presented with stories and histories, both the good and the bad.

Start in the Main Gallery and see the life-size "trenches" emblematic of the trench warfare of World War I. This large exhibit features six trenches filled with personal artifacts and suffused with the sounds of war, thus dramatically transporting you back in time to experience the horrible conditions our soldiers lived and died under. Next stop in front of a diorama that appears to be an ordinary war scene. You will soon realize that it's depicting the carnage inflicted when a howitzer shell veered off course and destroyed a French farmhouse. The "crater" is filled with a poignant reminder that "collateral damage" is a euphemism for killing innocent men, women, and children.

Walk around and explore. Above you is a World War I biplane, next to you is a French tank with a hole in its side after being taken out by a German tank. Use the many touch screens to explore the battles of World War I and the personalities of the war. Walk the lengthy Chronology Wall and try to piece it together in your own mind. And be sure to leave time to see the film *No Man's Land*, which screens in the Horizon Theater.

Overall, this is a powerful place. Plan on being humbled, educated, and changed by this experience. Plan, too, on coming away filled with pride. Current exhibits include a reminder of how appreciative the French were when we

The Liberty Memorial soars 217 feet above the National World War I Museum in Kansas City, Missouri. The two sphinxes at the base of the tower shield their eyes, one from the unknowns of the future, the other from the horror of battlefields past. Photo courtesy of National World War I Museum and Liberty Memorial

arrived. Our boys landed in the middle of France's darkest hour, and France effusively showed its thanks. But it was the US who was returning the favor. "Lafayette, we are here," said US army colonel Charles E. Stanton at the tomb of Lafayette. This destination tells you the rest of that story.

Hours: Regular hours: Tues–Sun: 10 a.m. to 5 p.m., Mon: closed. Summer hours (Memorial Day–Labor Day): Sun–Fri: 10 a.m. to 5 p.m., Sat: 9 a.m. to 5 p.m.
Website: www.theworldwar.org
Street address/GPS address: 2 Memorial Dr., Kansas City, MO 64108

John B. Mahaffey Museum Complex, Fort Leonard Wood, Missouri

- **US Army Engineer Museum**
- **US Army Military Police Museum**
- **US Army Chemical Corps Museum**
- **Military Vehicle Park**

Fort Leonard Wood hosts three commands that are essential to the functioning of the army—the US Army Military Police, the US Army engineering battalions, and the Chemical Corps. Museums on these three branches are found in one building, the handsome redbrick Mahaffey Museum Complex on Fort Leonard Wood.

Start your day with the Army Engineer Museum and explore the numerous exhibits that show their handiwork and explain their role in support of our frontline soldiers. Often confused with the Corps of Engineers (which they are not), the army engineers are combat-trained soldiers who build barracks, erect pontoon bridges, clear land mines, and even build defensive revetments. Dioramas with mannequins show them building bridges, riding combat bulldozers, and erecting other structures.

The Chemical Corps Museum is your next destination. Maps, photographs, and dioramas depict the chilling effects of chemical weapons on World War I soldiers, and how the army learned to defend against them. There is an extensive collection of gas mask and chemical suits and a Doomsday Truck that was designed, presumably, to protect the last surviving humans against anything toxic left in the air after a major biochemical attack.

Last stop is the Military Police Museum, with surprising facts and info—for instance, we all know that MPs directed traffic and picked up soldiers who'd had one too many, but did you know they also controlled Checkpoint Charlie in Berlin during the Cold War (there is a section of the Berlin Wall here for you to see), directed traffic over the battle-damaged World War II bridge at Remagen, and escorted celebrities who traveled overseas to entertain our soldiers?

A key part of any visit here is the large and excellent outdoor display of tanks and armored vehicles, complete with combat bulldozers and—you guessed it—MP vehicles. The Military Vehicle Park is anchored by six fully restored World War II–era barracks themed to show a soldier's life during our nation's conflicts. The Vehicle Park has an armored bulldozer, an armored steam shovel, several self-propelled and towed artillery pieces, tracked vehicles for combat engineers, multiple rocket launchers, a Vietnam-era RPB river boat (with an "MP" on the side), a Huey, and more. Each piece has been fully restored to its period colors and markings and is in tip-top condition.

All of the three museums use well-built dioramas and tableaus to tell their stories of these specialized commands. Be sure to visit the three gift shops in the main building.

Hours: Mon–Fri: 8 a.m. to 4 p.m., Sat: 10 a.m. to 4 p.m., Sun: closed
Website: www.wood.army.mil/museum
Street address/GPS address: 495 S. Dakota Ave., Fort Leonard Wood, MO 65473

Montana

The story of air defense is the focus of Montana's superb destination—but not in the expected way. Rather than jets, the Big Sky state will make you remember the early days of computers.

Malmstrom Air Force Base Museum and Air Park, Great Falls, Montana

Hands down, this is one of the nicest airparks in the nation. The lawns are beautifully manicured, the aircraft are nicely painted and well maintained, and the museum has all sorts of one-of-a-kinds in it. Let's break it down.

Malmstrom Air Force Base has a storied history that includes a major role in our Cold War network of air-defense assets. In the 1950s, it was a key hub in a sophisticated radar network that linked computer centers to combat jets that were sent up to shoot down an invading Soviet bomber. The base changed missions a few times and evolved into an air-refueling base and then changed hats again and became a missile base. Today Malmstrom is an active ICBM missile base. But let's not get ahead of ourselves.

As tempting as the outdoor airpark is, you should start your visit in the small museum itself because there's something here that you won't find anywhere else. It's a computer. The US Air Force was one of the first wide-scale users of computers, and SAGE was its name. SAGE[9] was actually a network of computer centers that processed signals from hundreds of air defense radar stations and stitched them together to paint a picture of the air environment. This picture was fed into radar scopes that displayed information to controllers who used it to direct our pilots to an enemy bomber. Sounds pretty ordinary today, but it had never been done before until SAGE came along.

Be that as it may, SAGE was actually a four-story *building*, the most interesting parts of which are on display here—the magnetic hard drives, the vacuum tubes, the display console with the radar scopes (they were manned by airmen affectionately called "scope dopes"), and more. The museum has launch control panels, a radar controller's station, and an astonishingly complete wall of aircraft models touted as one of the largest collections in the nation. But SAGE surely marks the dawn of the computer age and that alone makes this an important stop for the tech minded.

Next, walk the 8-acre outdoor airpark and enjoy the crisp, clean Montana air. Take the path in and among the various objects, including an F-100 Voodoo fighter jet, a UH-1 Huey helicopter, a KC-97 air refueler, a B-25 Mitchell bomber, and a Minuteman III ICBM, as well as several other fighters and interceptors that were used during the early years of the Cold War. Nicely, there are also period military cars and trucks mixed in to add texture and human interest.

Located on an active air force base, access is nonetheless fairly easy. Stop at the visitor center and show your driver's license and you'll be given a pass and directed to walk over to the museum.

Hours: Mon–Fri: 10:00 a.m. to 4 p.m., Sun, Mon: closed
Website: www.malmstrom.af.mil
Street address/GPS address: 90 Whitehall Dr., Great Falls, MT 59402

Nebraska

Nebraska football is a perennial favorite, but it's the Cold War that brings us here. General Curtis LeMay, the cigar-chomping commander in chief of Strategic Air Command, loved Omaha, Nebraska—so much so that he made it headquarters for the largest and deadliest bomber fleet the world has ever seen.

Strategic Air Command and Aerospace Museum, Ashland, Nebraska

Coming out of the death and destruction of World War II, no one wanted a World War III—and certainly not with atomic bombs. To that end, a concept called MAD —Mutually Assured Destruction—evolved. The United States and the Soviets intentionally maintained international striking forces so vast and so dispersed that one could never knock out the other, thus assuring that anyone trying a surprise attack would be thoroughly annihilated by the response. Strategic Air Command was the heart and soul of America's half of MAD.

At its Cold War peak, Strategic Air Command had more than 2,000 nuclear bombers (B-47s and B-52s), fighters, and missiles. Add to that the Navy's submarine-launched SLBMs and you have what was called the nuclear triad. The Soviets might knock out one leg or the other, but never all three. In a nutshell, that's the story told at the Strategic Air Command Museum— and how grandly they do it. A soaring facade of glass and steel greets you,

An Atlas missile, left, and a Thor bracket the entryway to the Strategic Air Command Museum in Omaha, Nebraska. Photo courtesy of Strategic Air Command and Aerospace Museum

around which are the tools of SAC—a B-1A supersonic bomber, a Thor ICBM, and an Atlas ICBM. Go in the main entrance and walk along the interior displays. Among the permanent exhibits is an outstanding study of the Martin Bomber Plant, where the B-29 *Enola Gay* was manufactured, and an exhibit on the Doolittle Raiders, one of whom was from Nebraska. There is a cockpit trainer for the B-52 (you can sit in the seats and manipulate the controls), a life-sized fallout shelter that your parents might have built, and a splendid cutaway of a KC-10 tanker showing the crew stations and how air-refueling systems worked.

The impressive number of aircraft on display include a SR-71 in a rakish pose slicing through the sky, a rare U-2 (they were famous—or infamous— for their overflights of the Soviet Union, overflights that helped us map out targets), a B-47 with the SAC shield slashing across the nose, one of the few remaining B-36 Peacemakers, a B-52, a supersonic B-58 Hustler shown with a weapons pod, a British Vulcan bomber, an EC-135 Looking Glass airborne command post, a B-17, and a B-29. One of our favorite exhibits is called Courage from Above and tells the story of the strategic bombing campaign of World War II. There is more—various missiles and rockets—so give yourself plenty of time to see it all. With 300,000 square feet this is a large museum, so you may wish to take a break in the SAC Lunch Café.

Hours: Daily: 9 a.m. to 5 p.m.
Website: www.sacmuseum.org
Street address/GPS address: 28210 W. Park Hwy., Ashland, NE 68003

Nevada

Nevada plays a vital role in our national defense—but largely a secret one. Consider Area 51, the Tonopah Test Range, Groom Lake, Alternate Emergency Landing Sites, atomic weapons testing—they fascinate us, they contribute to our national security, and they are an important part of our national story, but they are off-limits. Thankfully, there are a few wormholes through which we can slip and get a glimpse of this secret world . . . almost.

The Best Formerly Secret Military Sites: Nevada National Security Site (aka The Nevada Test Site), Las Vegas, Nevada

Remember watching atomic mushroom clouds on TV with Walter Cronkite narrating? The Nevada Test Site was where those atomic bombs were detonated, but that's all over now. The Nevada Test Site is no longer used and it's totally off-limits—except for this official, but little-known, tour.

For those adventurous few inclined to see this place, special tours will take you out to ground zero. They are run once a month by the Department of Energy departing from the Atomic Museum in Las Vegas at 7:30 a.m. and returning around 4 p.m. You'll see the moonlike landscape of Frenchman Flats where atomic bombs were detonated, you'll drive through the weathered buildings where the atomic workers once lived (Mercury, Nevada; now a ghost town), you'll visit the enormous Sedan crate that was formed by an underground atomic blast, and you'll see the ever-so-spooky ruins of "Main Street USA," where several average American homes were built to see if they could survive a blast (one was far enough away and did).

This is a once-in-a-lifetime opportunity to see one of the most restricted areas in the world and to connect with our past. Military tests conducted here included the blast from the Atomic Annie nuclear cannon, several air-dropped bombs from Strategic Air Command bombers, and tower "shots" around which soldiers trained in the business of atomic warfare. You must book this tour through the Department of Energy website, and be quick about it because seats fill up fast. (They say they will occasionally honor requests for special charters if you can put a group of 25 together.)

Tour Information: Monthly tours by reservation
Contact: (702) 295-0944 or (702) 295-0661
Email: Brenda.Carter@NNSA.doe.gov or HandorPM@nv.doe.gov
Street address/GPS address: 232 Energy Way, N. Las Vegas, NV 89030

National Atomic Testing Museum, Las Vegas, Nevada

Can anything in Las Vegas be odd? Perhaps not, but a museum dedicated to America's atomic bomb tests might come close. The National Atomic Testing Museum, located just off the Strip, is filled with examples of the weapons that were nuclearized and tested at the nearby Nevada Test Site. Among them—an atomic artillery shell, a backpack bomb, and an atomic UDT satchel, plus all sorts of atomic bombs, most of which are on display.

What makes this museum come to life, though, are the farcical posters and riotous exhibits that focus on the way we as a nation poked fun at the bomb. Did you know that Las Vegas bartenders served an Atomic Cocktail? Have you ever seen one of those old Civil Defense films? You will see it all here and, suffice to say, this is a trip back in time that is well worth a stop.

Hours: Mon–Sat: 10 a.m. to 5 p.m., Sun: 12 to 5 p.m.
Website: www.nationalatomictestingmuseum.org
Street Address/GPS Address: 755 E. Flamingo Rd., Las Vegas, NV 89119

Area 51

Yes, we're listing Area 51, but let's be honest. No one wants you anywhere near it much less to drive up to the gate. But if you're up for it and want to get close, read on. The best thing to do is drive out of Las Vegas to the "Extraterrestrial Highway" (SR 375). Take SR 375 toward Rachel and watch for the two large mailboxes. That's where you'll find the dirt road that will get you as close as you can get. You'll eventually see a sign that says "Warning. US Air Force Installation." Time to stop; that's as far as you can (or want) to go. But look around and take it in. You might see that unmarked truck everyone talks about (manned with MPs) or spot the fake trees that are disguised thermal and motion detectors. If you see contrails above you, chances are those are air force test pilots or fighter pilots in training. And around you? Most of those 3 million acres are Area 51, meaning—you're here!

If you get lost go into Rachel ask some locals where the road is. Better yet, tours are available from Las Vegas, most of which include a drive past McCarren Airport, where they will point out the mysterious all-white planes (with no other markings) of Janet Airline. Those are the planes that take employees out to Area 51.

Tours: See www.vegassightseeing.com or www.vegas.com. Look for Adventure Photo Tours.

Tonopah Test Range, Nevada

Nevada's Tonopah Test Range is home to secret flight testing and all sort of black projects—and to our much-loved F-117 Nighthawks stealth fighters of Gulf War I fame. Unlike the aircraft kept at Davis-Monthan, the F-117s at Tonopah are kept in a semistate of readiness which means they are flown in the sky every once in a while. Take NE 6 east out of the town of Tonopah until you come to the rocket. Stop and enjoy. It points to the Tonopah Test Range.

Website: www.http://ttr.sandia.gov/
Address: Tonopah, NV 89049

New Hampshire

We've come to love an imaginative museum in Wolfeboro, New Hampshire, but we can't help recommending the submarine USS *Albacore* to you, too. These are the two excellent—but different—military destinations in New Hampshire, both of which have things you'll find nowhere else.

Wright Museum of World War II, Wolfeboro, New Hampshire

You know you've arrived when you drive up to the Wright Museum—a World War II Stuart tank busting through a brick wall tells you that. Voted the Best 20th Century History Museum in New England, the Wright Museum differs from other military museums in one fascinating regard—rather than a museum about World War II per se, it is a museum about the home front and how Main Street USA was *affected* by World War II. Yes, they have the heavy stuff here—tanks and jeeps and APCs and rifles and even a mocked-up barracks—but what makes this a must-see destination are the glimpses of Main Street USA presented in the context of a world war. The Home Front Gallery has a full-scale 1940s living room complete with Mom at the piano over which is a picture of her son in a sailor's uniform. Next to that is a diorama depicting an American kitchen with a mom in a headdress as she feeds a reluctant baby in a high chair. Next to that is a dentist's office (look at those tools!), then a gas station, then a full-scale soda fountain with a soda jerk in period clothes. Everything you see is absolutely authentic down to the salt and pepper shakers and the Coca-Cola signs in the background. Here and there you'll find a period washing machine, some 1940s bicycles, and all sorts of posters, newspapers, and magazines from the era.

From the Home Front Gallery, walk through the Time Tunnel to the Military Gallery. Here you'll discover an exceptionally well-maintained collection of

For a trip back in time, visit the Wright Museum in New Hampshire, where everything is 1940s and entirely authentic, down to the uniform on the soda jerk. Notice the artifacts scattered throughout the diorama—everything here is authentic, which is the aim of this excellent destination. Photo courtesy of Wright Museum of World War II

drivable vehicles that include a World War II Sherman tank, halftracks, a jeep, an ambulance, and other wheeled vehicles. One thing to note—the Pershing tank owned by the museum is the only remaining tank from the ever-so-timely capture of the bridge over the Rhine River at Remagen.

This destination is a trip down memory lane for those who lived the home front during the war, a step back in time for the rest of us, and a place for all of us to honor the sacrifices of families and soldiers alike. Founded by David Wright, an avid collector of armored vehicles and a former marine, the Wright shows us that war has never been confined to the soldiers on the battlefronts. War affects mothers and fathers, brothers and sisters, and that's why we rate this as a top destination. Take a long look at the period clothing and the dioramas and imagine what it was like to have a son out on some remote island in the Pacific or poised to land on the D-Day beaches. The Wright makes us remember those days and in so doing reminds us to remember our soldiers today, too.

Hours: See website
Website: www.wrightmuseum.org
Street address/GPS address: 77 Center St. (Rt. 28), Wolfeboro, NH 03894

Albacore Park, Portsmouth, New Hampshire

Since the end of World War II, submarine commanders and designers alike have yearned for a submarine that could travel as fast underwater as it did on the surface. Drawing heavily on aeronautical engineering for her control surfaces and on wind-tunnel testing for her shape, out of that curiosity came a teardrop-shaped hull and the USS *Albacore*. She was launched in 1953 and her sea trials confirmed the design expectations—*Albacore* gave the Navy a giant leap forward in speed and underwater maneuverability. At a time when attack subs patrolled at top speeds of 18 to 24 knots, she raced along at 33 knots, and, with her radical X-shaped tail and various dive planes and brakes, she could turn on a dime. The results changed submarine design forever, and to this day, all submarines incorporate design principles that trace back to the *Albacore*.

If you're in the neighborhood, pull over and see Albacore Park in Portsmouth, New Hampshire. Although a smallish destination, it is a historically significant one. The *Albacore* is exhibited out of water so you can see her sleek, torpedo-shaped hull and the "X" array for her tail and propellers. You're welcome to tour her hull, where audio tapes play next to key locations as you navigate the interior compartments. A small gift shop and museum is located next to the submarine. You can also walk the Memorial Gardens, dedicated to those who were lost at sea.

Hours: Daily: 9:30 a.m. to 5:30 p.m.
Website: www.ussalbacore.org
Street address/GPS address: 600 Market St., Portsmouth, NH 03801

New Jersey

Like many of the states along our eastern and western seaboards, the military sites in New Jersey reflect not only the state's seagoing heritage, but also its role in coastal sea and air defense. Here we find destinations that include a great World War II battleship, a museum with a surprising 9/11 connection, and a Cold War radar station that only the most skilled can even attempt to see.

Battleship New Jersey Museum and Memorial, Camden, New Jersey

Name almost any island in the Pacific campaign and the battleship *New Jersey* was there. The Marshall Islands. Truk. New Guinea. The Philippines. Okinawa. Iwo Jima. Now fast-forward to Korea (she was there), and then fast-forward again to the bombing of the US Marine Corps barracks in Lebanon (she fired her 16-inch guns on Syrian antiaircraft guns). Are you getting the picture? No battleship has more decorations than the *New Jersey*. In a word, she was a warrior, and now you can walk her decks.

Anchored on the Camden, New Jersey, side of the Delaware River (just across from Philadelphia), the *New Jersey* towers as an icon of sheer power. Painted battleship gray, she is 887 feet long, 108 feet wide, and 11 stories tall from the waterline to mast. Her interior compartments have been fully restored and she is fully operational (plumbing, heating, food). There are video screens

The USS New Jersey *is anchored on the Delaware River across from Philadelphia. From bow to stern she is nearly the length of three football fields—and you can explore nearly every deck. Photo courtesy of Battleship* New Jersey *Museum and Memorial*

and exhibits throughout, each telling one aspect or more of her storied history or explaining the workings of a ship at sea. The *New Jersey*'s restoration allows her to host overnights for the Boy Scouts, the Girl Scouts and any other group interested in life at sea.

A real treat is to step inside a turret. An engineering feat of impossible size and explosive power, a 16-inch gun sits atop a 5-story iron structure that weighs 239,000 pounds and requires a crew of 80 sailors to fire. Six 110-pound bags of gunpowder are fed into the breeches behind a 2,700-pound projectile that can be shot 20-plus miles with near pinpoint accuracy. A 90-minute self-guided tour takes you through the ship, including a stop inside the gun deck of Turret #3.[10]

Hours: Daily: 9:30 a.m. to 5 p.m.
Website: www.battleshipnewjersey.org
Street address/GPS address: 100 Clinton St., Camden, NJ 08103

The Best Formerly Secret Military Sites: Nike Air Defense Missile Battery NY-56, Sandy Hook, New Jersey (Gateway National Recreation Area, New York/New Jersey)

The Gateway National Recreation Area in New York/New Jersey is an absolute treasure trove of former military forts and military sites to discover and explore. Plan a day for this lengthy driving trip around New York harbor in a two-state trip that includes coastal gun batteries, old forts, an air terminal—and a Nike missile battery.[11] Let's take a look.

The Sandy Hook Nike Battery NY-56, Fort Hancock, New Jersey

Any enemy ship attacking New York City would have to first navigate the passage between Sandy Hook, New Jersey, and Fort Tilden, New York. To block them, forts were built on both sides of the entrance, each with menacing gun batteries. Over time, the guns gave way to missiles, but the idea was the same—to protect New York City. The Sandy Hook Nike Battery NY-56 is on the New Jersey side of the entrance directly next to Fort Hancock. The missiles there were once part of an interconnected array of surface-to-air missiles that surrounded the New York metro area. The missiles are now gone but as a result of a herculean effort by a band of civilians, Nike Battery NY-56 has been preserved. Head out to Sandy Hook and take the road to Horseshoe Cove. It's pretty scruffy at first, and you'll notice fences on either side of the road walling off the areas have not been restored, but you'll eventually come to two restored Nike missiles. Drive just past the ranger station and park and get up close and personal with an incredible piece of US history—a pair of US Army Surface-to-Air missiles. Feel free to explore the area on your own or check out the NY-56 web site for guided tours. (Tours run sporadically in the warmer months.)

Fort Hancock, Fort Tilden, and the Gun Emplacements: While you're here, explore the old forts on both sides of the harbor. They are now part of the Gateway National Recreation Area. You'll see the guns that were built to block passage into New York harbor. Tours are conducted on select weekends from April to November. Check the National Park Service's website for more information.

Sandy Hook Nike Site tours: www.ny56nike.weebly.com
Maps for Fort Tilden, Fort Hancock, and the Nike missile site: https://www.nps.gov/gate/planyourvisit/maps.htm
Hours: Apr 1–Oct 31: Daily: 5 a.m. to 9 p.m.; Nov 1–Mar 31: Daily: 5 a.m. to 8 p.m.

The Best Formerly Secret Military Sites: Fire Control Tower 23, Cape May Point State Park, New Jersey

Drive out to Cape May to the Cape May Point Park. Here you'll find one of the best examples of a World War II fire control tower. Built in 1943, Tower 23 was one of the 15 towers that formed a defensive perimeter around the approaches to Delaware Bay. Tower 23 remains and has been restored and refurbished, including a spiral staircase inside. It is open to the public.

Hours: Daily: 10 a.m. to 4 p.m.
Website: www.capemaymac.org/world-war-ii-lookout-tower

Lakehurst Maxfield Field, Joint Base McGuire-Dix-Lakehurst, Lakehurst, New Jersey

One can be forgiven for thinking that the dirigible *Hindenburg* only lives in yellowed newspapers and black-and-white newsreels. After all, the great tragedy occurred back in 1937 and no one flies dirigibles any more precisely because of the horrendous inferno. Well, nothing could be further from the truth. The *Hindenburg* lives on at Joint Base McGuire-Dix-Lakehurst, in Trenton, New Jersey. There you will find an anchor chain placed on the ground where the command capsule came to rest and burned.

To see the *Hindenburg* crash site, reserve a spot on the weekly Wednesday tour that originates at the nearby Cathedral of the Air. A guide will explain the

In New Jersey you can walk up to the exact spot where the Hindenburg *came crashing down to the ground and burned after exploding in the air. Photo courtesy of WikiCommons*

events of that day in a brief 30-minute walk that goes around the crash site, and then you'll be taken into the 20-story-tall, 900-foot-long Hangar One, where you'll see remnants of *Hindenburg*—charred members of the airframe, twisted dinner utensils—and so on. The hangar contains a nearly full-scale model of an aircraft carrier and other curios but the centerpiece of this tour is the *Hindenburg*, and through this visit a piece of history will come to life.

Because this tour takes place on an active military base, you will need identification and cannot be a foreign national to enter.

Tour Information: Tours are conducted every Wednesday and on the second and fourth Saturday of the month. Reservations must be made two weeks in advance.

Website: www.navair.navy.mil/nawcad/lakehurst

Street address/GPS address: 3021 McGuire Blvd., Trenton, NJ 08641

Naval Air Station Wildwood Aviation Museum, Cape May, New Jersey

The little-known Naval Air Station Wildwood Aviation Museum is a very impressive military destination on the Jersey shore with at least one exhibit you won't find anywhere else. Read on.

The Wildwood Aviation Museum is housed in an original World War II–era hanger located on the grounds of Cape May Airport. This little-known museum has an impressive 92,000 square feet of history, heroes, and spectacular hardware. "How did we not know about this place?" wrote one reviewer, and we wonder that, too.

To start your day, a beautifully maintained F-14 Tomcat greets you as you drive up. Behind it sits Hangar #1, which is full of exhibits to educate and entertain. There's a flight simulator, experiments that explain the physics of flight, and a control tower where you can listen to live chatter between controllers and airplanes in the sky. Best of all, they have 26 airplanes and helicopters inside and out, including a classic World War II TBM Avenger torpedo bomber, a Cobra and a Huey combat helicopter, a nicely restored MiG-15, an F-16B Fighting Falcon, and a HH-52 rescue helicopter in the colors of the Coast Guard.

By far, the most unusual exhibit is called All Available Boats. Did you know that 300,000 people were evacuated from Manhattan *by water* during the collapse of the twin towers on 9/11? Yes, people raced away by foot and car but little known to most, they evacuated by water, too. The placard on this special Coast Guard exhibit says it all: "On the morning of September 11, 2001, as the World Trade Center tragedy unfolded, thousands of men and women who were on or near the waters of New York harbor, converged in any way possible. Answering the Coast Guard's radio call for all available boats, hundreds of vessels raced across the Hudson and East Rivers."

This exhibit gives you a whole new perspective on 9/11—and what it means as a civilian to answer the call. Listen to first-person accounts and view photos from this impressive sealift. You will again see the best in us, which is reason enough to make this a weekend destination.

Hours: See website
Website: www.usnasw.org
Street address/GPS address: 500 Forrestal Rd., Rio Grande, NJ 08242

While You're in the Neighborhood

Radar Station Texas Tower 4, Barnegat Inlet, New Jersey

One of the most unusual stories of the Cold war is witnessed by those who charter a dive boat and make a very risky 110-foot dive to see the barnacle-encrusted remains of an offshore radar station called Texas Tower 4. Built to give us early warning of a surprise Soviet bomber attack, Tower 4 was erected like an oil rig (hence the name) 120 miles out in the Atlantic Ocean squarely in the middle of the eastern hurricane track. For years, airmen served at sea watching their radar scopes, and for years "Old Shaky" shook and twisted and "danced" against the pounding of the waves. Flawed thinking and a powerful hurricane finally did it in. The three-legged radar platform collapsed in 1961 in the middle of a storm on a cold January night. All 28 souls on board perished. Her remains are where they sank, and if you have the training, it's a piece of history fast being lost to the ravages of the sea.

New Mexico

Two words sum up the destinations in New Mexico: The Bomb. The atomic bomb was developed in Los Alamos, New Mexico. Technologies and techniques related to the use of the bomb were developed and tested at White Sands Missile Range at Las Cruces, New Mexico. Finally, atomic bombs were "stockpiled" at Kirtland Air Force Base in Albuquerque, New Mexico. There are other things to see in this state, but nothing matches the bomb.

Bradbury Science Museum, Los Alamos, New Mexico

In 1942, the Manhattan Project scouts went looking for a site where their scientists could work in secrecy to develop the bomb. Nothing could be more isolated than a city on top of a remote mesa so they bought up land for what would become the Los Alamos Laboratory. Ground was broken and the lab was built and people started to arrive, and it all remained hush-hush until the bomb was dropped on Hiroshima and the secret got out.

Ironically, it was the very secrecy of the Manhattan Project that led to the Bradbury Museum. During those early years of Los Alamos, someone recognized that the story of what they were doing might simply disappear unless they started to collect their papers and store them for posterity. The lab's chief, Norris Bradbury, thought that was a good idea and told them to stuff what they had in a room in a nearby ice house until they realized they had a museum.

The Bradbury Science Museum is organized by galleries with each gallery telling one part of this complex story. The Defense Gallery, for instance, explains the role of nuclear weapons in our national security, how new bombs are tested in this environmentally sensitive age, and how bombs continue to be safely stockpiled. It uses informative displays, touch screens, graphics, and an abundance of artifacts to tell that story.

Start at the main entrance and visit the display called the Lab to view a short film about the activities of Los Alamos today. Then head right and begin a counterclockwise walk through the museum. You'll start in the History Gallery to learn how Los Alamos came about and then go into the Research Gallery for the science of atomic energy. Next comes the Defense Gallery with the story of how the atom was weaponized, with a fascinating section on the differences between an "atomic" bomb and a "nuclear" bomb. The Defense Gallery Theater shows a short film of stockpile stewardship.

This museum is aware of the good and bad of the bomb and it will challenge you to read, experience, learn, and debate. The museum is not limited to the museum, either. The entire city was once a secret city, so a walking tour lets you see where the men and women of the Manhattan Project worked, lived, and breathed. Note the audio prompts as you walk about. Use your cellphone to hear information on your self-guided tour.

Hours: See website
Website: www.lanl.gov/museum
Street address/GPS address: 1320 Central Ave., Los Alamos, NM 87544

New Mexico Museum of Space History, Alamogordo, New Mexico

To understand the contents of this special destination you have to close your eyes and take yourself back to a time

The New Mexico Museum of Space History is seen against a backdrop of rugged New Mexico foothills. The sort of human-endurance testing that opened the door to space flight was conducted here in New Mexico. That unusual story is told at this fascinating destination. Photo courtesy of New Mexico Museum of Space History

long before the internet and long before space shots. In a sense, you have to imagine a time before the wheel, before fire—because here in New Mexico is where our nation did some incredibly dangerous but incredible important animal testing (including a chimpanzee named Ham) and human testing. On the verge of supersonic flight and space, our scientists had to ask some very hard questions. For instance, what would happen to a pilot if he or she had to eject on the other side of the sound barrier? How many g-forces could a human sustain on a rocket booster that was thundering into space? Could a pilot bail out from 100,000 feet and if so what would happen as he fell? Would his body explode as it passed through the sound barrier? Indeed, could a human survive in space?

The answers came from animal and human testing conducted at nearby Holloman Air Force Base, much of it overseen by the great air force medical researcher Dr. John Stapp. Stapp allowed himself to be strapped into a rocket sled that was accelerated to 632 mph (i.e., the speed of a jet) and "crashed" into a series of water barriers sufficient to put 46g-forces on him. Stapp survived and became the fastest human alive, but more importantly he gave the

Air Force's human factors people the key pieces of data they needed to design safer cockpits and better lap belts.

Human and animal testing helped us get into space, and this impressive facility in New Mexico tells that story. You start on the top floor and wind your way past enormous video walls and interactive exhibits. The section called Rockets showcases civilian and military uses of rockets with inert shapes displayed along the walls. Living and Working in Space displays space suits, space food, and the things humans need to survive in that vacuum. The most impressive display centers around an enormous video wall and speaks to the early probes into space. Called Icons of Exploration, here you will find scale models of *Sputnik* and *Explorer*, the first satellites, and the crowning touch—a piece of moon rock—symbolic the success that came out of those years of animal and human experiments.

The Stapp Outdoor Air Park has a walkway that winds through a number of large artifacts, including the rocket sled Stapp rode to 46 g-forces, the Little Joe launch booster that was used to test the escape mechanism for the Apollo flights, rockets, radar-tracking displays, and other artifacts.

Hours: Wed–Sat, Mon: 10 a.m. to 5 p.m., Sun: 12 to 5 p.m., Tues: closed
Website: www.nmspacemuseum.org
Street address/GPS address: 3198 State Route 2001, Alamogordo, NM 88310

The Best Formerly Secret Military Sites: Trinity Site, Socomo County, New Mexico

Impossible as it may seem, it is *not* impossible to stand at the spot where an atomic bomb was detonated. Spooky, yes, crazy, yes, but there is a little-known twice-a-year tour that will take you out to Trinity Site, where the scientists from the Manhattan Project successfully set off the first atomic bomb. To get there you have to enter the highly restricted US Army White Sands Missile Range and travel in a caravan of cars accompanied by an armed escort. The line of cars will be miles and miles long but no one is denied. The trip takes about six hours (be sure to have a full tank of gas; no stops) and there are hazards out there, including slightly elevated radiation levels, the pos-

Want to stand where an A-bomb was detonated? You can. This obelisk marks the spot. And, contrary to urban lore, the site is not contaminated. Photo courtesy of WikiCommons

sibility of snakes, and the possibility of unexploded ordnance (this is an active test range). However, said the White Sands base commander: "We have travelers from as far away as Australia who travel to visit this historic landmark." An obelisk in the middle of the desert marks ground zero.

Open to Public: First Saturday in April and October. Tours start at the Tularosa High School parking lot next to the athletic field. Be there between 6:30 and 7 a.m. Contact the Alamogordo Chamber of Commerce or visit https://www.nps.gov/whsa/learn/historyculture/trinity-site.htm.

The National Museum of Nuclear Science & History, Albuquerque, New Mexico

The National Museum of Nuclear Science has a comprehensive display of nuclear weapons, most of which can be seen in the museum's 9-acre outdoor display called Heritage Park. Although a bit scruffy in places (with dust and weeds), you can see the progression of nuclear bombers from the post-war B-29, to the B-47, the first jet bomber, to today's B-52. Notice the white painting on the underbelly of the B-52. This reflective paint was designed to help prevent the bomber from bursting into flames by warding off the thermal pulse when a nuclear bomb detonated. Notice, too, the array of the fighter jets. At one time or another, all of these jets were on strip alert with nuclear air-to-air missiles and tactical bombs at the ready (fighter jets could carry the B43 atomic bomb).

Next are the ICBMs and cruise missiles. Here you can walk around the Titan II, the Minuteman, the Polaris, and the MX missile, or study the Hound Dog and Snark nuclear cruise missiles. Like the bombers and fighters, all of these missiles carried nuclear warheads.

Two more artifacts deserve your time. The sail of the USS *James K. Polk* is here. It symbolizes the part played by submarines in the triad of nuclear deterrence (nuclear bombers, nuclear ICBMs, and submarine-launched nuclear missiles—SLBMs). The *Polk* was a fleet ballistic missile carrier that had 16 Polaris (later Poseidon) SLBMs inside her hull. You can't miss Atomic Annie, one of the few remaining examples of the huge, 280mm cannon built to nuclearize the US Army, Annie was disassembled, put on a train, and sent to the Nevada Test Site, where she successfully fired a live nuclear artillery shell. The small A-bomb inside successfully detonated.

The museum itself is smallish but has some fascinating exhibits, some of which are terribly poignant. The display on "criticality" is a reminder of the terrible risks involved when exploring the atom. A Los Alamos scientist dropped a screwdriver into a plutonium pile, which pushed a block of beryllium into a sphere and created a reaction that bathed him in radiation. He died some days later—slowly—from radiation exposure.

Hours: Daily: 9 a.m. to 5 p.m.
Website: www.nuclearmuseum.org
Street address/GPS address: 601 Eubank Blvd. SE, Albuquerque, NM 87123

White Sands Missile Range Museum, Las Cruces, New Mexico

To do a deep dive into the development of missiles and rockets and other air-delivered weapons, you need go no farther than the White Sands Missile Range Museum located next to the legendary White Sands Missile Range. For starters, there's nothing like having hundreds of thousands of acres and hundreds of square miles of open desert with no humans, animals, or national monuments to get in the way. Misfire a missile and you blow up a rock. Accidentally drop a bomb and you blow a hole in the sand. That's why they built the White Sands Missile Range here in Las Cruces. They could test to their hearts' content.

And test they did. When you arrive at the Missile Range Museum, you'll be greeted by more than 50 missiles and rockets that were tested or refined here. Notable among them is the Patriot missile, which saw action defending against Scud missiles during Operation Desert Storm, an Intermediate Range Ballistic Missile (IRBM) called the Redstone, a nuclear air-to-air missile called the Genie (the idea was to shoot one into a formation of Russian bombers and let the shock waves knock out a dozen in one blast), the Nike Ajax and Nike Hercules air-defense missiles, and a V-2 rocket like the ones Adolf Hitler used to rain terror down on England (they were reverse engineered here). Did you know that our strategic bombers carried nuclear-tipped missiles to blast open corridors through which they would fly to their targets inside the Soviet Union? You can see a USAF Hound Dog here too, just like the ones carried by our B-52s.

Stories and artifacts abound inside the museum. Here you'll find a number of cutaways of missiles and rockets showing their engines and their explosives. There are launch control panels and artifacts from the early years of White Sands. Other exhibits speak to the ongoing mission at White Sands and the ever-changing threats our nation must counter. In a sense, by understanding the story behind each of the weapons you get an understanding of the evolving threats our nation has faced and how we used technology to overcome them. In a nutshell, that's the story of White Sands—that the threat never ends and the enemy's technologies constantly evolve, and that new technologies will continue to be developed here and tested here.

Base access is required to get in. You must present a valid driver's license and go through a brief security screening.

Hours: Mon–Fri: 8 a.m. to 4 p.m., Sat: 10 a.m. to 3 p.m., Sun: closed
Website: www.wsmr-history.org
Street address/GPS address: US Hwy. 70, White Sands, NM 88002

New York

Like California, New York is a state rich in military destinations. From the Hudson Valley to Long Island, three branches of the military are represented here at destinations you know, some you don't—and one you've been walking past every day.

Intrepid *Sea, Air & Space Museum,* New York, New York

The star of New York City isn't Broadway. It's the *Intrepid* Sea, Air & Space Museum, or so we'd like to think. What's bigger than a space shuttle called the *Enterprise* or a swing-nosed supersonic jetliner called the *Concorde*? What does a theater on Broadway have that compares to an 872-foot-long, 27,000-ton aircraft carrier jammed with supersonic jets, high technology missiles, and agile combat helicopters?

Well, a theater on Broadway provides inspiration, that's what. Today's jaded New Yorkers want big visuals, *grand* stories, and the latest technologies—and, you guessed it, *Intrepid* rises to the occasion. Inside her hangar decks are large, high-definition screens with interactive content explaining the latest air and space technologies. There are audio tours, iPhone apps, immersive exhibits, and dioramas that engage all the senses. There is the mind-blowing 4-D theater, the stomach-churning G-Force Encounter, and the hands-on Exploreum, where you and your kids get into Hueys and bubble canopies and space capsules.

Commissioned at the height of World War II, the *Intrepid* was an old straight-deck carrier later converted to a more generous angled deck. She fought extensively in the Pacific (the Gilberts, Marshall Islands, Peleliu, Truk, the Philippines, and more), where she survived hits by torpedo and four kamikazes. After the war she went on to support the conflict in Vietnam and

A sidewalk view of New York's Intrepid *Sea, Air & Space Museum, New York, New York. Photo Courtesy of Department of Defense*

later was part of the ships positioned to recover our early space shots. She was retired in 1974 and eventually moved here to be a floating museum.

Crammed on her hangar deck and on the flight deck are warbirds beautifully restored covering all the major conflicts going back to the first carrier-born aircraft. Some notables not often seen elsewhere—an F9F Cougar jet fighter and an FJ-3 Fury fighter, both flown in the 1950s, a Soviet Mig-17 and MiG-21, the A-12 CIA spy plane, cousin to the SR-71, and an Israeli Kfir, which was used as an adversary aircraft in our own training exercises. Notice the paints on these planes. The staff picked colors and markings most representative of the periods in which these planes served.

After exploring the *Intrepid*, walk down to the Cold War guided-missile submarine USS *Growler*. The *Growler* is displayed with a restored sea-to-surface Regulus missile on deck elevated and ready for flight, and its interior compartments are open for your visit. The *Growler* was one of the first missile-carrying submarines and a predecessor to the SLBM-class subs. Be sure to leave time to explore her compartments.

What else? How about a supersonic jet called the *Concorde* and a space shuttle called *Enterprise*? Yep. They're both here too. *Intrepid* is one of the best one-stop-shopping destinations for the full spectrum of military assets and civilian airplanes.

Military ceremonies at the Intrepid Museum. Many of the destinations in this guide are used by the military for ceremonies as well as educating their soldiers. Photo courtesy of Department of Defense

Yes, Broadway has it stars, but the *Intrepid* is a celebration of air, sea, and space writ large. The restorations are impeccable, the variety of exhibits is interpretative and stimulating for visitors of all ages, and the knowledge to be found goes deep. The *Intrepid* is at Pier 86 on the Hudson River at 46th Street and Twelfth Avenue. Arrive early and stay late. There is ample parking, plenty of taxis, and lots to see. Tickets required; see their website for the latest exhibits on display.

Hours: Daily: 10 a.m. to 5 p.m.
Website: www.intrepidmuseum.org
Street address/GPS address: Pier 86, W. 46th St. & Twelfth Ave., New York, NY 10036-4103

West Point Museum, US Military Academy, New York

Like the Naval Academy, the US Military Academy is a military destination in and of itself, but what makes this extra special is the museum. This is the oldest military museum in America, with displays and exhibits that show us the parallels between military history and American history. The Revolutionary War? Here you can see the links from a chain that was stretched across the Hudson River to block the British fleet. Also here? George Custer's last message from the Battle of Little Bighorn, the cannon that fired the first American shot of World War I, plus an excellent history of the Manhattan Project (it was run by the US Army) and a replica of the bomb dropped on Nagasaki (remember, the US Air Force was then the US *Army* Air Force). And so it goes. Two great histories intertwined like strains of DNA.

A visit requires access to the campus. Check the website for current requirements.

Hours: 10:30 a.m. to 4:15 p.m.
Website: www.westpoint.army.mil/museum.html
Street address/GPS address: 2110 New South Post Rd., West Point, NY 10996

Cradle of Aviation Museum, Garden City, New York

The Cradle of Aviation Museum takes its name from Long Island's aviation legacy. After all, Charles Lindbergh took off from Roosevelt Field, which is on Long Island, and both Grumman and Republic Aircraft were here, makers of some of the most iconic warbirds of World War II. In fact, among the 75 warbirds in this fine museum almost all of the Grumman "cats"—the F-4 Wildcat, F-6 Hellcat, and the F-14 Tomcat—plus a Grumman F-11 Tigercat (painted in the colors of the Blue Angels) are in the air above you as you walk into this glass-and-steel masterpiece.

Your visit here is somewhat of a clockwise walk through a history of flight starting with hot air balloons and the mere dream of flight and continuing through commercial airliners and combat aircraft, and on into space. There are eight exhibit halls chock-full of beautifully staged dioramas, most with aircraft and helicopters. There is a planetarium and a domed theater that will overwhelm your senses (and give you a bit of vertigo), and they're right next to the café, where you can stop for a cold drink while you contemplate landing on Mars in some distant future (the wall murals in their Red Planet Café depict the landscape of Mars).

The inventory of aircraft will amaze, including the Grumman cats plus the Republic Thunderchief and Thunderbolt. There are also an A-10 Warthog, an A-6 Intruder, and an F9F Panther, with10 different cockpits to sit in, plus 30 different hands-on exhibits—but who is counting? In any event, plan on spending a half day here and enjoying every minute of it. There's also a nice museum shop for a special souvenir.

Hours: Tues–Sun: 9:30 a.m. to 5 p.m.; Mon: closed
Website: www.cradleofaviation.org
Street address/GPS address: Charles Lindbergh Blvd., Garden City, NY 11530

The Best Formerly Secret Military Sites: Brooklyn Army Terminal, Brooklyn, New York

Some 27 million tons of war matériel—and 2.2 million soldiers—began their journeys to the combat fronts of World War II from this waterfront terminal officially known as the New York Port of Embarkation.[12] Today it is the Brooklyn Army Terminal and it's home to private enterprise, but this once-thriving terminal still has its signature railroad tracks and loading docks and the 5-ton cranes that worked the 10-foot by 10-foot balconies picking and packing ammunition and 2-ton cargo pallets as if they were mere matchsticks.

The best way to see this is to go on the tours run by turnstilestours.com. During their two-hour walk they will give you a history of the soldiers who assembled here and the longshoreman who made this hub work. They will take you into the atrium of Building B—which is considered a marvel of cantilevered engineering—to see where the cranes (no longer working but still there) worked the concrete balconies from which supplies were routed, picked, and packed.

If you let your imagination run wild, you can still see those young soldiers lined up with their duffel bags waiting to board their ships with cigarettes jauntily hanging from their lips. One of the largest embarkation points during the war, the Brooklyn Terminal was a place in constant motion with steam rising from engines, cranes lowering tanks into cargo holds, and soldiers eager to take on Hitler.[13]

Tours: Tours offered the first and third Saturday of the month by www.turnstilestours.com. They also offer a tour of the Brooklyn Navy Yard.
Website: www.bklynarmyterminal.com
Street address/GPS address: 140 58th St., New York, NY 11220

Cranes plucked supplies from the balconies here at the Brooklyn Army Terminal as 2.2 million soldiers embarked on ships to fight World War II. Tours take you inside. Photo courtesy of WikiCommons

Old Rhinebeck Aerodrome, Red Hook, New York

Hangar doors open. Wood propellers are pulled. Engines blossom to life with a puff of blue smoke. A biplane takes to the skies. A long-forgotten era—including World War I—comes to life just miles up the Hudson River from New York City at the Old Rhinebeck Aerodrome. A grass airstrip, old hangars, and even older airplanes will greet you, as will the quiet of a summer pasture with the distant sound of aircraft engines. This is an effortless trip back in time when the first fragile wood-and-cloth airplanes took to the skies. You don't need an invitation to come here—just arrive. But check the website for air shows and biplane rides. There is almost always something going on each and every weekend through late fall.

Hours: Daily: 10 a.m. to 5 p.m.
Website: www.oldrhinebeck.org
Street address/GPS address: 9 Norton Rd., Red Hook, NY 12571

While You're in the Neighborhood

The Museum of American Armor, Old Bethpage, New York

The Museum of Armor maintains a beautiful collection of restored World War II military vehicles that is open for your inspection in Old Bethpage, New York. They have an M4 Sherman tank, an M5 Stuart tank, an M20 escort, a Bofurs 40mm antiaircraft gun, and a dozen other restored military vehicles all painted army green.

But what they excel at is what they call the Armor Experience. The Armor Experience is a team-building exercise and a history lesson in one. You and your group put on army uniforms and load into tanks and trucks, and your "column" heads into the woods on a combat patrol facing an uncertain outcome. Local reenactors in period uniforms—Allied and German—bring the event to life. Your column comes onto a French village occupied by the Germans, and you attack. Chaos ensues, your column reacts, and all sorts of lessons are learned. Each Armor Experience takes about two hours. Most of them are booked by young-adult groups or corporations as team-building exercises, so form a group and book your own event.

Recently relocated to Old Bethpage Village, the museum is open five days a week. Check their website for directions, dates, and ticket information.

Hours: Wed–Sun: 10 a.m. to 4 p.m., Mon, Tue: closed
Website: www.museumofamericanarmor.com
Street address/GPS address: 1303 Round Swamp Rd., Old Bethpage, NY 11804

Empire State Aerosciences Museum, Schenectady, New York

For those who live in upstate New York, consider a visit to the Empire State Aerosciences Museum. This small destination has some two-dozen warbirds, including Soviet MiGs, Century-series jets (F-101, F-102, and F-105), an exceedingly rare Navy RA-5 Vigilante, plus plenty of modern military aircraft, including an F-14 Tomcat and an A-10 Warthog. Best of all—and one of the reasons we recommend this destination to you—on display here is a large scale model of the Japanese aircraft carrier *Akagi*. Why is that notable? A little history is in order.

The *Akagi* was one of the six Japanese aircraft carriers that participated in the sneak attack on Pearl Harbor. After Pearl Harbor, it continued to wreak havoc throughout the Pacific until in 1942 the *Akagi* sailed to Midway, where she was engaged by our own forces. Three SBD Dauntless dive bombers from the USS *Enterprise* peeled off and dived on the *Akagi,* one of which scored a direct hit with a 1,000-pound bomb. The bomb detonated in her hangar bay, which was filled with fueled aircraft, and a fire broke out that they could not control. The Japanese ultimately scuttled her.

It would be months before the last Japanese aircraft carrier from Pearl Harbor was sunk (the last was the *Zuikaku*), but sinking the *Akagi* was a significant victory for America on the long road to Tokyo. A large-scale model of the *Akagi* is on display here, and we thought that alone made this military destination particularly special.

Hours: Fri–Sunday: 10 a.m. to 4 p.m., Mon–Thurs: closed. (Open Tues–Sun through Labor Day.)
Website: http://www.esam.org/index.html
Street address/GPS address: 250 Rudy Chase Dr., Glenville, NY 12302

The 10 Best Military Experiences: American Airpower Museum, Farmingdale, New York

First a disclaimer: This is not just a museum destination. Yes, the American Airpower Museum is a museum and it does have displays and there is an excellent collection of warbirds here that includes a beautiful A-10

Warthog, an F-111 Aardvark, a B-25 Mitchell, and an A-6 Intruder (and plenty more), but what makes this worth your while is the museum's C-47 D-Day Flight Experience. Unlike any other ride in a C-47, on this flight you'll be part of a D-Day parachute "drop" reenacted by volunteers who will fly with you fully dressed as World War II paratroopers. You will start in the briefing room, where you and your paratroopers will plan your mission. From there, you'll board the plane and your C-47 will lumber down the runway and take off and bounce through the air with the roar of engines—and a sense of urgency. Your reenactors will prepare for their jump and talk to you as they line up (but they do not go out the door).

This is a fabulous way to get to know the iconic C-47 (a DC-3 in civilian life) plus a powerful way to relive history and to understand the role of our paratroopers. But this is also serious stuff, so you will be briefed on safety protocols and escorted in and around the aircraft.

Hours: Thurs–Sun: 10:30 a.m. to 4 p.m., Mon–Wed: closed
Website: www.americanairpowermuseum.com
Street address/GPS address: 1230 New Hwy., Farmingdale, NY 11735

North Carolina

North Carolina is the birthplace of aviation, and Kill Devils Hill certainly deserves a place on your bucket list even if it doesn't make our guide to military destinations. By all means, take that long walk up the hill to the monument and remember that day when powered flight became a reality. What *did* make our list, however, will make your day. There's a destination that will immerse your in the world of military special forces, there's a rugged battleship awaiting your inspection, and a special quirky destination with an unusual connection to New York City.

Airborne & Special Operations Museum, Fayetteville, North Carolina

The soaring facade tells you something special is inside, and this museum doesn't fail. You enter the building under a canopy of paratroopers descending through a majestic 5-story atrium and then

Paratrooper Iron Mike has just hit the ground in Occupied Europe. Now he stands in front of the Special Operations Museum in North Carolina. Photo courtesy of Airborne & Special Operations Museum

pass through one realistic exhibit after the other. Consider the extraordinary detail of the Blackhawk Down Mogadishu exhibit. Delta Force soldiers are huddled against a shell-scarred wall as they plan their break out under enemy fire. One man is wounded, two are scanning the streets. Across the way is a bullet-ridden Technical, the rotor of the downed Super 61, and a wall of Mogadishu images. This is so real, so detailed, that you can feel the tension in the air—how will they *ever* make it?

That's the sort of powerful displays you'll find throughout this immersive museum, so plan your day carefully so you can take it all in. The best way is to navigate your visit by galleries. Start with the first parachute jump in 1940 depicted in the Early Airborne Gallery and then continue through the World War II Gallery, the Korea and Cold War Gallery, the Vietnam Gallery, and a gallery focused on today's ever-evolving Contingency Operations. As you walk through the exhibits, you'll see large artifacts placed in realistic battlescapes with mannequins in combat poses. There is a jeep coming out of a World War II glider, a tank moving forward with paratroopers landing behind it, a Huey coming in for a landing in a Vietnam LZ, a combat team

The soaring facade of the Airborne & Special Operations Museum in Fayetteville, North Carolina, tells you you're in for something rather extraordinary. The exhibits inside don't fail. Photo courtesy of Airborne & Special Operations Museum

on a Humvee, special operators of the skids of a Little Bird, and an ever-so-spooky Iraqi war "hide-sight." All of the hardware are the real deal—tanks, helicopters, and Humvees.

The museum tops it all off with an uber-realistic 4-story video theater called the Vista Dome. Forget IMAX when you enter this one. The 24-seat Pritzker Simulator rocks and rolls you as you watch incredible footage (some of it animations) of the intense situations our special operators face. Two movies run all day—*Army on the Move* and *Experience the Legend*. You'll "jump" out of a cargo plane into a stomach-churning HALO jump (High Altitude Low Opening parachute jump), rope down into hostile urban territory from a helicopter gunship, race through enemy streets in a Ranger Buggy, deploy into a hot LZ in Vietnam, and fly into Normandy with the 101st Screaming Eagles.

Taken together, this destination is an action-packed portrait of the variety of dangerous missions our special forces are asked to undertake. And because it's located adjacent to Fort Bragg (the training base for our airborne and special forces soldiers), don't be surprised if the person next to you is a soldier from the base. There is a well-stocked gift shop for a souvenir. And check their website—many of the exhibits are temporary.

Hours: Tues–Sat: 10 a.m. to 5 p.m., Sun: 12 to 5 p.m., Mon: closed
Website: www.asomf.org
Street address/GPS address: 100 Bragg Blvd., Fayetteville, NC 28301

Carolinas Aviation Museum, Charlotte, North Carolina

We could have been picky and said that this was a civilian destination, but then we remembered that the main exhibit here is the Airbus that ditched in the Hudson River. That's right—the Miracle on the Hudson plane. Here's the story: Bird strikes choked off two engines as US Airways Flight 1549 departed from LaGuardia. The captain saw the Hudson, reached it, and successfully ditched. Everyone survived, but no one knew what to do with the plane until someone suggested that it ought to complete its trip to Charlotte, North Carolina. The idea was approved, and the plane was reassembled here and put on display.

The Miracle on the Hudson plane has finally come home—and it's here at the Carolinas Aviation Museum in Charlotte, North Carolina. Photo courtesy of WikiCommons

The Carolinas Aviation Museum is essentially a large hangar filled with airplanes loosely organized in groups according to how they were used. There are civilian airplanes, commercial airplanes, military airplanes, and helicopters. The military aircraft include the Vietnam-era CH-46 Sea Knight and a variety of fighters (AV-8B Harrier, A-4 Skyhawk, A-7 Corsair, plus an F-14 Tomcat). The commercial airplanes include the Miracle on the Hudson Airbus displayed next to a handsome DC-3 in the colors of old Piedmont Airlines and an Eastern Airlines DC-7. If a trip back in time to the good old days when a stewardess served hot meals and passengers wore coat and tie appeals to you, this is the area for you.

The Miracle on the Hudson plane is certainly the centerpiece here, but the rest of the museum has plenty of military aircraft to enjoy. Each airplane is presented with an informative placard and most of them have a small exhibit area with handsome visuals of that aircraft in use.

Hours: Mon–Fri: 10 a.m. to 4 p.m., Sat: 10 a.m. to 5 p.m., Sun: 1 to 5 p.m.
Website: www.carolinasaviation.org
Street address/GPS address: 4672 First Flight Dr., Charlotte, NC 28208

The 10 Best Military Base Tours: Seymour Johnson Air Force Base, Goldsboro, North Carolina

Home to our F-15E Strike Eagles and KC-135 tankers, Seymour Johnson offers a comprehensive base tour on the last Thursday of each month. Depending on how busy they are that day, you'll see a maintenance hangar for the jets, talk to the maintainers and/or some pilots, see a Strike Eagle up close, or possibly go inside a tanker. On almost all tours, you'll stop at the base BX for lunch (bring money; it's a Subway).

Tours are booked through the Goldsboro Wayne Travel and Tourism Bureau. You need 15 people to get the full tour; less than 15 and you'll have a windshield-only tour. This is an impressive base with a storied history, so make this a must-see destination.

Website: http://www.seymourjohnson.af.mil/Units/Public-Affairs/
Street address/GPS address: 1630 Martin St., Goldsboro, NC 27531

The 10 Best Military Base Tours: Marine Corps Air Station Cherry Point, Cherry Point, North Carolina

Want to see the home of our AV-8B Harriers? This is your place. MCAS Cherry Point flies the AV-8 Harriers and the EA-6 Prowlers, and it's a logistics support base for the new F-35B Lighting II fighters (the ones capable of vertical flight). Windshield tours take you around the base and are offered weekly on Wednesday morning. The tours last about two hours. You must request a seat by at least the Monday before the tour. Contact the public affairs office.

Website: http://www.cherrypoint.marines.mil/Public-Affairs/
Street address/GPS address: MCAS Cherry Point, NC 28533
(zip code is important)

While You're in the Neighborhood

USS North Carolina, Wilmington, North Carolina

The battleship USS *North Carolina* fought in virtually every campaign of the Pacific and earned no less than 15 World War II battle stars. She is a beautiful ship painted in a zig-zag camouflage gray-on-gray paint scheme. She was deactivated just after the war. Now she sits in quiet repose in Wilmington, North Carolina.

A self-guided two-hour tour will take you through her interior compartments, including a nicely restored chapel, a kitchen with simulated food, the bridge, the mess, the wardrooms, and so on. If a more detailed examination of the ship is your thing, consider the optional paid tours to see the engineering spaces and other difficult-to-access areas of the ship.

You access the *North Carolina* through a land-side pavilion.

Hours: Labor Day–Memorial Day: 8 a.m. to 4 p.m., Memorial Day–Labor Day: 8 a.m. to 7 p.m.
Website: www.battleshipnc.com
Street address/GPS address: #1 Battleship Rd., Wilmington, NC 28401

North Dakota

There are plenty of wide open spaces in North Dakota which means there's plenty of land for an ICBM—and an enterprising community who created a fun military destination crammed with artifacts and aglow with color.

The Best Formerly Secret Military Sites: Ronald Reagan Minuteman Missile State Historic Site, Cooperstown, North Dakota

The Oscar-Zero Missile Alert Facility and the November-33 Launch Facility are all that remain of the 150 Minuteman II intercontinental ballistic missile launch sites that were once spread out over a 6,500-square-mile area around the Grand Forks Air Force Base, North Dakota (yes, the same number of missiles as in South Dakota). Guides are here to take you to the topside facility or down the elevator to the Launch Control Facility. This is basically the same tour and has the same things to see as the South Dakota site, so if you went to one you can skip the other.

Hours: See website
Website: www. history.nd.gov/historicsites/minutemanmissile
Street address/GPS address: 555 113-1/2 Ave. NE Hwy. 45, Cooperstown, ND 58425

Fargo Air Museum, Fargo, North Dakota

This is a beautiful little museum with lots of flags and colors and lots of fun—and an intimidating 33-ton Minuteman II ICBM out front. But go outside. Colorful murals provide backdrops to a collection of nicely restored warbirds. Kids love the yellow DC-3, adults love the P-51 Mustang—and everyone loves the RQ-4 Global Hawk UAV. There is a Huey, T-6 Texan, and a B-25 Mitchell to round things out. This gem of a destination is located on the south side of Hector International Airport.

Hours: Tues–Sat 10 a.m. to 5 p.m., Sun: 10 a.m. to 1p.m., Mon: closed
Website: www.fargoairmuseum.org
Street address/GPS address: 1609 19th Ave. N., Fargo, ND 58102

Ohio

The list of Ohio destinations is short but impressive. The star of the state:
Wright-Patterson's National Museum of the US Air Force. Nothing tops this
sprawling complex with its hundreds of military warbirds, rockets, missiles,
and helicopters. See listing under Top 20.

National Museum of the US Air Force, Wright-Patterson Air Force Base, Ohio

This mecca of aviation covers military flight like no other. For
starters, there are some 360-plus planes and missiles on display,
which is probably some sort of record. Like the Smithsonian National Air &
Space Museum, the types and models of aircraft and space vehicles you'll see
span the entire history of flight—but here the story is 100 percent military.

*Some 19 acres of airplanes and displays are enclosed by these four massive hangars at the
National Museum of the US Air Force. Photo courtesy of Department of the Air Force*

There is a B-52 bomber, an F-117 Nighthawk fighter, a B-2 Stealth bomber, virtually every fighter flown from the P-38 to the F-22 Raptor; as well as guns, missiles, bombs, parachutes, and just about anything else related to the global mission of the Air Force. There is a collection of planes that have been designated *Air Force One* (you can walk through some of them), a 96-ton Titan IVB space booster, the first plane to fly back to North Vietnam to bring out our POWs, and the otherworldly XB-70 Valkyrie bomber. And so it goes. Hundreds of planes. Thousands of stories. And four enormous buildings.

To make sense of all this (and to plan your day) all of the objects on display are organized by galleries and each gallery is literally *packed* with airplanes. There is a gallery on the early experiments to use airplanes as weapons, a gallery on the biplanes of World War I, another on World War II, another on the Korean War, the Cuban Missile Crisis, Vietnam, the Cold War, and so on. The World War II Gallery is a good starting point and representative of the others in scope and detail. All told, some 70 specific aspects of the World War II air war are covered, including the Doolittle Raiders, the air wars over Europe and in the Pacific, Ploesti, Schweinfurt, Big Week, D-Day, the Hump, the Marianna's, and so on. Mannequins of pilots, crew members, and maintainers wearing period uniforms are incorporated into the aircraft displays. Warbirds flown by all of the combatants—British, German, Japanese, and American—are included as are each of the theaters of the war be it the Pacific, China-Burma-India, North Africa, or Europe. Some of the notable aircraft in this gallery include a Messerschmitt Bf-109, a Messerschmitt Me-163 Komet jet fighter, a Focke-Wulf Fw 190, a Mitsubishi A6M2 Zero, a Kawanishi N1K2 George, both the razorback and the bubble-canopy versions of the P-47 Thunderbolt, a rare P-38 Lightning, plus all of the expected warbirds from the P-51 Mustang to the B-17 Flying Fortress.

This organization and depth of storytelling continues in the Vietnam Gallery, the Cold War Gallery, and the others. Each gallery combines period aircraft with exhibits on specific operations from that conflict or that era. Wherever possible, cockpits are open, and in some cases the cargo planes and the larger passenger planes (like the presidential aircraft in the fourth building) are "walk-through aircraft." Some planes incorporate cutaways so you can see their belts of ammunition or how their bombs were carried in the bomb bay.

Those with a sharp eye will know in an instant that this B-52 was painted for the Vietnam conflict (back left). B-52s on nuclear ground alert had white underbellies. Those that flew over Vietnam were painted black, the better to blend in with the sky. Seen in the Vietnam display area at the National Museum of the US Air Force.

The outdoor airpark is where you'll find President Reagan's railroad-mounted ICBMs and where some of the larger aircraft are displayed, such as the 174-foot-long, 282,000-pound C-17 Globemaster cargo plane, the AC-130 Hercules gunship, or the electronics-laded EC-135 "Looking Glass" Cold War airborne command and control post. There is also a replica World War II airfield with a Nissan hut and a control tower. All that's required of you is to walk around it and be effortlessly transported back to England circa 1944.

Admission is free and there are dozens of audio programs to download and play as you walk the nearly 19 acres of display areas. And, yes, as you can see you can easily spend the day here, but don't worry. There is an enormous cafeteria, a digital 3D theater, and a gift shop that rivals anything anywhere. Be forewarned—if you see it here, buy it here; most of the items won't be found in your local stores.

Hours: Daily: 9 a.m. to 5 p.m.
Website: www.nationalmuseum.af.mil
Street address/GPS address: 1100 Spaatz St., Dayton, OH 45431

Oklahoma

Here we find the big guns. Main battle tanks. Self-propelled 155mm howitzers. Surface-to-air missiles. Wheeled cannons. This state has one of the most impressive collections of weapons we've ever seen—and a variety of destinations.

Fort Sill National Historic Landmark and Museum, Fort Sill, Oklahoma

This museum, plus the U.S. Army Field Artillery Museum, which follows, would each be worthy of a weekend trip, but the two together make for a visit unlike any other military destination on our list." Why is that? Because from the earliest days of our republic—long before airplanes flew or missiles were launched—there were long guns and muskets and wheeled howitzers and artillery pieces. And over the next two centuries, those weapons developed and improved and artillery would be a constant figure in our nation's conflicts—and that's the story told at these two destinations. An old fort from our frontier days, and our nation's history as seen through our artillery. First, some background on the collections.

Not too many years ago, these two destinations were one, but a collection focused on our nation's frontier years was clearly at odds with a collection focused on the evolution of artillery pieces. To give each one a chance to fully realize its potential, the artillery collection was pulled out of the fort and a Field Artillery Museum was established. Over the ensuing years, both collections grew and now we have two excellent destinations in one stop. First, Fort Sill.

There was a time when the US Army was called the cavalry and the Great Plains were largely Indian territory. Fort Sill is of that time, and this 142-acre destination has no less than 38 fully restored period buildings on the grounds. There are three cavalry barracks, a mess hall, a storehouse, and a kitchen all furnished just as they would have been in 1875 (uniforms and mess hall plates, etc.). As you move about the grounds, you'll get a feel for what it was like to live on the Great Plains at a time when refrigeration was a block of ice and you ate what you caught. Life was hard but also gracious, and the quiet here lets

The US Army's nuclear 280mm cannon was nicknamed Atomic Annie. This incredible weapon can be seen at three of our destinations, including here at Fort Sill. Photo courtesy of Department of Defense

you reflect on those early days. Indeed, wander the streets and imagine yourself, without any effort, in the 1800s.

All self-guided tours start at the visitor center, where you watch a short movie on the history of Fort Sill. Notice the tableau showing how all of the buildings were organized back in the day, plus display cases with period guns and uniforms, mannequins and busts, and hundreds of faces from the 1900s photographed and displayed in oversize prints. Next walk outside and see the Field Artillery schoolhouse, the Calvary Barracks (1870), the Post Chapel (1875), or the Quartermaster buildings. There is an interpretive center, a World War I exhibit, and the well-liked Warrior's Journey and Native American Gallery, which focuses on the life of Native Americans before there were reservations. Most of all there are thousands of small artifacts tucked in here and there, some as innocent as a pantry filled with knives, forks, and spoons (from the 1860s), others as colorful and as moving as a collection of ceremonial Indian headdresses.

A cellphone-based audio tour lets you walk the grounds at your own pace, but be sure to visit Geronimo's grave site before heading over to the Field Artillery Museum for part 2.

Hours: See website
Website: www.http://sill-www.army.mil/.
Street address/GPS address: 435 Quanah Rd., Fort Sill, OK 73503

US Army Field Artillery Museum, Fort Sill, Oklahoma

The second part of your visit should be spent outside. Well, mainly outside. The US Army Field Artillery Museum has more than 70 artillery pieces, self-propelled guns, and other military weapons and vehicles from World War I, World War II, Korea, Vietnam, and up to the present day. Take the winding, twisting path through Artillery Park and see the equipment our soldiers use. Each artifact is on a concrete pad and painted with period colors and insignia. Among them, a beautifully maintained and somewhat rare M40 Long Tom Gun, a T97 Self Propelled Howitzer, a Vietnam-era M56 self-propelled 90mm gun, plus rocket launchers, many, many more howitzers, and artillery pieces American, German, and Soviet. A very special item? You have to see—and perhaps can't miss—one of the last remaining M65 280mm cannons dubbed Atomic Annie. This 84-ton monster of a gun had a 27-foot-long barrel that fired a 15-kiloton *atomic* artillery shell 20 miles. It was successfully tested during a live-fire demonstration in 1953 at the Nevada Test Site. Twenty were made; less than a half dozen remain. And be sure to visit the white Nike missiles. There was a time with these impressive missiles ringed our cities ready to shoot down an invading Soviet bomber. Wander about and let your imagination go wild.

Inside the museum are dioramas with even more artillery pieces—particularly the very old ones—plus period ammo, combat gear, and other military artifacts seen in action complete with mannequins in uniforms. The dioramas depict scenes as far back as the Revolutionary War—see the wheeled guns—and as current as today's war on terror.

Try to schedule your visit to coincide with the Living History days. The local reenactors bring to life these incredible pieces in uniforms from the Revolutionary War to World War II.

The enormous 240mm howitzer located at Fort Sill Field Artillery Museum.
Photo courtesy of Department of Defense

Hours: Tues–Sat: 9 a.m. to 5 p.m.
Note: All persons over the age of 16 must fill out FS Form 118a and pass a background check at Fort Sill Visitor Control Center before entering Fort Sill.
Website: www.sill-www.army.mil/famuseum
Street address/GPS address: Corral Rd., Fort Sill, OK 73503

Stafford Air & Space Museum, Weatherford, Oklahoma

If you can't make it to the US Space and Rocket Center in Huntsville, Alabama, this is the stop for you. Jam-packed with beautifully designed displays and numerous artifacts, the Stafford museum covers the major milestone of powered flight with an emphasis on space travel. (US Air Force general Thomas P. Stafford, the museum's namesake, was raised in Weatherford, Oklahoma. A former test pilot, he became a NASA astronaut and made several historic space flights, including the first meet up in space with Soviet cosmonauts.)

Perhaps what distinguishes this museum most is its collection of engines. To see the difference between a Goddard rocket engine and a Saturn F-1 speaks volumes about the energy required to lift a human into orbit. Goddard's liquid-fueled rocket climbed just 41 feet and could be hauled around by a couple of men. The F-1 engine weighs 18,000-pounds, five of which were under the first stage of the powerful Saturn booster that lifted *Apollo* into space.

On the aviation side you can trace the evolution of flight from the Wright Brothers to the present day through a combination of replicas (the *Wright Flyer*), scale models (the X-1), and actual airplanes. There is a Cold War Russian MiG 21 Fishbed fighter, a US F-86 Sabre from the Korean War, an F-4 Phantom, and an F-16 Fighting Falcon on display (airplanes Stafford flew), plus a T-38 Talon, the first supersonic trainer. And who can miss the F-104 rocketing skyward at the entrance to the museum? Also at the Stafford is the actual simulator that was used to train the astronauts who piloted the space shuttle. A total of 20 air and space vehicles are on display.

Hours: Mon–Sat: 9 a.m. to 5 p.m., Sun: 1 to 5 p.m.
Website: www.staffordmuseum.org
Street address/GPS address: 3000 Logan Rd., Weatherford, OK 73096

Charles B. Hall Memorial Park, Tinker AFB, Oklahoma

Charles B. Hall was the first African American to shoot down an enemy aircraft in World War II and the first African American to receive the Distinguished Flying Cross. The Charles B. Hall Memorial Park at Tinker Air Force

Base is an outdoor airpark open to the public with a dozen or so well-maintained World War II and Cold War aircraft. Among them—a somewhat rare B-47 bomber, the weather-gathering WB-29 model of the B-29 bomber (it provided the first area forecast of an impending tornado), a B-52 bomber, a B-1B bomber, an A-7 Corsair fighter, and an F-105 fighter, to name a few of the more notable ones. Here and there among the planes are statues and memorials, among them a powerful depiction of Rosie the Riveter. Exit on Airport Depot Boulevard off I-40.

Hours: Daily: 7 a.m. to 6 p.m.
Website: http://www.tinker.af.mil/About-Us/Charles-B-Hall-Air-Park/
Street address/GPS address: Tinker Air Force Base, Oklahoma City, OK 73145

Oregon

You can hear the wind blow through the pine trees and smell the salt water in the air. That's the beauty of Oregon—a natural beauty—and these two destinations will keep you far from cities while you explore our military legacy, and the splendid outdoors.

Evergreen Aviation & Space Museum, McMinnville, Oregon

Quietly nestled among the pine trees of McMinnville, Oregon, is a peaked-roof building holding some of the most interesting military artifacts in the nation. Part civilian and part military, the Evergreen Air & Space Museum has a beautiful SR-71 displayed with canopies up, a fleet of MiGs (MiG 17, MiG 21, MiG 23, and the sleek but intimidating MiG 29), a group of planes from Douglas Aircraft including the big AD-1, a Skyraider, and an A-4 Skyhawk, the later two of Vietnam fame, plus an outstanding collection of modern fighters, most of which are Air Force models. There is a Titan II ICBM standing 103 feet tall vertically slicing through the floors of the museum with a viewing area down by the main engines in the bottom of the Cold War "silo."

The centerpiece, of course, is the Spruce Goose. With its eight engines and 320-foot wingspan, it dwarfs everything around it. To illustrate just how

Halfway between Portland and Corvallis, Oregon, is the Evergreen Museum, with its unique collection of warbirds and missiles, including the one-of-a-kind Spruce Goose. Seen here: A Titan missile rising through the floors of the main building. Photo courtesy of Evergreen Aviation & Space Museum

big it is, Evergreen parked a DC-3 under one of its wings. It scarcely overlaps two engines.

Founded by Delbert Smith, the entrepreneur who started Evergreen Airlines, the Evergreen Museum is just south of Portland and worth every minute of the drive. The museum staff will tell you the story of each airplane they have; many of their 250 docents flew or worked on the planes (or helicopters) you're interested in.

Hours: Daily: 9 a.m. to 5 p.m.
Website: www.evergreenmuseum.org
Street address/GPS address: 500 NE Captain Michael King Smith Way, McMinnville, OR 97128

While You're in the Neighborhood

The Tillamook Air Museum, Tillamook, Oregon

During World War II, there was an ever-present fear of a second Japanese attack, this time against the mainland. To guard against that, the Navy ran coastal patrols using a fleet of blimps. Naval Air Station Tillamook was home to some of those airships—these beautiful, 252-foot-long lighter-than-air reconnaissance blimps that were able to sustain flight for up to three days.

The Tillamook Air Museum is what's left of those days, and it's worth a visit if only to see what a US Navy airship hangar looks like. The museum is in Hangar B, which is a behemoth of a structure. Measuring 192 feet high, 1,072 feet long, and 296 feet wide, it encloses no less than 7 acres. The hangar is in the record books as the largest free-standing, clear-span wood structure in the world.

In addition to the hangar, the museum has a small assortment of fighter jets, including an F-14 Tomcat, an A-7 Corsair, and an A-25 Invader. The exhibits inside tell the Tillamook story using photographs from the era.

And, however off the beaten path this destination is, they made it easy to find. At the turnoff from OR 101, there is an A-4 Skyhawk fighter jet and on the side of the hangar it says "Air Museum."

A café serves food from 11 a.m. to 2 p.m.

Hours: See website
Website: www.tillamookair.com
Street address/GPS address: 6030 Hangar Rd., Tillamook, OR 97141

Pennsylvania

Not counting the national parks in Pennsylvania—and you should certainly visit Valley Forge—Pennsylvania has an amazing array—and range—of destinations. From the old navy yard in Philadelphia to the all-new Museum of the American Revolution (also in Philadelphia) to the Heritage Trail, this state is brimming with American military history.

US Army Heritage and Education Center (US Army Heritage Trail), Carlisle, Pennsylvania

Many of our favorite destinations went to great lengths to build immersive, interactive, digitally enhanced exhibits. The Army Heritage Center took a different route.

Here you will be immersed in a physical world. We're talking about a long, wonderfully designed walk through American history called the US Army Heritage Trail. Superb in detail and authenticity, you will walk past (and into) a full-size Revolutionary War blockhouse, a full-size Civil War winter encampment, a rabbit warren of World War I trenches, a Yorktown redoubt, the split-rail fences along the road at Antietam, a World War II waypoint, and a cluster of full-size World War II barracks just like the ones our recruits lived in during basic training. You will see tanks, helicopters, wheeled cannons, and antiaircraft guns, and more all in combat settings.

A cluster of World War II barracks is but one of the many life-size military and combat battlescapes on the Heritage Trail at the US Army Heritage and Education Center. The battlescapes begin with the Revolutionary War and continue to present day. Reenactors often stage weekend encampments along this outdoor walk. Photo courtesy of US Army Heritage and Education Center

The Heritage Train is a 1-mile walk with 14 waypoints that begins at the Education Center. What will you see along the way? There is an M42 twin 40mm Bofors self-propelled gun and an 8-inch M1 howitzer called the defender of Pusan at the Korean War stop. The Cold War installation features an intimidating M60 Patton main battle tank next to a Cobra attack helicopter. The Vietnam Fire Support Base has a pair of 105mm howitzers sighted against some distant target with a Huey sweeping in on a resupply mission. And then there is the German pillbox. Close your eyes and see the machine guns raking the beaches of Normandy or firing on the battlefields of Belgium. Suddenly you realize how preciously thin the divide is between life and death.

The trail winds around until it returns you to where you started for the second part of your day. Inside the Education Center is another walk, this one through a series of visually engaging displays that follow the life of a soldier from the Spanish-American War to the current war on terror. There are tableaus with scale models of battlescapes as well as large artifacts and dioramas with soldiers in period uniforms. Oral histories are available and play through your cellphone as a kind of self-guided tour. And be sure to see the in-depth and rather intense exhibit called Courage, Commitment and Fear: The American Soldier in the Vietnam War. With it is a short film here called *Our Journey through War*.

So enjoy the outdoors. Crawl over berms. Walk through the trenches. Feel the wood, touch the steel. The World War II obstacle course is sure to wear out a car full of kids who have been cooped up in the backseat. And check for reenactment days. All manner of groups like to come out here and encamp around these fascinating structures.

The trail is open for walking from dawn to dusk. Entry into the buildings follows the hours of the Education Center.

Education Center Hours: Mon —Sat: 10 a.m. to 5 p.m., Sun: 12 to 5 p.m.
Website: www.ahec.armywarcollege.edu
Street address/GPS address: 950 Soldiers Dr., Carlisle, PA 17013

The Museum of the American Revolution, Philadelphia, Pennsylvania

Each year, millions of us make the journey to Philadelphia to see Independence Hall and the Liberty Bell, but there was

"Liberty now has a country," said the Marquis de Lafayette. The recently opened Museum of the American Revolution tells the story of our battle for independence. Photo courtesy of Museum of the American Revolution

always something missing. Yes, it was fascinating to walk around the city and visit these places, but where was the *story*? That problem has now been solved in the form of the all-new Museum of the American Revolution. Walk down the cobblestone streets past the food trucks selling mouthwatering steak sandwiches and enter an architectural masterpiece. Opened in 2017, everything you want to know about the seeds of the American Revolution—and its outcomes—are here. Exhibits challenge you to remember those times 200-plus years ago by asking questions about the origins of the ferment, how you might have managed the "messy process" of a revolt against a king to whom generations of your own family had pledged their allegiance long before you were born, or how you might have otherwise conducted the war if you had been a general. Emotional, tricky stuff, yes—and the museum makes that point time and again as the displays and exhibits artfully help you see the Revolution the way it was, warts and all.

Start in the theater up front in the Main Gallery and view the 15-minute overview of the Revolution and then work your way through the many, many exhibits. The museum uses old letters, scale models, full-sized dioramas, panoramas, and interactive video kiosks to tell the many stories of the Revolution. Crowd favorites include the recreation of Boston's Liberty Tree, where the leaders of the Revolution discussed their cause and made plans, and the full-sized Privateer that raided British ships. Be sure to see the collection of the weapons of the Revolution, George Washinton's command tent, as well as scenes and stories depicting some of the major battles of the war. You will end up your visit in the Battlefield Theater with its sights, sounds, and motions.

After an hour or so on your feet, the Cross Keys Café is a welcome break for a cold drink and a sandwich. And don't miss the gift shop for period coffee mugs, busts, and other gifts you won't find anywhere else.

Hours: Daily: 10 a.m. to 5 p.m., extended summer hours
Website: www.amrevmuseum.org
Street address/GPS address: 101 S. Third St., Philadelphia, PA 19106

The Navy Yard Walking Tour, Philadelphia, Pennsylvania

Sometimes the best things in life are hidden in plain sight. That's certainly true when it comes to Philadelphia Navy Yard. In the middle of one of the nation's busiest cities, nestled between an international airport, an oil refinery, and a football stadium, is the historic Philadelphia Naval Shipyard, a place where scores of military ships were once built or repaired.

At its World War II height, the Philadelphia Navy Yard employed some 40,000 workers and turned out more than 50 ships while repairing more than 500. There were barracks, officers quarters, mess halls, and officer and enlisted clubs—the yard was a military city unto itself—but the need diminished in the decades after the war and the Navy pulled out in 1995. Thankfully, the yard was successfully converted to civilian use with a keen eye toward preserving its storied military history and the classic military buildings, grounds, and docks that made it up. Today you can stroll through those same grounds and explore the former admirals and officers quarters, each a masterpiece of Georgian architecture now fully restored and occupied by various private companies. Be sure to walk around the Navy docks and see the still-active Reserve Basin where mothballed destroyers and freighters are tied up side by side like toys. The old Marine Parade Grounds are here, too.

A one-hour walking tour starts at the end of Broad Street. Follow the designated trail signs as you wind your way through this special part of our nation's naval history. Be sure to dress according to the weather.

Hours: Mon–Fri: 6 a.m. to 8 p.m.
Website: www.navyyard.org/information-and-directions/
walking-tour-visitors-guide
Street address/GPS address: 4747 S. Broad St., Philadelphia, PA 19112

South Carolina

South Carolina is a navy town (Naval Weapons Station Charleston is here). Oh, and South Carolina is an air force town (three air bases here). And did we say that South Carolina is an army town (Fort Jackson is a major training base) *and* a marine corps town (Parris Island inducts new marines). All four facts are true—South Carolina plays an important role in our nation's defense and has a tremendous military legacy. It also has Patriots Point.

Patriots Point, Mount Pleasant, South Carolina

You might be in Charleston for the architecture or the beautiful beaches or a round of golf, but be sure to head across the bridge to Mount Pleasant and Patriots Point. A perennial favorite for tourists and veterans alike, Patriots Point is a multiship complex anchored by the aircraft carrier USS *Yorktown*. A World War II veteran, the USS *Yorktown* fought in almost every major battle in the Pacific theater, earning no less than 11 battle stars. She was then recommissioned for Vietnam and earned 5 more battle stars before being sent out on one more mission, this time to be part of the fleet of ships stationed in the ocean to recover *Apollo 8*. Only then was she allowed to step down to enjoy life as a floating museum.

Start your visit on the *Yorktown* and work your way through the extensive exhibits on her hangar deck. Read about her battles and the men who served on her. Take in the video clips and explore the World War II warbirds and the B-25 Mitchell that's here. Next, take Tour 1 (self-guided) and explore her interior compartments. In the main, the restorations let you see the ship the way she was with

A visit to an aircraft carrier typically begins here, on the hangar deck. All five CVs in this guide use this cavernous space to display aircraft and dioramas, show videos, and offer rides in their simulators. Seen here: The Yorktown *at Patriots Point. Photo courtesy of author's collection*

only a few displays placed here and there. Mannequins can be seen dishing food in the galley and preparing for patients in the medical spaces.

The aviation buff will find almost every aircraft or jet every deployed on a Navy aircraft carrier, including World War II–era planes such as the F6F Hellcat, the FG-1 Corsair, the TBM Avenger, and the SBD Dauntless. Vietnam-era jets include the F-4 Phantom, the A4 Skyhawk, and the A6 Intruder. There is also an F-14 Tomcat and an F/A-18 Hornet, plus dozens of other ones, including helicopters and large artifacts. Be sure to walk through the Medal of Honor Museum (on the hangar deck) before disembarking.

Next, visit the destroyer the USS *Laffey* and learn her D-Day story. The *Laffey* screened the landings on Utah Beach, protecting the soldiers as they fought their way ashore. After that, she moved down to Cherbourg, where she shelled the German gun emplacements. As if that wasn't enough, she next moved to the Pacific, where she nearly went under. They call her the ship that would not die because she was hit by no less than six kamikazes and four bombs—but survived. The *Laffey* was repaired and went on to fight in Korea, and then she served during the Suez crisis and even patrolled the Mediterranean during the Cold War.

To help you visualize the confines of the spaces on a ship (and the various crew functions), the interior compartments of many of the ones in this guide are populated with mannequins. Here sailors dish out pancakes and eggs on the aircraft carrier USS Yorktown *at Patriots Point. Photo courtesy of author's collection*

Next walk down to the USS *Clagamore*. Although the *Clagamore* doesn't have the battle history of the *Laffey*, it does tell an important story. Follow her history by reading the onboard displays that talk about the Cold War arms race and the constant improvements that had to be engineered into submarines like the *Clagamore*. Weapons systems were always being upgraded to new capabilities, and the silent service was no exception.

Finally, get ready for the land-side exhibits. New to Patriots Point is the incredibly immersive Vietnam Experience. This 2.5-acre outdoor park has a very realistic Brown Water Support Base and a Marine Artillery Fire Base. (In 1965 the US Navy reinstituted its brown water operations and began patrolling the Mekong River with a fleet of river boats that included the agile PBRs— Patrol Boat, River.) The Brown Water Support Base seen here reimagines those operations in a full-scale diorama that incorporates a 31-foot PBR with grenade launchers and a full complement of guns. Next to it is the Marine Artillery Fire Base, which reimagines a fire base at Khe Sanh and delivers the same reality with mannequins, a 105mm howitzer, sandbags, medical MASH tents, and three of the iconic helicopters of Vietnam, the Huey, Sea Knight, and Sea Horse. Note the landscaping. Realism was one of the objectives, and these are incredibly detailed battlescapes.

This is one of the most visited military destinations in the nation so come early. There is a gift shop that you must pass through as you leave (how clever) and a few places to grab a sandwich or an ice cream on the *Yorktown*.

Hours: Daily: 9 a.m. to 6:30 p.m.
Website: www.patriotspoint.org
Street address/GPS address: 40 Patriots Point Rd., Mount Pleasant, SC 29464

South Dakota

South Dakota has always played a major role in maintaining the stalemate that has kept the two superpowers coasting along in neutral. It was home to one of Strategic Air Command's earliest nuclear bomber bases and later got ICBMs. Each of our destinations in South Dakota tells part of that Cold War story.

South Dakota Air & Space Museum, Rapid City, South Dakota

The South Dakota Air & Space Museum is inextricably linked to its neighbor, Ellsworth Air Force Base. Ellsworth Air Force Base began as a World War II training base that stamped out B-17 pilots and navigators with production-line-like regularity. When the war came to an end, it became a bomber base in its own right, starting with a wing of B-36 intercontinental bombers and then a wing of supersonic B-1B Lancers. Ellsworth eventually entered the missile age with a wing of Titan ICBMs, followed by Minuteman missiles, followed by the more-advanced Minuteman IIs.

The South Dakota Air & Space Museum tells that story, and more. A series of creme-colored hangars form the main museum, with a B-1B bomber and a Minuteman II missile there to greet you as you arrive. Inside, backlit displays are filled with histories and tableaus. You'll find aircraft cockpits, crew stations, and artifacts that cover more than 100 years of aviation history. There is a miniature scale model of the World War II raid on Ploesti, a command console for the missiles, and an F-104 cockpit trainer, to name some of the things to see. Notice the backlit displays, too. There is so much to absorb here.

Next walk the outdoor airpark. The incredibly beautiful Black Hills Mountains provide a stunning backdrop to a display of more than 30 well-maintained aircraft, including a World War II–era B-29, a Vietnam-era B-52, a Huey, an FB-111 Aardvark, a EC-135 tanker, an F-100, an F-102, an F-105, and more. The aircraft are painted in period colors and with period markings. The black underbelly of the B-52, for instance, tells you this plane was flown over Vietnam, and was not part of the nuclear force. Seen from the ground, black blends in with the sky. White was the coating put on B-52s with a nuclear mission.

Interestingly, the museum offers a daily bus tour that departs from the museum and takes you around Ellsworth Air Force Base and stops at the old Minuteman II training silo. You'll go down 30 feet and look through portholes to see the missile and have the entire operation explained to you. During the tour, you'll get a windshield view of a strategic bomber base and pass several points of interest, including the security force's guard dogs and the flight line (if it's open). And don't be surprised if you see a B-1 bomber taking off or landing. This is an active-duty base.

Museum Hours: See website
Website: www.sdairandspacemuseum.com
Street address/GPS address: 2890 Davis Dr., Ellsworth AFB, SD 57706

The Best Formerly Secret Military Sites: Minuteman Missile National Historic Site, Philip, South Dakota

To see this ICBM missile site, you have to visit two places. The first is the launch silo, where the missiles were kept underground and ready to go 24/7. The second is the launch control facility, which is where the keys were. In this South Dakota complex, the Delta-09 missile silo and Launch Control Facility Delta 01 make up the excellent Minuteman Missile National Park.

For your visit here, start at the park's visitor center and take in all of the exhibits and displays, being sure to watch the various films on the need for ICBMs and the stakes of the Cold War. Here's where you will take the Launch

The view looking down a missile silo in South Dakota. Seen here: The warhead of a Minuteman ICBM. Photo courtesy of Minuteman Missile National Historic Site, National Park Service

Control Facility Delta 01 Tour. You must be able to climb two completely vertical 15-foot ladders but if that's no problem, park rangers will take groups of six down the elevator 31 feet to see the launch control panel where they would enter the launch codes and turn the keys. Nuclear war would begin here.

Next, drive down the road 15 miles and see the Delta-09 Silo. Look through the glass viewing cap to see an inert Minuteman II. No park rangers are needed for this part. Just one glance and you can imagine the furious explosion of heat and energy as a Minuteman rose into the sky taking with it a W62 nuclear warhead with a 170 kiloton yield (Hiroshima was 14 kilotons).

The Minuteman II National Historic Site is run by the National Park Service and it is well laid out and very well organized. A total of 150 ICBM missiles were once based in South Dakota.

Hours: Daily: 8 a.m. to 4 p.m.
Delta-01 Tours: require advanced reservations—see website
Website: www.nps.gov/mimi/index.htm
Street address/GPS address: 24545 Cottonwood Rd., Philip, SD 57567

The Best Military Base Tours: Ellsworth Air Force Base, Rapid City, South Dakota

This is a one-of-a-kind opportunity to tour an active-duty bomber base attached to the granddaddy of our air commands, the US Air Force Global Strike Command. On this tour you will see the impressive, swept-wing B-1B supersonic nuclear bomber and meet an aircrew. Tours run on the second and fourth Friday of the month, April through October. Depending on the activity that day, stops usually include a visit to a B-1B with time set aside to talk to the airmen. You will also stop to buy your own lunch as you see the rest of the base facilities.

Arrangements must be made through the Ellsworth Public Affairs office but if fewer than 15 people sign up, it will not go, so call first. (This tour is apart from the silo tour offered by the nearby South Dakota Air & Space Museum.)

Website: http://www.ellsworth.af.mil/Home/Public-Affairs/
Street Address/GPS Address: 1940 EP Howe Dr., Ellsworth Air Force Base, SD 57706

Texas

You can be picky in Texas. There are more than enough excellent military destinations to choose from with something for everyone no matter what conflict you study or what branch of the military fascinates you most.

The National Museum of the Pacific War, Fredericksburg, Texas

After winding your way through the beautiful Hill Country of Texas, you begin to wonder what on Earth is a museum dedicated to the war in the Pacific Ocean doing in a dusty, landlocked town miles from the nearest seas? It's a beautiful place no doubt—Texas wineries abound and the scenery is ruggedly handsome. It's also a town filled with wonderful people and conveniently located equidistant from Austin and San Antonio. But that's not the answer. As it happens, Fredericksburg, Texas, is the birthplace of US Navy Fleet Admiral Chester W. Nimitz, our World War II commander in chief of the Pacific Fleet. Nimitz is from this charmingly small town and rose through the ranks to command some two million sailors and five thousand ships all with one distinct mission: defeat Japan. Thus, this excellent museum.

First, let's go back in time. The Pacific campaign was a lengthy, distant, island-hopping campaign across an ocean three times the size of the Atlantic. There was combat in Guadalcanal on one side of the Pacific, Wake Island on another, and more combat out to the Philippines. Bloody battles were fought in places with names that were foreign to the average American and in conditions alien to our soldiers. In the Pacific, heat, poisonous snakes, diseases, and bullets all claimed lives.

So, how did we do it? How did American marines, sailors, soldiers, and airmen carry the battle to Japan? One could answer that question by putting up a series of maps and photographs and video clips—but everyone's done that. Not here. The people of Fredericksburg wanted a museum that would let you *experience* the story.

There are three distinct "campuses" on the 6 acres that make up this excellent destination. The first is the main museum and the crown jewel, called the

A submarine "surfaces" through the lawn in front of the National Museum of the Pacific War. This sort of imaginative staging repeats throughout this superb destination. Photo courtesy of author's collection

George H. W. Bush Gallery. The Bush Gallery greets you with a stone wall that forms an undulating wave behind which a Navy submarine literally rises out of the ground (Admiral Nimitz was first and foremost a submariner). Behind the submarine is the museum itself. The local stone used in the construction of the building not only makes for a harmonious whole but also imparts a distinctive look to this destination. After paying your admission fee, you will follow a twisting, turning path through a series of multimedia exhibits that take you from the seeds of war in the Pacific, to the unconditional surrender of Japan. There is a display or diorama explaining all of the battles on each of the islands using a combination of mannequins, large-scale artifacts like tanks or artillery pieces, foliage, special lighting, video displays, and other visual graphics. Along the way you will pass video walls, use touch screens, listen to your audio wand, and see hundreds of artifacts, including Japanese and American warplanes, combat artillery pieces, and, incredibly, one of the Japanese mini-subs that was captured in Hawaii.

After touring the Bush Gallery, head over to the Pacific Combat Zone. Here you will find an enormous plaza imprinted with a map of the Pacific

Volunteers use flamethrowers as they reenact the assault on a Pacific island. Reenactments such as these are carried out at the National Museum of the Pacific War. Photo courtesy of National Museum of the Pacific War

Ocean connecting the TBM aircraft hangar, the PT boat base, and the one-of-a-kind 2.5-acre outdoor amphitheater. Visit the TBM hangar first and see a restored torpedo bomber like the one that President George H. W. Bush flew. Then go to the PT boat base to see PT-309 being readied for a night patrol in the Pacific. After that, head outside to the amphitheater. The land before you is sculpted to represent a Pacific island, and it's used by the museum for its twice-monthly reenactments. You will literally feel the earth shake as "marines" maneuver across the topography and storm objectives complete with live explosions, armored vehicles, and flamethrowers—and you will feel your heart break as young actors become casualties of war.

Finally, there is Nimitz Museum itself, which is inside the old Nimitz Hotel. The Nimitz Museum tells the story of the Nimitz family and how a young boy from this landlocked part of Texas grew up to become the commander in chief of the Pacific forces. The Nimitz Hotel has been beautifully restored and has exhibits throughout.

You could easily spend the weekend here, and many people do. There are plenty of motels and excellent restaurants in town and so very much to enjoy in the area. But first and foremost, let it sink in. Linger and explore and let this destination remind you of the great sacrifice our men made to end this war.

The reenactments in the Pacific Combat Theater are performed twice monthly, March through November. Tickets are required and dates are posted on their website.

Museum Hours: Daily: 9 a.m. to 5 p.m.
Reenactments: 10:30 a.m. and 2 p.m.
Website: www.pacificwarmuseum.org
Street address/GPS address: 340 E. Main St., Fredericksburg, TX 78624

Lone Star Flight Museum, Houston, Texas

An excellent collection of beautifully restored World War II–era warbirds anchors this newly relocated military destination. Formerly on Galveston Island, after suffering one too many hurricanes, the Lone Star Flight Museum tossed in the towel and moved lock, stock, and barrel to Houston. They reopened in 2017 with two 30,000-square-foot hangars and 20 top-notch military aircraft and helicopters.

You'll begin your visit through the Arrival Hall and go either right or left into, respectively, the Heritage Hangar or the Waltrip Hangar. Among the aircraft in these hangars (the locations and specific planes may change): a B-17 Flying Fortress, a B-25 Mitchell, an SBD Dauntless, an F6F Hellcat, an F4-U Corsair, a P-47 Thunderbolt, an AD-1 Skyraider, and more. The $38 million facility includes the Texas Aviation Hall of Fame, simulators, cockpits to sit in, touch screens, interactive exhibits that focus on military pilot training in Texas (home to the USAF's pilot training bases), and more.

Many of their aircraft are flying models. Qualified pilots will take you up in the B-17, the B-25, the T-6, the SBD, or one of their World War II trainers. A restaurant is slated to open soon.

Hours: Tues–Sun: 9 a.m. to 5 p.m., Mon: closed
Website: www.lonestarflight.org
Street address/GPS address: 11551 Aerospace Ave., Houston, TX 77034

USS Lexington *Museum on the Bay, Corpus Christi, Texas*

This has to be on your list if for no other reason than to launch off a carrier deck in an F/A-18 Hornet and fly a mission ending with a nerve-wracking carrier landing. Really? Well, almost. The $180,000 flight simulator on the *Lexington* has full motion control and incredible graphics allowing you to come as close to the real thing as possible, short of becoming a naval aviator.

But that's not why you're here. The USS *Lexington* is a touchstone of US history. The *Lexington* saw combat during World War II, spending 21 months in theater with an impressive record of Japanese planes shot down, enemy ships sunk, and countless days making sure our soldiers and marines got ashore. She's an angled-deck carrier now but during the war she was a straight-deck carrier, which was something else. During your visit, stand on the fantail and try to imagine what it was like to be an exhausted, 28-year-old navy fighter pilot coming in from a combat mission bouncing around in an F6F Hellcat looking down at that tiny deck and seeing a wall of parked airplanes at the end, hoping—*believing*—that the arresting cables would stop you before you plowed into them (and, yes, some did crash that way). That's a straight-deck carrier (she was modified in 1955).

You'll start your visit in the hangar deck and see some of the 20 perfectly maintained aircraft. You'll find such expected carrier icons as the F-4 Phantom, the A-6 Intruder, the F-14 Tomcat, the F/A-18 Hornet, and the A-4 Skyhawk, but add to that list the F9F Cougar, the F2 Banshee, the A-3 Skywarrior, the A-7 Corsair, and a fun-to-see T-2 Buckeye trainer jet (it's the trainer many Navy pilots flew back when they first trapped on a carrier). Walk around the hangar deck and the flight deck and read not just the facts on these planes but their combat histories, too. The decks are open and the ship is welcoming with docents ready to tell you a story or two.

Most of the ship can be seen on a self-guided tour, but they do have some interesting options. If you love the grit of the interior compartments, try the Hard Hat Tour. There's a Flight Operations Tour, too, if that's more your cup of tea. (Both require an extra fee.)

Either way, when you're topside, be sure to look landward and enjoy the spectacular view of Corpus Christi. The *Lexington* has received more than five million visitors since it opened to the public.

Hours: Daily: 9 a.m. to 5 p.m.
Website: www.usslexington.com
Street address/GPS address: 2914 N. Shoreline Blvd., Corpus Christi, TX 78402

The 10 Best Military Experiences: Ox Hunting Ranch/Drivetanks.com, Uvalde, Texas

Leave it to our friends in Texas to do things big. In this case, we're talking about a vast, remote, 18,000-acre cattle ranch that has been converted to an every-growing guest ranch dedicated to the majesty of the outdoors be it hunting, fishing, shooting bows and arrows, birdwatching, giraffe watching, kayaking, jet skiing —or, in this case, driving a real tank.

A visitor fires the main gun on a Sherman tank during an outing at the Ox Ranch in Texas. They will also let you fire the main gun on a Soviet T-34 or a British Scorpion. Photo courtesy of Ox Hunting Ranch/Drivetanks.com

In 2016 the Ox Hunting Ranch launched Drive Tanks and put out a barn full of 30- and 60-ton tracked vehicles for you to choose from. There is a beautifully restored World War II Sherman tank, a Russian T-34, a British Scorpion, a British Chieftain, and a German Leopard tank. Essentially, you pick a tank, request a date, arrive by car, helicopter, or jet, and take your tank out for a spin. Your instructor will brief you on the history of the tank, train you in its operations, and go over important safety protocols. When you're done, out you go to rumble and roar over obstacles, streams, and other challenges ideally suited to show off the tank's muscle (there are more than 100 miles of dirt roads on the property). And get this. Unique in all of America, they let you fire the big gun on the Sherman, the Russian T-34, or the British Scorpion FV1. Repeat—you can load the main gun, pull the trigger, and hear and feel the shock as the shell shoots out of the barrel. (And these are the *main* guns. The M4 Sherman has a 76mm gun, the T-34 has an 85mm gun, and the Scorpion fires a 76mm gun.)

If tanks and tracked vehicles are more what you want, they have a range where you can fire almost any weapon the US Army owns, and some they don't. The have an M134 minigun (a Gatling gun that fires 6,000 rounds a minute), flamethrowers, machine guns of all types, AK-47s, and rifles all the way down to your grandfather's World War II M1 carbine.

The ranch is owned by internet entrepreneur Brent Oxley. Passionate about customer service and quality, Oxley and his team have thought of everything. They offer lodging for their overnight guests in their World War II–themed "barracks," they serve chef-prepared meals—or guests can come in for just a day trip and meet up with their hosts and guides. Most important of all—this is a professional operation. Tanks and guns are serious business, and military enthusiasts and armored buffs alike consider this to be the best in class. Located about an hour and a half from San Antonia, they recently added a 5,800-foot runway that will take a decent-size corporate jet.

Hours: See website for reservations
Website: www.drivetanks.com and http://www.oxhuntingranch.com/
Street address/GPS address: 1946 Private Rd. 2485, Uvalde, TX 788801

The 10 Best Military Experiences: Wings of Freedom/Collings Foundation, Stowe, Massachusetts/Houston, Texas

They say that behind every great private collection of warbirds is a passionate collector—and that says it all about the Collings Foundation. Incorporated as a nonprofit by cash register entrepreneur Richard F. Collings, the Collings Foundation has a stable of World War II–era and Vietnam-era warbirds that are available for a once-in-a-lifetime flying experience.[14]

From their private airport in Stowe, Massachusetts (and at air shows across the nation), Collings offers up what they call the "Wings of Freedom" flights. Choose between a B-17 Flying Fortress, a B-24 Liberator, a B-25 Mitchell, or a P-51 Mustang. Before you go up, you'll receive an extensive preflight briefing that covers the plane's history, what to expect in the sky, the dos and don'ts of being a passenger in a World War II warbird, plus important safety procedures. All of this comes from pilots, many of whom are former military aviators. All flights are operated under an FAA program called the Living History Flight Experiences.

What's really special about the Collings Foundation is their one-of-a-kind Vietnam Memorial Flight Experience. From their air base in Houston, Texas, Collings offers an amazing opportunity to fly in a no-kidding, red-hot Vietnam-era F-4D Phantom or an A-4 Skyhawk. Procured from the boneyards at Davis-Monthan Air Force Base, Collings completely overhauled both airplanes and put them into service as "civilian-operated jets." Before your intense, 40-minute flight, you will be briefed on the flight envelope of a high-performance jet, receive appropriate safety protocols and emergency procedures, and hear a little history about the jets. Your pilots will be former Navy or Air Force fighter pilots with thousands of hours in the sky.

Importantly, those in the know consider Collings to be a top-notch, professional, safety-conscious organization. In the end, you'll experience firsthand what it's like to be a combat fighter pilot, including those g-forces front seaters have felt for decades.

Hours: You will arrange your hours when you book
Website: www.collingsfoundation.org/events/category/wings-of-freedom-tour
Street address/GPS address: You will arrange your meet point when you book.

The Frontiers of Flight Museum, Love Field, Dallas, Texas

Although technically not a military site, there's a lot to love about this spot just minutes from downtown Dallas. First of all, Love Field is where Southwest Airlines got its start, something that will be absolutely obvious to you when you arrive. Why? You can't miss the tail of the Southwest Boeing 737 cleverly rammed into the side of the building.

After getting over that incredible sight—worth the trip by itself—go inside and enjoy the selection of perfectly restored warbirds, biplanes, and modern jets. There's a T-38 Talon (our first supersonic jet trainer), an A-7 Corsair, plenty of civilian biplanes and sport planes, plus the other half of the 737 open for a cockpit tour. Other things to capture your imagination—a piece of moon rock, a display that shows how Alexander Calder painted an entire Boeing 727 during his commission for "Flying Colors," a Tomahawk cruise missile, an SR-71 cockpit simulator that was used to train pilots (the only one ever built), and a display showing you what a real "black box" looks like. There are plenty of other military aircraft outside, including an F-16B two-seat trainer, a Huey, and an F-105 fighter.

Civilian, maybe, but this is a well-designed museum filled with fascinating military artifacts and airplanes in every corner. The Museum Store has a nice selection of one-of-a-kind gifts, as well.

Hours: Mon–Sat: 10 a.m. to 5 p.m., Sun: 1 to 5 p.m.
Website: www.flightmuseum.com
Street address/GPS address: 6911 Lemmon Ave., Dallas, TX 75209

Cavanaugh Flight Museum, Addison, Texas

This well-stocked museum in Addison, Texas, greets you with a deep inventory of warbirds, military vehicles, and helicopters presented without much fanfare but beautifully preserved. Although it lacks the interactive displays and dioramas of other destinations, the Cavanaugh nonetheless has four hangars crammed with World War I, World War II, Korean- and Vietnam-era aircraft plus a few tanks and military vehicles tucked in the corners. In the main there is little more than an informative placard or an occasional artifact (a weapon, an ejection seat, and so on) next to the model on display, but the variety of aircraft more than makes up for it. German, Russian, British, and American models are exhibited, P-47s, Spitfires, and Heinkels included. Interestingly, there is a small "car show" here, too, with cars from the 1950s next to the planes.

The stock-in-trade here is a warbird ride. In addition to the usual T-6 Texan, T-28 Trojan , P-51 Mustang, and Stearman biplane (all on display, too), the Cavanaugh offers flights in the huge AD5-W Skyraider, the 0-2 Skymaster, the F4-U Corsair (FG-1D), and the bubble-canopy OH-13D Helicopter.

Qualified pilots brief you on the dos and don'ts and safety procedures and then take you up for a 30-minute flight. Some aircraft have dual controls, which means that if you booked with an optional CFI, you can manipulate the flight controls.

During the air show season, some of their planes may be on the air show circuit, so give them two weeks' notice if you want a specific airplane.

Hours: Mon–Sat: 9 a.m. to 5 p.m., Sun: 11 a.m. to 5 p.m.
Website: www.cavflight.org
Street address/GPS address: 4572 Claire Chennault, Addison, TX 75001

While You're in the Neighborhood

1st Cavalry Museum, Fort Hood, Texas

An extensive and well-designed outdoor display of armored vehicles makes this stop more than worthwhile. Some 60 tanks, armored bulldozers, howitzers, artillery pieces—and more tanks—can be found in the outdoor tank park in front of the 1st Cavalry Museum. A long, winding walkway weaves in and around an M1E1 Abrams main battle tank, an M3 Stuart tank, an M4 Sherman, an M41 Walker, an M47 Patton, an M60 Patton, towed and self-propelled howitzers, a Soviet T55 and a T72 main battle tank, antitank guns, an Honest John surface-to-surface missile (it had a nuclear warhead), plus army helicopters and much, much more.

There is also a modest array of indoor exhibits that tell the history of the 1st beginning with its frontier days of the US Cavalry, through the Indian Wars, Vietnam, and up to today. This museum is located on base so bring ID and proof of insurance for your auto.

Hours: Mon–Fri: 9 a.m. to 4 p.m., Sat: 10 a.m. to 4 p.m., Sun: 12 p.m. to 4 p.m.
Website: www.museumsusa.org/museums/info/15952
Street address/GPS address: 2218 Headquarters Ave., Fort Hood, TX 76544

American Undersea Warfare Center in Seawolf Park, Galveston, Texas

This attractive outdoor naval park in Galveston is home to the submarine USS *Cavalla* and the destroyer USS *Stewart*. This is a beautifully maintained pocket park with well-manicured grounds. And both ships have fascinating stories.

Let's start with the *Cavalla*. A classic, Gato-class World War II–era submarine, the USS *Cavalla* had perhaps the most spectacular maiden combat voyage of any submarine in naval history. After departing Pearl Harbor, and while under way to her station in the Phillipines, on June 19, 1944, she spotted some Japanese ships, one of which was the aircraft carrier *Shokaku*. *Cavalla* maneuvered into position and fired a spread of six torpedoes, three of which found their mark. The *Shokaku* shuddered from the explosions (and eventually sank). The *Cavalla* immediately came under fire from enemy depth charges and survived but when it was over, it was a triumph: one of the Japanese aircraft carriers that participated in the sneak attack on Pearl Harbor was gone.

The USS *Stewart* was no lightweight either. A veteran destroyer escort, the *Stewart* screened countless Atlantic convoys against German U-boats and did one tour out to Pearl Harbor. She is one of the last surviving examples of a World War II destroyer escort and today serves alongside the *Cavalla* as a memorial to the many Texans who lost their lives at sea.

You can walk through the interior compartments of both ships and explore them to your heart's content. You will come away with a good feel for life on a navy ship as well as a deeper appreciation for the service of our naval sailors.

Hours: Daily: 9 a.m. to 6 p.m.
Website: www.americanunderseawarfarecenter.com
Street address/GPS address: 100 Seawolf Pkwy., Galveston, TX 77554

USS Texas (Battleship Texas Foundation), LaPorte, Texas

As a World War I–era battleship, this is indeed a classic straight-bow dreadnaught. The USS *Texas* served in both World War I and World War II. Interesting fact—during World War II she escorted convoys across the Atlantic and then provided gun support for the D-Day invasion.

Self-guided tours are available, or you can take the 3.5-hour Hard Hat tour and see the pilot house, the ammo handling room, and more.

Hours: Daily: 9 a.m. to 5 p.m.
Website: www.tpwd.texas.gov/state-parks/battleship-texas
Street address/GPS address: 3523 Independence Pkwy. S., LaPorte, TX 77571

National Vietnam War Museum, Weatherford, Texas

This start-up museum has already accumulated some interesting artifacts, including a UH-1 Huey and a 34-ton Vietnam-era landing vehicle tracked

(LVT). The founders have also erected a half-scale replica of the Vietnam Memorial and have landscaped two contemplative gardens. Don't expect a lot of pizzazz here, but do come if you want a quiet moment remembering the events of 50 years ago.

Hours: Daily: 9 a.m. to 1 p.m.
Website: www.nationalvnwarmuseum.org
Street address/GPS address: 12685 Mineral Wells Hwy., Weatherford, TX 76088

Museum of the American G.I., College Station, Texas

Armored and tracked vehicles are the staples at the Museum of the American G.I. You'll find well-restored tanks that include two variants of the M4 Sherman battle tank, plus an M5 Stuart tank and an M24 Chaffee. Seen shoulder to shoulder, they present an impressive—and intimidating—array. Around them are a half-dozen wheeled vehicles (jeeps and trucks), plus a M18 Hellcat tank destroyer, a M8 Greyhound APC, and others.

Most of this collection is from World War II, but be sure to notice the Vietnam-era Cobra attack helicopter and the always-fascinating PBR patrol

PBRs (Patrol Boat River) anchor Vietnam exhibits at the UDT Museum, Patriots Point, the Russell Museum, and the Museum of the American G.I. Photo courtesy of author's collection

boat also from the Vietnam conflict. This is a living-history museum, meaning they routinely start the engines and put everything in motion. Watch for their annual Living History Weekend.

The museum is the brainchild of tank collector and military hardware expert Brent Mullins. As of this writing there were six more tanks and other vehicles in restoration.

Hours: Check their website for hours. They are generally open Wed through Sun 10 a.m. to 5 p.m., but this changes based on the season.
Website: http://americangimuseum.org/
Street address/GPS address: 19124 Highway 6 South, College Station, TX 77845

The Texas Forts Trail Region

Like Kentucky's Bourbon Trail or Alabama's Robert Trent Jones Golf Trail, the Texas Forts Trail has unified the state's various military destinations into a single 650-mile driving loop. Choose the Military Theme to see dozens of forts and museums as well as military monuments and sites from as early as the Mexican War for Independence to the Civil War to World Wars I and II, Korea, and more. Be sure to get your free travel guide online.

Website: www.texasfortstrail.com/plan-your-adventure/historic-sites-and-cities

The 10 Best Military Experiences: Commemorative Air Force, Dallas, Texas

The Commemorative Air Force (CAF) is a loose, national confederation of warbird owners organized by "wings" (aka "air bases" or "squadrons") located in a dozen or so states. Many of their pilot/owners are qualified and approved to offer flights called "Living History Flight Experiences." To find a wing near you use the directory on the main website. This also tells you what aircraft are available where. You will usually have your choice of small trainers, large bombers, or agile fighters, most of them World War II-era.

The CAF is well known on the air show circuit. They own the much-loved and historically significant B-29 called *Fifi* that flies as part of their seven-plane CAF AirPower History Tour. Check their website for links to the local wings and for up-to-date information on flyable aircraft (it changes).

Hours: See website for local operators and their hours
Website: https://commemorativeairforce.org/
Street address/GPS address: See website for the wing nearest you

Utah

Utah isn't the first state that comes to mind when you plan a trip to some undiscovered military destinations, but it should be. For one, you might discover Wendover Air Force Base. Wendover was once a beehive of airmen training for World War II bombers, but today it sits still and silent, a largely untouched World War II air base ready to transport you, without any effort on your part, back in time. Hill Aerospace Museum is here, too, and while unknown to even some of the locals, it has one of the largest outdoor displays of military aircraft in the West. Either way, recalibrate your signals and plan a weekend here. Ghost town or airpark, Utah has some spectacular military destinations.

Hill Aerospace Museum, Ogden, Utah

Nestled between the Great Salt Lake and the ski resorts of Snowbasin is a nondescript building that is actually the Hill Aerospace Museum. Anywhere else and you'd think you'd made a wrong turn and had arrived at an office park, but the airplanes give it away. This excellent museum has on display more than 100 beautifully maintained aircraft spanning the entire history of military flight from biplanes to the supersonic SR-71.

Start your visit inside the museum and explore the Hadley Gallery. In the center section are World War II- and Korea-era aircraft. On one side, you'll see a P-51 Mustang and a P-38 Lightning wedged in between a B-17 Flying Fortress and a B-24 Liberator. On the other side are the Korean planes—a pair of F-84s, an F-86, an A-26, and more.

The trainers are located to the extreme right. Here you'll find a T-33, a T-37, and a T-38 trainer, the latter being the first supersonic Air Force trainer. To the far left are the World War I biplanes and scouts. All of them have been restored with period markings.

"Walk-through" airplanes and helicopters are found at many destinations. Seen here: A Marine Corps CH-46 Sea Knight of the HMM-161 "Greyhawks" at Patriots Point. Photo courtesy of author's collection

From the Hadley Gallery go back to the Lindquist Stewart Gallery and be surrounded by modern jets. Here you'll see the SR-71 spy plane, the Century-series jets—the F-100 Super Sabre, F-101 Voodoo, F-102 Delta Dagger, F-104 Starfighter, and F-105 Thunderchief—plus Vietnam-era planes such as the F-4 Phantom and the OV-10 Bronco. Farther in are the modern jets, including a rugged A-10 Warthog, the variable-wing F-14 Tomcat, an F-15 Eagle, and an F-16 Fighting Falcon.

In front of the museum is an exceptionally good outdoor airpark Take one side of the walking path to see the heavy bombers beginning with Word War II and going up to the present day. There is a B-29, a B-47, a B-52, a KC-135 tanker, and a B-1. On the other side are a mix of cargo planes and a few more fighters—a C-45, a C-119, a C-123, a C-131 cargo plane, and so on, mixed in with another F-4 Phantom and an F-16 Fighting Falcon.

Plan your day when you come here. There are about 30 acres to walk with some 100 aircraft on display. There is a theater and a gift shop and the planes have been beautifully restored to period colors and markings. Located adjacent to very active Hill Air Force Base (F-16s and F-35s), you might see some aircraft taking off or landing, adding to the fun of being here.

Hours: Mon–Sat: 9 a.m. to 4:30 p.m., Sun: closed
Website: www.hill.af.mil/Home/Hill-Aerospace-Museum
Street address/GPS address: 7961 Wardleigh Rd., Building 1955, Hill Air Force Base, Ogden, UT 84056

The Best Formerly Secret Military Sites: Historic Wendover Airfield, Wendover, Utah

This is the perfect outing to experience a true World War II air base and in so doing be transported back some 70 years. Let us explain.

At the height of World War II, this remote air base on the salt flats desert of Utah was buzzing with activity. There were more than 19,000 civilian and military personnel training and being trained here to fly B-17s and B-24s, not counting the totally secret activities of the 509th Composite Group, which was itself training to drop the A-bomb. Before it was over, Wendover

Part ghost town, part restored World War II air base, Wendover Air Field remains as it was in the 1940s when it was a training base for B-17 and B-29 bomber crews. Photo courtesy of WikiCommons

Airfield produced more than 1,000 aircrews and had more than 600 buildings on the base.

All that is long gone, of course, but the old air base is still here. A diligent group of volunteers is working to preserve many of the 90 original buildings so all of us today can see a World War II airbase exactly as it was in 1943. The old officers club has been completely restored and converted to a museum and gift shop, and the control tower is in excellent shape and nearly open. Park your car and get out and walk these dusty grounds. Let your imagination run wild. See those young flyboys walking around those distant barracks and hangars. With some advance notice they will even take you over to the *Enola Gay* side of the field, where the actual B-29 hangar is still standing and you can see the loading pit for the A-bomb. But call ahead. TSA restricts their movements on that side of the airport, so they need to know when you want to go. Other buildings are undergoing restoration.

Old and worn down in some places and completely restored in others, Historic Wendover Airfield is part ghost town, part living history. Either way, it's a one-of-a-kind connection to our past, a place to feel life the way it was when America was at war. It's located 120 miles west of Salt Lake City, and you'll pass the legendary Bonneville Salt Flats on the way.

Hours: Mon–Fri: 11 a.m. to 4 p.m., Sat: 9 a.m. to 5 p.m., Sun: closed
Tours: http://www.intermountainguidenevada.com
Website: www.wendoverairbase.com/museum
Street address/GPS address: 345 Airport Way, Wendover, UT 84083

While You're in the Neighborhood

Thiokol Rocket Garden, Brigham City, Utah

There's nothing but desert hardscrabble out here—that is, until you see some pointy-looking objects in the distance. No, it's not a mirage. You've stumbled upon an outdoor rocket "garden" erected by the same Thiokol people who made our space boosters and rockets (now a company called ATK). There are some 20 different missiles, some of them pointing left, some of them pointing right, some pointing straight up, including a Patriot missile. For the missile aficionado there's a space shuttle reuseable solid rocket motor, a Polaris booster, a 12,000-pound solid rocket demonstration motor for the US Army, an Army Spartan motor, a TX-31 Loki antiaircraft rocket battery, various iterations of the Air Force Falcon air-to-air missile, a TX-140 Hermes, a US Army Hawk missile, a US Army surface-to-surface Lacrosse antitank missile, the Nike Hercules, a Hellfire missile, the Sidewinder air-to-air missile, an Army wire-guided TOW missile, and more.

It's an unusual place. It's out of the way. There's no museum or guides. But it's ever so interesting. Use a map. It's about 25 miles out of Brigham City.

Website: www.utahsadventurefamily.com/atk-thiokol-rocket-display
Street Address/GPS Address: UT 83, Promontory, UT

Virginia

You can easily spend a week in Virginia visiting military sites and still not take it all in. Our recommendation? Start by enjoying the incredibly immersive, beautifully staged exhibits in the National Museum of the Marine Corps and then work your way around to the other museums. You'll stop at the Quarter-masters Museum, the Transportation Museum, Nauticus, the Armored Foundation, and more. As one of our military friends said, Virginia has an abundance of riches. We agree.

The National Museum of the Marine Corps, Triangle, Virginia

One doesn't think of the ramrod-straight, tough-as-nails marines as being artistic, but they'd be dead wrong. Just visit the newly reopened National Museum of the Marine Corps for proof of that. As you walk into the soaring atrium, you're surrounded by a swirl of helicopters, Harriers, Dauntlesses, and Corsairs zooming down to help their buddies on the ground—and inside the exhibit area it only gets better. A doorway turns into a portal and you discover that you're inside the belly of a Marine helicopter that's just landed in a hot LZ. As you come out the other end, you unhappily find yourself in the middle of firefight complete with the sights, sounds, flashes, and smells of combat (yes, the smells are here, too). If those experiences

The architectural design of the National Museum of the Marine Corps evokes the image of the flag-raising on Iwo Jima. Photo courtesy of Department of Defense

don't tell you this is not your grandmother's museum, than how about hoisting a 40-pound rucksack on your shoulders and having a drill sergeant in your face? Enter a soundproof booth for that experience.

But we're ahead of ourselves. You start your visit in the Leatherneck Gallery which is overwhelming in size and action. It's impossible to miss the 211-foot spire piercing the glass-and-steel atrium and the 3-story superstructure suggestive of an amphibious assault ship and representative of the tie between the Navy and the Marines. Here, too, is the first of the museum's many hyper-realistic, heart-pounding dioramas. Look for the amphibious tractor breeching a wall of logs put up by the Japanese on Tarawa. There is a wounded Marine to the left: Look at the painful grimace on his face. The Marine Corps use face casting to capture these realistic expressions. Each mannequin's face adds a sense of personal determination, courage, and spirit—and often pain—to a story. They are cast from real people.

Inside the museum, the World War II Gallery is up first. Be sure to see the two flags raised over Iowa Jima—they are both on display—and the exhibit on the Pacific air war complete with a Mae West life vest worn by a pilot. There is an M3 Stuart tank next to a 75mm howitzer next to an exhibit on the various weapons of the war, including weapons used against us by the enemy. Before you leave, be sure to spend a moment watching the films and newsreels from the 1940s. Each island in the Pacific campaign has an exhibit and each one is staged with combat action, foliage, Marines, lighting, and large scale objects.

The Vietnam Gallery is next, and it's every bit as compete as the World War II Gallery. Again, the dioramas are stunning and incredibly realistic. You can't miss the one on the Siege of Khe Sanh, or the incredibly immersive experience called the Battle of Hill 881 South (the audio you'll hear is chilling). The curators used lighting, foliage, landscaping, and body casting to create these incredibly realistic battlescapes. Note the A4 Skyhawk hanging from the ceiling and the M50 self-propelled 6-barrel 106mm rifle called "the ontos" compete with Marines advancing alongside.

This architectural masterpiece of a museum has an impressive 120,000 square feet of interactive exhibits and dioramas that showcase the weapons, artillery, aircraft, and landing craft of the Marines with histories and stories associated with each. They cover conflicts back as far as the first days of the Marines, through Korea, Vietnam, and to the current war on terror. Ultimately, being

The lobby of the National Museum of the Marine Corps. Photo courtesy of National Museum of the Marine Corps

a Marine is the theme here—accepting duty over all else, making sacrifices for one's brothers, for one's company, for the corps, for the nation. You'll learn about Guadalcanal and the Solomon Islands and other battles, but you'll feel something more here, too—pride and honor among them.

Crowds do form during the middle of the day, so it's best to come early and have lunch in the Tun Tavern. Built to resemble the iconic 1775 Philadelphia tavern, the Tun serves up a hearty meal all day. (There's also the more convenient Devil Dog Diner for a quick meal.)

So, yes; the Marines do use imagination and creativity to make their history come to life—just look down at your feet and see the "sands" of some distant Pacific island or the "mud" of a patch of ground in Southeast Asia. And what about that strikingly familiar silhouette of this ultramodern museum? What does that remind you of? As the brochure puts it, "the museum's soaring design evokes the image of the flag-raisers of Iwo Jima." Creative? Artistic? The *marines*? Enough said.

Hours: Daily: 9 a.m. to 5 p.m.
Website: www.usmcmuseum.com
Street address/GPS address: 18900 Jefferson Davis Hwy., Triangle, VA 22172

National Maritime Center Nauticus Featuring Battleship Wisconsin and the Hampton Roads Naval Museum, Norfolk, Virginia

Several years ago, the city leaders of Norfolk decided that a beautifully built waterfront museum that combined several themed destinations would result in a nautical center of gravity that would become a must-visit destination for tourists and families alike. The result is Nauticus, a multipurpose jewel of a building located on the Norfolk waterfront adjacent to the battleship *Wisconsin*. Nauticus is a nautical-themed museum with educational displays and interactive exhibits colocated with the Hampton Roads Naval Museum—and the battleship *Wisconsin*.

Like the *New Jersey*, the *Wisconsin* was one of our nation's ultrafast, ultrapowerful Iowa-class battleships. She could zip through the seas with the speed of a destroyer yet weighs an otherwise sluggish 52,000 tons and carried a crew of 1,900. The *Wisconsin* has three massive gun turrets, each with three 16-inch guns capable of firing a 2,700-pound shell 20-plus miles with near pinpoint accuracy. She served in the Pacific theater of World War II, in Korea, and in Operation Desert Storm. Proving the seaworthiness of a large ship, in 1944 she and an entire task force of several hundred ships sailed directly into a Pacific hurricane that was packing 180 mph winds and generating monster seas. Three ships went down, several more were damaged, and 790 men were lost—but the *Wisconsin* sustained a mere two injured seamen. After the Gulf War she was decommissioned and moved here in 2010 as a museum ship.

The Nauticus *complex houses the Hampton Roads Naval Museum and the great battleship USS* Wisconsin. *Photo courtesy of Nauticus*

Start your visit on the *Wisconsin*. Her weather decks have been beautifully restored, and her interior compartments have exhibits that will tell you much about her service at sea. Optional guided tours take you into the engine room and throughout the ship, but most visitors elect the self-guided options.

Nauticus is the shoreside museum next to the *Wisconsin*. Here you'll find numerous military and science exhibits (many oriented toward schoolchildren), including the visually fascinating SOS Station. SOS Station shows how weather patterns form and sweep across our planet (oftentimes on unpredictable storm tracks). It uses a suspended Earth across which the magic of special effects dramatically creates weather phenomena that sweep across the globe.

The Hampton Roads Naval Museum is your final stop. It's up a flight of stairs and has one of the finest collections of model ships this side of Annapolis. Note the *Monitor* and *Merrimack*. These Civil War enemies were the first ironclad ships to do battle (it was a stalemate); however, the *Monitor* introduced an idea that revolutionized warships. No, it was not armor plating—rather, it was the turret. The main gun on the *Monitor* was mounted in a turning 320-degree turret that was placed inside a protective shell called a barbette. It is through this idea of a turret that we can directly connect the *Monitor* to the 16-inch gun turrets on the *Wisconsin*.

Hours: See website
Website: www.nauticus.org
Street address/GPS address: 1 Waterside Dr., Norfolk, VA 23510

The Best Formerly Secret Military Sites: Military Ghost Ships. James River Reserve Fleet, Fort Huger, Virginia

The spooky ships anchored in the middle of the muddy-brown James River near Newport News are actually part of our National Reserve Fleet of merchant ships. They sit there waiting to be called up but until they are, they truly look ghostly. The best views are from the Fort Huger side of the river. Head toward Smithfield, Virginia, to VA 10 and follow the Civil War Trails signage to the Isle of Wright Country Museum/Fort Huger. Drive down to the river and behold ghost ships.

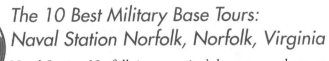

The 10 Best Military Base Tours: Naval Station Norfolk, Norfolk, Virginia

Naval Station Norfolk is our nation's largest navy base, as well as a major naval air station, and because of its size, more than a few people have asked to see it up close. To that end, Naval Station Norfolk has designated Tidewater Tours as the official tour operator for the base. You will board a bus and be taken around the base, visiting the piers with the ships, the Naval Air Station and the jets, the airpark (where they have a display of decommissioned aircraft), and the old, historic part of the base. This is a 45-minute windshield-only tour, meaning once on base you are not allowed to get off the bus—but don't worry; its wonderfully panoramic and covers all the major areas.

You might also consider taking the cruise ship *Victory Rover,* which sails up and down the Elizabeth River. You'll have an excellent view of the ships from the water side. This tour departs from the Nauticus Museum (see listing under Virginia).

Website: https://www.visitnorfolk.com/things-to-do/tours/ tour-norfolk-naval-base/
Street address/GPS address: 9079 Hampton Blvd., Norfolk, VA 23505

US Army Transportation Museum, Fort Eustis, Virginia (Newport News)

After cussing you out, an army drill sergeant will relentlessly pound a message into your head. *Keep moving soldier!* Well, it's a message not lost on anyone in the military—mobility is essential to an army and this 6-acre museum explains how our US Army uses every possible air, sea, land, and rail transportation asset to keep its soldiers moving. It's an interesting story with an unusual assortment of objects, not all of them usually associated with the army.

Your visit to the Transportation Museum starts in the 1950s-looking redbrick building, where you will find dozens of dioramas explaining the many unusual ways the Army Transportation Corps has moved men and matériel. For instance, in 1944, just days after D-Day, army tugboats—yes,

A Vietnam gun truck seen at the Transportation Museum in Fort Eustis, Virginia. Photo courtesy of WikiCommons

army tugboats—were used to position the coastal breakers called Mulberries off the Normandy coast of France. The Mulberries only lasted a few days—a terrific storm blew them apart—but during those critical days they performed spectacularly, allowing cargo ships to dock and unload supplies for our troops. How about an army *train* that supplied the city of Berlin with food, coal, and other necessities during the Cold War? Did you know that the Transportation Corps had gun trucks, too? Gun trucks were like the Gatlin gun-totting AC-130 Puff The Magic Dragons aerial gunships—they were trucks bristling with guns that were placed in supply convoys in Vietnam to lay down fire if convoys were attacked. The one on display here was known as Eve of Destruction (the soldiers painted names on their trucks like pilots did on their planes), and it is one of the few left today.

Now head out to the vehicle park for a kaleidoscope of shapes and sizes. The park is divided into four pavilions, one each for land, sea, rail, and air transportation. In the shed dedicated to wheeled vehicles, you'll see rows and rows of jeeps and the many variations and modifications made to them. Perhaps more impressive is the rugged 6×6 wheeled transporter displayed with an M4 Sherman tank mounted on its back. Beyond it is an even larger and quite ominous-looking 8×6 wheeled transporter (seemingly out of the *Terminator*) with an M60 Patton tank. More to today's war on terror, the third transporter here is a 6x8 with one of the new, heavily armored Mine Resistant Ambush Protected (MRAP) vehicles (they replaced Humvees).

In the aviation section there are a few fixed-wing aircraft like the Caribou small cargo plane, plus numerous helicopters. There is the futuristic-looking heavy lifter that wraps its steel legs around an object called a CH-54 Skycrane helicopter—and a small, one-man helicopter called an Aerocycle. There are tried-and-true helicopters like the Huey, Choctaw, and the Chinook, but also failures like the H-25 Mule, a twin-bladed helicopter. The black-and-gold Blackhawk was assigned to the Military District of Washington, D.C. The Transportation Corps also took care of dignitaries.

Farther down the path is the train shed, where you'll find an assortment of locomotives, utility cars, and boxcars. One of the locomotives was designed for narrow-gauge track, and another was built not to ride our own rails but to move supplies across the tracks of a post–World War II Europe. As many as a dozen other railroad cars are exhibited, odd ones, many to repair tracks, others to move goods.

The watercraft area is next. The largest boat here is the LARC—the Light Amphibious Resupply Cargo vehicle used for beach supply in Vietnam. It can carry no less than five tons. Around it are an assortment of experimental designs including an amphibious car and several service boats like tugs, barges, and J-boats (J-boats were shaped like patrol boats but were used to transport supplies on rivers).

There is a small gift shop here, and a full tour will take you about two hours. And note this: A third of the visitors here will be soldiers. Soldiers are brought here to appreciate the extremes the US Army Transportation Corps will go to get their mission done, which is why a visit here makes for a fascinating destination for all of us.

Guided tours are available but they require advance reservations.

Hours: Tues–Sat: 9 a.m. to 4:30 p.m., Sun, Mon: closed
Website: www.transportation.army.mil/museum/index.htm
Street address/GPS address: 300 Washington Blvd., Besson Hall, Fort Eustic, Newport News, VA 23604

US Army Quartermaster Museum, Fort Lee, Virginia

You'd never think to create a museum devoted to, what—a quartermaster? But think again. How does an army move? Who gets the fuel to the tanks on the front lines? What about food? Supplies? Uniforms? The answer is, the quartermaster—quartermasters run the supply chain for the army, and the history of that service is on display in this small but endlessly fascinating museum in Fort Lee, Virginia.

Step inside and start learning abut this little-known branch of the army. Did you know the quartermasters train the army's parachute riggers? Or that in addition to getting water and fuel out to the troops, the quartermasters are the ones who test the water for bacteria and other biology? Did you know that General Grant's personal effects were carried around in an ambulance? Did you know that Eisenhower had his own mobile living quarters that he used when he was on the road during World War II? Yes, the quartermasters keep them both on the move. Eisenhower's van is here. As is Grant's personal luggage transport, the Rucker Ambulance.

The much loved and iconic Bell UH-1 Huey can be found at destinations across America. Photo Courtesy: Department of Defense

Plan your visit around these unique large-scale artifacts and then tour the rest of the displays and exhibits for an overview of the military as viewed behind the scenes. There is a Huey to show how quartermasters use air assets for aerial delivery of supplies, a field kitchen complete with sandbags showing food delivery, an amphibious landing craft called a DUKW being unloaded after D-Day, an exhibit showing how the quartermasters train war dogs, and another on how they stabled horses during those early years. Each diorama uses realistic landscaping and mannequins plus an array of facts and figures. In the McNamara Supply Gallery, for instance, you'll learn than by D-Day plus three days the quartermasters had delivered ashore 750,000 food rations. In all they would deliver hundreds of thousands of *tons* of food, clothing, ammunition, and fuel over the Normandy beaches. Yet another gallery is filled with facts and figures on the fuel pipeline they installed during Iraqi Freedom.

In a nutshell, this is a collection of beautifully rendered dioramas telling a story not well known to the general public. While you're visiting, be sure to look closely at the faces of the mannequins. These are some of the finest examples of face and body casting anywhere, a technique few museums do as well as it's done here.

Hours: Mon–Fri: 10 a.m. to 5 p.m., Sat: 11 a.m. to 5 p.m., Sun: closed
Website: www.qmmuseum.lee.army.mil
Street address/GPS address: 1201 22nd St., Fort Lee, VA 23801

While You're in the Neighborhood

American Armored Foundation and Tank Museum, Danville, Virginia

They say the average visitor spends more than two hours here, and when you see the long, cavernous, 330,000-square-foot hall filled with tanks and artillery, you'll believe it. The inspiration of founder and collector William Gasser, the Tank Museum is now one of the largest and most extensive collections of tanks and artillery pieces in the world (more than 120 of them, to be precise). With the tanks and artillery pieces positioned side by side, you're in for a lot of walking, but what a treat. Shermans, Pershings, Pattons, German tanks, British—

they're all here in one giant space. There are period military uniforms (more than 300 of them), flamethrowers, bazookas, and machine guns (150 of those), plus all sorts of small-arms weapons (more than 65 of them). And that just scratches the surface. There are detailed dioramas showing tanks and vehicles in combat scenes or in military uses specific to their function, plus thousands of badges, flags, pennants, helmets, and military toys.

Be sure to visit on demonstration days. They fire the big guns, light the flamethrowers, have radio-controlled tank battles, and so on. The schedule of events is listed on the website. The facility has no heat or air-conditioning, so wear clothing appropriate to the weather.

Hours: See website
Website: www.aaftankmuseum.com
Street address/GPS address: 3401 US Hwy. 29, Danville, VA 24540

Virginia War Museum, Newport News, Virginia

Although small and somewhat limited in scope, the Virginia War Museum has some very special artifacts, and it's the perfect weekend destination for you if artillery and tanks are your thing. There are numerous display cases and exhibits on such topics as war posters, military uniforms, women in the military, African Americans in the military, and small arms. Around you'll see a Gatling gun, an M5 Stuart light tank in World War II battlefield dress, a German 88 gun from World War II, an Iraqi antiaircraft gun captured during the Gulf War, a battle tank from World War I, plus several examples of towed artillery pieces.

What makes this destination special, though, are four artifacts that each come with a backstory that speaks volumes about the last 100 years. First, there is a blood chit carried by our airmen in the Pacific that would be their means of bartering for their lives if it ever came to that. Anyone who helped them could redeem the chit for a cash reward from America.

Next, there is a sobering display with a piece of the wall from Dachau, the German concentration camp, and a display with a piece of the wall from a German stalag where American POWs were kept.

Finally, and on a happier note, the museum has a piece of the Berlin Wall, which is a fitting statement about all the reasons we do so much to keep our own freedoms. Be sure to visit here if you're in the neighborhood.

Hours: Mon–Sat: 9 a.m. to 5 p.m., Sun: 12 to 5 p.m.
Website: http://www.warmuseum.org/index.php
Street address/GPS address: 9285 Warwick Blvd., Newport News, VA 23607

American Civil War Museum, Richmond, Virginia

This is actually a collection of three destinations. The first is Historic Tredegar Iron Works in Richmond, which was a major industrial and financial resource to the Confederacy during the Civil War; the second is the White House of the Confederacy, where Jefferson Davis lived, also in Richmond (tours available); while the third is the Museum of the Confederacy in Appomattox, Virginia, which is ground zero for all things Confederate. All of these buildings have been restored and contain exhibits inside.

Hours: Daily: 10 a.m. to 5 p.m.
Website: www.acwm.org
White House & Museum of the Confederacy
Street address/GPS address: 1201 E. Clay St., Richmond, VA 23219
American Civil War Museum–Appomattox
Street address/GPS address: 159 Horseshoe Rd., Appomattox, VA 24522

Washington

The state of Washington has some of the most interesting military destinations in the nation. One can't overlook the nearly pristine collection of warbirds and vehicles at Paul Allen's Flying Heritage and Combat Armor Museum in Everett, or the amazing story of undersea warfare told in Keyport, Washington.

Flying Heritage and Combat Armor Museum, Everett, Washington

This marvelous collection of mint-condition warbirds and combat vehicles is worth a visit by any measure but to see a MiG-29 puts it over the top. Founded by Microsoft billionaire Paul G. Allen, the Flying Heritage and Combat Armor Museum has an extensive collection of warbirds all meticulously restored and maintained in perfect flying condition.

The Flying Heritage & Combat Armor Museum's collection includes a rare LCVP "Higgins Boat." Some 1,089 were used on D-Day. LCT-595 was tasked with launching amphibious tanks during the first wave at Utah Beach. The flag (foreground) was flown on one of the first vessels into combat on that historic day. Photo © 2017 Vulcan Inc. + Affiliates.

As of this writing there are 25 well-curated aircraft on display, including the world's only airworthy Focke-Wulf Fw 190A German fighter, the last Fw 190D-13 at all, the world's only surviving Nakajima Ki-43 type Ib Oscar, and one of only three flying de Havilland Mosquitos.

Additionally, there are 26 military vehicles on display, all painted as if they just rolled off the production line. There's a Sherman tank, an M48 Patton tank and M60 Patton tank (there were several tanks named after Patton), an M1A1 turret trainer, a Type 95 Japanese tank, a Soviet T-34 tank, plus artillery pieces and antiaircraft pieces and more.

The MiG-29UB Fulcrum is certainly one of the coolest jets in the world and just to see one is fascinating. This particular MiG was a frontline fighter for the Ukrainian Air Force and is finished in a light gray/dark gray camo paint. There is also a full-size replica of *SpaceShipOne*, the first private aircraft to put a human in suborbital flight twice within a two-week period and winner of the 1994 X Prize. (The actual prize-winning aircraft is in the Smithsonian National Air & Space Museum; the X Prize team had six additional aircraft built from the same molds. This is one of them.)

An ever-growing museum, an additional 60 new military vehicles (tanks, half tracks, and other army vehicles) were being prepared for release into the museum collection at the time of this writing, so be sure to check the website for updates. And don't ignore the many interactive displays inside the museum. There are eight enormous 98-inch screens that challenge your understanding of wars and the causes of war. Swipe them with your hands, move data left and right. The centerpiece is the Conflict Simulator Command Center. This one poses questions and scenarios and forces you to make "decisions," the consequences of which are played out on the monitors.

Hours: Tues–Sun: 10 a.m. to 5 p.m., Mon: closed
Website: www.flyingheritage.com
Street address/GPS address: Paine Field, 3407 109th St. SW, Everett, WA 98204

US Naval Undersea Museum, Keyport, Washington

US Naval Undersea Museum consists of 18,000 square feet of exhibits and artifacts that tell the story of naval undersea submarine warfare. Located in the Pacific Northwest on Puget Sound's Kitsap Peninsula, you'll know you've arrived when you see the handsome white building with a collection of undersea submersibles in front and the sail of the submarine USS *Sturgeon* standing guard by the entrance.

Start inside the main building. Among the museum's seven permanent exhibits is a fascinating collection of torpedoes, including cutaways that let you see how the propulsion, fusing, and ranging technologies have evolved over the decades. Another dedicated exhibit focuses on undersea mines and how they work. After that, follow the curving path through the displays and see highly visual exhibits that explain how nuclear subs carry and launch ICBMs, and one on the complex physics of the oceans and how the Navy lives and fights in this incredibly hostile environment.

The fascinating story of underwater combat is told here at the Naval Undersea Museum in Keyport, Washington. Photo courtesy of Department of Defense

Another part of the "undersea" story is undersea rescue. The exhibits on this topic are large-scale objects, including the deep-sea rescue submersibles and research craft. You'll see the diving bells and hard hats worn by underwater salvage experts.

Nearby Naval Base Kitsap is a fascinating complex but also a highly secured navy base. It is the navy's third-largest base and home to our Ohio-class nuclear submarines as well as various surface ships, including some of our aircraft carriers.

And what about that sail in front? The USS *Sturgeon* was a nuclear attack submarine that served our nation during the Cold War before being retired. The 37 Sturgeon-class fast attack submarines that were built carried Tomahawk cruise missiles, the over-the-horizon Harpoon anti-ship missile, the SUBROC nuclear antisubmarine ballistic missile, plus an assortment of advanced torpedoes. Because almost anything to do with a submarine like this is top secret, little of it was left when it was taken out of service, little that is except the sail, which was salvaged and is here.

This is a beautiful part of the Northwest with spectacular vistas of the sound. Many people spend a weekend here, and you should too. Hotels and good restaurants can be found in the Keyport area.

Hours: Wed–Mon: 10 a.m. to 4 p.m., Tues: closed
Website: www.navalunderseamuseum.org
Street address/GPS address: 1 Garnett Way, Navy Region Northwest, Keyport, WA 98345

Museum of Flight, Seattle, Washington

With Boeing next door, the Museum of Flight understandably celebrates civilian aviation—but it doesn't ignore the military side, either. At the Museum of Flight, you'll be immersed in both worlds as you navigate an inspiring glass-and-steel complex that spreads across two campuses and features 175 airplanes.

You'll start your visit in the East Campus in what is no doubt the granddaddy of all aviation display areas. From the entrance, go to your left into the Great Gallery and be amazed by its 3 million cubic feet of space and some 50 military and civilian aircraft. As you walk in you'll be surrounded by civilian sport planes, experimental aircraft, aircraft from the early years of aviation, and, in the back, some military types. Go to your left and find the F-4 Phantom and a Mig-21 placed next to each other, adversaries over Vietnam but friends here in retirement. Elsewhere, a civilian DC-3 hangs over the M-21. The M-21 is a CIA variant of the SR-71/A-12 spy plane that was made to carry the D-21 supersonic drone at the SR-71s hypersonic speeds (three times the speed of sound). That made the M-21 the mothership of all motherships, but the D-21 proved to be tricky, and on the fourth test it crashed into the M-21 after separation, destroying both planes. The project was abandoned and this is the only surviving model. (It's on the main display floor seen paired with the drone and is one of those fabulous one-of-a-kinds that make visits to museums unexpected treats.)

Next, cross back through the museum's main entrance for the Personal Courage Wing and enter this beautifully lit pavilion. Here you'll find 28 superbly restored World War I and World War II warbirds each surrounded by curving murals and period dioramas that hit the spot. Both galleries contain aircraft flown by all of the adversaries. For instance, the World War II Gallery has a German Messerschmitt Bf-109, a Japanese Nakajima Ki-43 Oscar, a British Spitfire, and five American classics: a P-47 Thunderbolt, a P-51 Mustang, a FM-2 Wildcat, a FG-1 Corsair, and a P-38 Lightning. Placards tell a story about each.

From here walk the Memorial Bridge over to the Aviation Pavilion in the West Campus. In a sense, this is the history of the Boeing Company. Here you will find the first Boeing B-727 trijet made, the first Boeing 737, and the first Boeing 747. Next to them is the latest from Boeing, a 787 Dreamliner. Against the windows is a sleek Concorde supersonic passenger jet.

The military aircraft here celebrate Boeing's contributions, too. There is a Boeing B-17 Flying Fortress, a Boeing B-29 Superfortress, and a Boeing B-47 Stratojet nuclear bomber. (The ever-so-familiar Boing B-52 will soon be installed in a special Vietnam exhibit. Check the museum's website for details.) Around the edges are fighter jets, including an AV-8C Harrier and four of the Grumman jets—an F9-F Cougar, an A-6 Intruder, an EA-6B Prowler, and a F-14 Tomcat,

As hard as it is to imagine, there's even more to see here, including a Space Gallery and the Red Barn, the "garage" where Boeing was born. But here's the important point: Across the board the restoration work is nothing short of perfect. The period finishes and markings are beautifully done, many aircraft are displayed with drop tanks or appropriate weapons stores, and the settings are colorful and informative. The flight simulators are top-notch, the movies in the theater zoom you across time and space, and the glass-and-steel exhibit halls are beautiful. Give yourself a few hours to see it all, and take a break in the Wings Café. And, as always, the gift shop is stocked with things you don't see in the local big-box store, so if you see it here, buy it here.

Hours: Daily: 10 a.m. to 5 p.m.
Website: www.museumofflight.org
Street address/GPS address: 9404 E. Marginal Way S., Seattle, WA 98108

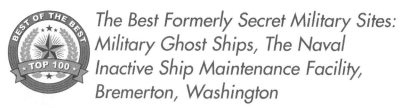

The Best Formerly Secret Military Sites: Fort Casey's Gun Batteries, Whidbey Island, Washington

A well-preserved example of our World War II coastal defenses can be found inside the Fort Casey State Park on Whidbey Island, Washington. The guns are pointing out toward Admiralty Inlet, and the old fort remains. One bonus feature: The jets from next-door Naval Air Station Whidbey routinely overfly the state park, giving you a 50-yard-line view of naval air training.

Hours: Daily: 8 a.m. to dusk
Website: www. parks.state.wa.us/505/Fort-Casey

The Best Formerly Secret Military Sites: Military Ghost Ships, The Naval Inactive Ship Maintenance Facility, Bremerton, Washington

On most mornings, the bows of these mothballed ships will loom up out of the mist and take you by surprise. Where are the gates? Where are the guards? Relax: This is a navy town. Take the waterfront drive and you'll come face-to-face with aircraft carriers and destroyers (although that varies depending on what ships are there in any given year). Seven ships are here as of this writing.[15]

West Virginia

The prospect of a nuclear attack led to the creation of a doomsday scenario that anticipated the need for underground bunkers to ensure that key elected officials survived to govern in the post-war period. In the language of the formerly secret *Emergency Plans Book*, these bunkers were called continuity-of-government bunkers. The only continuity-of-government bunker to be opened to the public is here in West Virginia.

This statue honors the SEALs and their Medal of Honor recipients in a moving tribute to selflessness. Photo courtesy of National Navy UDT-SEAL Museum

The Best Formerly Secret Military Sites: The Greenbrier Bunker, Hot Springs, West Virginia

A well-known destination, but well worth it, this formerly secret continuity-of-government bunker was hidden for years but is now a top tourist attraction. Located on the grounds of the swank Greenbrier resort, this sprawling underground complex carved out of the side of the mountain was designed to provide Congress with a post–nuclear war "home" from which the nation might be governed. It was supposed to be utterly secret lest the Soviets target it and end it all, but the 7,000-foot-long runway at the otherwise unused local airstrip gave it away. The bunker was eventually acknowledged, shut down, cleaned up, and opened to the public.

The official tour takes you through enormous steel doors into a tunnel that seems longer than a football field, at the end of which is a 112,000-square-foot bunker for 1,100 people. There is an auditorium with green seats for 470 people, rows and rows of high school–like lockers, a hospital, a broadcast center (to communicate to outside survivors), a dormitory with bunk beds for 1,100, and a kitchen with tons of emergency rations, all of which are on display.

Tours last about 90 minutes and depart from the lobby at the Trellis Lobby. As you walk around think not only of the expense but also that we have several unacknowledged continuity-of-government facilities still in operation. Just in case.

Hours: Daily: 9:30 a.m. to 3:30 p.m. (subject to change)
Website: www.greenbrier.com/Activities/Bunker-Tours
Street address/GPS address: 300 W. Main St., White Sulphur Springs, WV 24986

Wisconsin

Two destinations beckon—a base tour with a major display of army tracked and wheeled vehicles and the well-known home to the Experimental Aircraft Association with their collection of warbirds in Oshkosh.

The 10 Best Military Base Tours: Fort McCoy, Fort McCoy, Wisconsin

Fort McCoy is a major US Army training center, so to go on base you need to arrive during their posted open houses or schedule your own tour during a weekday. Either way, there are some fascinating things to see here. For one, there is a Commemorative Area, which is a cluster of World War II–era barracks that depict life as a solider in the 1940s, and an Equipment Park, with some 70 army tanks, APCs, howitzers, and helicopters. The World War II area consists of a restored administrative building, a World War II dining hall, and old barracks with period uniforms, foot lockers, and even a potbellied stove. You can go inside the old barracks and visualize the way it was those many years ago, then stop in the adjacent History Center for more detailed information.

Artillery pieces and tanks can be found at dozens of destinations, including towed howitzers like this one in Pennsylvania. Photo courtesy of Army Heritage Trail

The Equipment Park is exhaustive and extensive. Among the military vehicles are fire trucks, command trucks, reconnaissance vehicles, armored personnel carriers, and supply trucks. Tanks include an M60 Patton, an M4 Sherman, an M1 Abrams, a rare, experimental TE95 main battle tank, plus a 155mm self-propelled howitzer, a 105mm towed howitzer, an M110 8-inch self-propelled howitzer, and loads of others.

Access and hours are posted in the website and vary according to which area you want to visit. Open houses allow access to them all. Tours for 15 or more can be set up for any weekday with advance notice.

Website: www.mccoy.army.mil
Street address/GPS address: 100 E. Headquarters Rd., Fort McCoy, WI

EAA Aviation Museum, Oshkosh, Wisconsin

Military pilots and warbirders alike find a special place in their hearts for this grassroots organization that started out as a ragtag group of homebuilders of airplanes and morphed into one of the largest and most respected pilot-oriented organizations in America. Although by definition a civilian group, the Experimental Aircraft Association embraces warbirds and military aircraft, and at their annual fly-ins and air show they draw hundreds of thousands to see the latest bombers, fighters, and transports as well as World War II and Vietnam-era aircraft lovingly restored.

The key military component of the newly renamed Aviation Museum (formerly the Airventure Museum) is the Eagle Hangar. An enormous, colorful, 120-foot wall mural depicts the continents on our planet to visually show us that World War II was indeed a world war. With that as a backdrop, here you will find a small but pristine collection of warbirds anchored by the rare World War II–era P-38 Lightning. The twin-tailed, twin-engine Lightning was fast and agile and generally outmaneuvered the Japanese fighters it encountered in the Pacific theater so much that our top aces racked up 30 and 40 aerial victories (Richard Bong held the top spot at 40 planes confirmed). Other aircraft in the hangar include the perennial favorites—the P-51 Mustang, a B-25 Mitchell, an F4-U Corsair, a British Mosquito, a Bf-109 Messerschmitt made in Spain, and more.

Two more things to note: The Timeless Voices of Aviation is a fascinating collection of oral histories that cut across all aspects of flight but most vividly contains first-person accounts of combat as told by military pilots and aircrews. True, too, for the art and photography collections held by the EAA. Here again, mixed into the pictures and paintings of civilian aviation are many images that visualize war scenes from America's conflicts.

Hours: Daily: 10 a.m. to 5 p.m.
Closed: New Year's Day, Easter, Thanksgiving, Christmas Eve, and Christmas Day
Website: www.eaa.org/eaa-museum
Street address/GPS address: 3000 Poberezny Rd., Oshkosh, WI 54902

THE BEST-OF-THE-BEST LISTS

THE TOP 20 BEST-OF-THE-BEST MILITARY DESTINATIONS IN AMERICA

IT BEGINS WITH THE FIRST STEP AND ONLY GETS BETTER

The Smithsonian National Air & Space Museum in Washington, D.C., sits on top of every list of the most popular and most-visited museums in the nation. They have more airplanes, more exhibits, and more displays than any other in their field—and they cover the full width and breadth of their specialty, including military aviation. That puts them on top of our list, too, but they are closely followed by several other excellent "national" museums and specialized destinations that drill down into their subject areas with more depth and nuance than a museum as vast as the Smithsonian could ever hope to. Between the two—destinations that range far and wide and destinations that go deep—you have countless opportunities to spend more than a few weekends in the full richness of the finest military destinations in America. But, if time is an issue, here's a short list—our annual Top 20 Best-of-the-Best.

1. **Smithsonian National Air & Space Museum, Washington, D.C.**
   If it set a record or established an aviation milestone, it's probably on display at the Smithsonian. Think of the *Wright Flyer*, the *Bell X-1*, and the first jet aircraft to take off and land on an aircraft carrier. That's what makes the Smithsonian a must-visit military destination. But that's not the only thing. Here you'll find plenty of *everything*—military aircraft, drones, helicopters, missiles, rockets, and history.

2. **The National Museum of the Marine Corps, Triangle, Virginia**
   Battles. Hardware. People. Few places bring history to life like the National Museum of the Marine Corps. All the battles, and all of the specialties—air, sea, and land—are to be found here in this newly renovated destination. Plus they have some of the most realistic combat landscapes and dioramas anywhere.

3. **National World War I Museum and Liberty Memorial, Kansas City, Missouri**
   The story of World War I, and the memory of the soldiers who fought the Great War, are honored here in Kansas City. You enter this incredibly beautiful destination by walking across a glass pedway that arcs over 9,000 red poppies, each representing 1,000 deaths during the war. A powerful start to a powerful museum.

4. **National World War II Museum, New Orleans, Louisiana**
   Owing to the many years of tireless work by the determined scholar and author Stephen Ambrose, the National World War II Museum storytelling has become of the highest order. A campus with multiple pavilions, this destination will keep you fascinated for the better part of a weekend.

5. **National Museum of the US Air Force, Wright-Patterson Air Force Base, Ohio**
   This sprawling mecca of aviation covers military flight like no other. For starters, there are some 300-plus aircraft on display covering every American conflict that used any sort of air asset. Like the Smithsonian National Air & Space Museum, the types and models of aircraft and space vehicles span the entire history of flight—but here the story is 100 percent military.

6. **The National Museum of the Pacific War, Fredericksburg, Texas**
   What on Earth is a museum dedicated to the war in the Pacific Ocean doing in a dusty, landlocked town miles from the nearest seas? As it hap-

pens, Fredericksburg, Texas, is the birthplace of US Navy Fleet Admiral Chester W. Nimitz, our World War II commander in chief of the Pacific Fleet. Nimitz rose through the ranks to command some two million sailors and five thousand ships all with one distinct mission: defeat Japan. Three "campuses" make up this excellent destination.

7. **Airborne & Special Operations Museum, Fayetteville, North Carolina**
The soaring facade tells you something special is inside, and this museum doesn't fail to deliver. Here you will journey through an action-packed, highly realistic portrait of the dangerous missions our special forces have been asked to undertake—from that first parachute jump in 1940, to today.

8. **National Naval Aviation Museum, Pensacola, Florida**
An F-14 pointing skyward tells you've arrived at the National Naval Aviation Museum at NAS Pensacola. In a nutshell, this is the history of naval aviation in all its afterburning glory, beginning with those first takeoffs and landings on makeshift aircraft carriers, all the way up to rockets blasting navy astronauts into space.

9. **USS *Alabama* Battleship and Memorial Park, Mobile, Alabama**
Spread across a campus the size of a small college is an impressive and well-maintained assortment of military aircraft, tanks, helicopters, a submarine (the USS *Drum*), a land-side building packed with military artifacts large and small—and, of course, the queen of the palace, the great battleship USS *Alabama*.

10. **National Infantry Museum, Columbus, Georgia**
This is one of the most alive, vibrant, and interesting military destinations in America. Using beautifully designed and utterly realistic landscapes, the curators of this museum have recreated some of the most famous battle scenes in American history, complete with the sights, sounds, *and confusion* of war. A $100 million masterpiece.

11. ***Intrepid* Sea, Air & Space Museum, New York, New York**
What does a theater on Broadway have that compares to an 872-foot-long, 27,000-ton aircraft carrier jammed with combat jets, high technology missiles, agile helicopters, a space shuttle, and the supersonic Concorde? The star of Broadway is the *Intrepid* Sea Air & Space Museum, or so we like to think.

12. **Pima Air & Space Museum, Tucson, Arizona**

    Sunshine rains down on this part of Arizona and brings vividly to life the exquisite colors and shapes of the more than 300 air and space vehicles displayed at the Pima Air & Space Museum in Pima, Arizona. In just one day you can experience the width and breadth of our aerospace history, including a visit to an ICBM missile silo *and* a tour of the nearby US Air Force boneyards.

13. **Flying Heritage and Combat Armor Museum, Everett, Washington**

    This marvelous collection of mint-condition warbirds and combat vehicles is worth a visit by any measure, but to see a MiG-29 puts it over the top. Founded by Microsoft billionaire Paul G. Allen, the Flying Heritage and Combat Armor Museum has an extensive collection of warbirds and armor all meticulously restored and in perfect working order.

14. **Museum of Aviation, Robins AFB, Georgia (near Macon, Georgia)**

    Visitors who discover the Museum of Aviation scratch their heads and wonder how something like this could have been here so long without them knowing about it. Well, they're not alone. Wear comfortable shoes. The Museum of Aviation consists of four large hangars with indoor and outdoor displays spread out across 51 acres with more than 85 military airplanes, cockpits, missiles, and helicopters.

15. **Pearl Harbor, Hawaii**

    Hawaii is a special military center of gravity, particularly when you realize that there are *four* important Pearl Harbor sites all within a few miles of one another. Start at the *Arizona* Memorial (the Valor in the National Monument) and then visit the Battleship *Missouri* Memorial, the *Bowfin* Submarine Museum, and the Pacific Aviation Museum. Each destination has a special message, a special meaning—and taken together they *are* the full story of Pearl Harbor.

16. **Air Zoo, Portage, Michigan**

    From the moment you walk into this celebration of flight, your senses will be pleasantly overwhelmed by the large-scale panoramas, beautifully painted warbirds, space capsules, and exquisite dioramas. Enjoy a collection of 50 aircraft, most of them warbirds. And what's the name? Well, when your airplanes are called Bearcats, Tomcats, Hellcats, Tigers, and Cougars, you have . . . a *zoo*.

17. **The Wright Museum of World War II, Wolfeboro, New Hampshire**

    Yes, they have the heavy stuff here—tanks and jeeps and APCs and rifles and even a mocked-up barracks—but what makes this a must-see destination are the dioramas of Main Street USA. Mom and pop's living room. A soda fountain. Bond drives. Voted the Best 20th Century History Museum in New England, the Wright Museum differs from other military museums in one fascinating regard—rather than a museum about World War II per se, it is a museum about the home front and how Main Street USA was *affected* by World War II. This is a seamless trip back to the 1940s.

18. **Palm Springs Air Museum, Palm Springs, California**

    The 59 aircraft on display at the handsome Palm Springs Air Museum are beautifully restored and ready for your visit—and visit you must. In addition to the spectacular buildings and well-staged displays, on open cockpit days you don't just *look* into a warbird, you *get inside* the plane and sit in the pilot's seat. The warbirds here span generations of military flight. Oh, and they offer warbird rides, too.

19. **The National Navy UDT-SEAL Museum, Fort Pierce, Florida**

    The National Navy UDT-SEAL Museum is all about the US Navy's special forces and the incredible missions they've undertaken since the first World War II frogman donned breathing apparatus. What makes a visit here so interesting is this—everything on display was actually used during training or on a mission, including combat; there are no replicas.

20. **US Army Heritage and Education Center (US Army Heritage Trail), Carlisle, Pennsylvania**

    Many of our favorite destinations went to great lengths to build immersive, interactive, digitally enhanced exhibits. Not so here. The Army Heritage Center took a different route. Here you will be immersed in a *physical* world. We're talking about a long, wonderfully designed 1-mile walk through full-size American battlescapes on the US Army Heritage Trail. Walk down into a World War I trench. Step inside a World War II barrack and see the old cots. Touch the split-rail fence at Antietam. And more.

THE 10 BEST MILITARY EXPERIENCES IN AMERICA

NOWHERE ELSE: THE BEST PLACES TO
FLY A PHANTOM, DRIVE A SHERMAN,
OR RACE A PT BOAT

They say to truly understand someone you need to walk a mile in their shoes. What was it like to be a young Lt. John F. Kennedy in command of a PT boat in the Pacific? Could you handle the claustrophobic feeling inside a Sherman tank? How about jinking in an F-4 Phantom fighter jet in the skies over Vietnam? Here are those undiscovered destinations that let you experience a Sherman tank, fly in a Vietnam-era Huey helicopter, take to the skies in an F-4 Phantom—and roar across a lake in a restored PT boat just like the one Jack had in the Pacific.

1. **(Tie) Ox Hunting Ranch/Drivetanks.com, Uvalde, Texas**
    Nowhere else: Drive one of *several* tanks. Fire the main gun. Spend the night in re-created World War II barracks or fly home in your own jet leaving from their private runway.

1. **(Tie) Wings of Freedom/Collings Foundation, Stowe, Massachusetts/ Houston, Texas**

   Nowhere else: Fly in a real F-4 Phantom fighter jet or a TA-4 Skyhawk jet. Highly trained professionals let you experience flight unlike anywhere else in the nation.

2. **PT-305, Lake Pontchartrain, Louisiana**

   Nowhere else: This is the only operating PT boat in the world. With the roar of three 1200-hp engines, you'll go out on Lake Pontchartrain and zip through the waves. The trip is coordinated through the National Museum of World War II in New Orleans.

3. **Army Aviation Heritage Foundation, Hampton, Georgia (South Atlanta Regional Airport)**

   Nowhere else: Fly in a Vietnam-era Huey or a Cobra helicopter—or both—from the same air base. The sheer physicality of a Huey in flight will leave you breathless.

4. **American Airpower Museum, Farmingdale, New York**

   Nowhere else: Fly in a World War II–era C-47 with a World War II para-trooper. You'll start in a briefing room and then fly with reenactors dressed in real World War II uniforms, ready to jump as you fly through the sky.

5. **California Overland Desert Excursions, Borrego Springs, California**

   Nowhere else: Take an army deuce-and-a-half out to the old training grounds for the invasion of North Africa. The sand in your teeth is half the fun.

6. **National Liberty Ship Memorial, Pier 45, San Francisco, California USS *Pampanito*, Pier 45, San Francisco, California**

   Nowhere else: Feel the engines come to life as you sail on the SS *Jeremiah O'Brien*, a true World War II Liberty Ship. Or walk down a few yards and squeeze through the 27-foot-wide hull of the USS *Pampanito*—a World War II electric-diesel submarine.

7. **USS *Kidd* Veterans Museum, Baton Rouge, Louisiana**

   Nowhere else: Visit a US Navy destroyer that displays true, World War II navy colors. Walk her decks. Examine the guns. Go back in time.

8. **Stallion 51, Kissimmee, Florida**

   Nowhere else: The only full-cockpit, dual-seat Mustangs with a certified CFI as your pilot, thus allowing you to take the controls and *fly* a P-51.

That's right—this isn't a cramped second seat, and your highly experienced pilot is also a licensed flight instructor, so you get to yank and bank the plane yourself.

9. **Drive A Tank, Kasota, Minnesota**

Nowhere else: Drive a tank. Crush a car. Plow through a house. Use an M4 Sherman tank plus other armored vehicle.

10. **Commemorative Air Force, Dallas, Texas**

This Texas-based organization has chapters across the US offering flight experiences in more than a dozen different types of warbirds based at airports in a dozen different states.

THE 10 BEST FORMERLY SECRET MILITARY SITES IN AMERICA

GHOSTS OF OUR NOT-SO-DISTANT PAST

It wouldn't do to ignore the forbidden fruits of our military history. Who among us wouldn't like to see the top-secret facilities on Plum Island or at Raven Rock or even that not-so-secret Area 51? We can't take you to those places (yet), but we can tell you about a few formerly secret or largely forgotten destinations that are more than worth a road trip.

1. **Historic Wendover Airfield, Wendover, Utah**
   This is the perfect outing to experience a true World War II air base and in so doing be transported, with no effort on your part, back to another place and time. Dozens of original World War II buildings dot the landscape, including the loading pit where they secretly trained the *Enola Gay* crew to carry the A-bomb.

2. **Nevada National Security Site (aka the Nevada Test Site), Las Vegas, Nevada**
   There was a day when we brazenly exploded atomic bombs out in the Nevada desert. Well, the Nevada Test Site is no longer, and the grounds are totally off-limits—except for this official but little-known tour that will take your breath away.

3. **Military Ghost Ships**
   Yes, Virginia, there *are* ghost ships and they can be seen in several places. Our favorites are found in the Navy Inactive Ships Maintenance fleet, but there's nothing wrong with the Navy Reserve Fleets. All are plenty spooky and easy to find. See listings by states.
   - **Middle Loch, Hawaii**
   - **Suisan Bay, California**
   - **James River, Virginia**
   - **Philadelphia, Pennsylvania**

4. **Pinal Airpark, Marana, Arizona**
   This former CIA airfield out in the remote Sonoran Desert was opened to the public a few years ago. Still visible are signage and barracks, but there's also a helicopter training base for the army and a spooky boneyard filled with silent, ghostlike jetliners.

5. **Trinity Site, Socomo County, New Mexico**
   Impossible as it may seem, it is *not* impossible to stand at the spot where the first atomic bomb was detonated in the 1940s. Spooky yes, crazy, yes, but there is a little-known tour that will take you out to Trinity Site, where the scientists from the Manhattan Project successfully set off the first atomic bomb.

6. **Brooklyn Army Terminal, Brooklyn, New York**
   Some 27 million tons of war matériel—and 2.2 million soldiers—began their journeys to the combat fronts of World War II from this waterfront terminal officially known as the New York Port of Embarkation.[1] Today you can see the signature railroad tracks and the cantilevered loading docks and the 5-ton cranes that worked the balconies picking and packing ammunition crates as if they were mere matchsticks.

7. **Abandoned Cold War ICBM Missile Launch Pads and Control Facilities**
   Want to see a real Intercontinental Ballistic Missile silo (ICBM)? Many have been shut down under various SALT treaties, active ones remain

off-limits, but there are three that are open to the public—and what a sight they are.

- **The Minuteman II National Historic Site, Philip, South Dakota**
- **Ronald Reagan Minuteman Missile State Historic Site, Cooperstown, North Dakota**
- **Titan Missile Museum, Sahuarita, Arizona**

8. **Abandoned Nike Air Defense Missile Batteries**

The threat of a Soviet air invasion was so real that at one time we had some 265 Nike surface-to-air missile sites around our largest cities.[2] Happily, tensions abated, the threat dissipated, and the Nike missile sites were shut down. However, four remain and all are worth a visit. Find one near you.

- **Nike Air Defense Missile Site SF-88L, Sausalito, California**
- **Nike Site HM-69, Homestead-Miami, Florida**
- **Nike Missile Site, Summit, Alaska**
- **Nike Air Defense Missile Battery NY-56, Sandy Hook, New Jersey**

9. **Abandoned World War II Fire Control Towers and Gun Batteries**

The fear of yet another surprise attack was very real during World War II. To guard against that, gun batteries and fire control towers lined our beaches on the eastern coast. The towers were the "eyes" for the gun batteries that would repulse such an invasion. Several towers still stand today, each an incredibly stark reminder of a war that is now 75 years in the rearview mirror

- **Fire Control Tower 23, Cape May Point State Park, New Jersey**
- **Nahant Fire Control Towers, Nahant, Massachusetts**
- **Fire Control Towers, Delaware Seashore State Park, Delaware/ Cape Henlopen, Delaware**
- **Fort Foster, Kittery Point, Maine**
- **Battery 234, Gulf Islands National Seashore, Fort Pickens, Florida**
- **Fort Casey's Gun Batteries, Whidbey Island, Washington**

10. **The Greenbrier Bunker, Hot Springs, West Virginia**

Well-known, but well worth it, this formerly secret continuity-of-government bunker was where our surviving officials would govern a decimated, radiation-soaked, post–World War III nation. Lucky them.

THE 10 BEST MILITARY BASE TOURS IN AMERICA

PLACES WHERE A SENSE OF DUTY PERVADES

Is the ultimate military destination a military base itself? Perhaps, but there aren't many opportunities left to witness our soldiers, sailors, marines, and airmen in their habitat (and it's only gotten harder since 9/11). Almost without exception, our military bases now require a security clearance to get in, and most of those once "routine" base tours have been canceled. That said, there are some good ones left and we list them below.

Note: Check the base's official website for any changes to the credentials requirements to get in. In almost all cases you must have a valid driver's license and you will have to go through a brief security check. In some cases (but not all), you must also be an American citizen. Finally, in addition to the tours listed below, most bases will create a familiarization tour for you if you have a group of 15 or more. Contact the Public Affairs Office at the installation that interests you.

1. **Seymour Johnson Air Force Base, Goldsboro, North Carolina**
   Home to our F-15E Strike Eagles and KC-135 tankers, Seymour Johnson offers a comprehensive base tour on the last Thursday of each month. On almost all tours, you'll stop at the base BX for lunch (bring money; it's a Subway).

2. **Fort Irwin, Fort Irwin, California (near Barstow)**
   Fort Irwin "Box Tours" are made available through the Fort Irwin Public Affairs Office. You will be taken on base to the observation deck overlooking "the Box," where military maneuvers take place often with simulated combat. The tour lasts about six hours, including a stop on base for lunch (bring money).

3. **MacDill Air Force Base, Tampa, Florida**
   MacDill Air Force Base runs a well-organized tour on the first and third Friday of the month. Stops typically include the air traffic control tower, the security forces' working dogs area, the explosive ordnance disposal units (EOD), and the flight line to see a tanker and perhaps meet the pilots or a boom operator.

4. **Naval Station Norfolk, Norfolk, Virginia**
   Naval Station Norfolk has designated Tidewater Tours as their official tour operator. You will board a bus that takes you around the base, including a visit to the piers, where the ships are, and to the Naval Air Station, where they have a display of decommissioned aircraft.

5. **Ellsworth Air Force Base, Rapid City, South Dakota**
   Home to the scary-looking B-1 bombers of the US Air Force Global Strike Command, base tours here run on the second and fourth Friday of the month, April through October. Depending on the activity that day, stops usually include a visit to a B-1B with time set aside to talk to the airmen. You will also make a stop to buy your own lunch as you see the rest of the base facilities.

6. **Marine Corps Air Station Cherry Point, Cherry Point, North Carolina**
   Windshield tours take you around the base and are offered weekly on Wednesday morning. The tours last about two hours. This is a great chance to see our AV-8B Harrier "jump jets."

7. **Vandenberg Air Force Base, Lompoc, California**

   Tours of the Vandenberg Air Force Base space port are offered on the third Tuesday of each month starting at 1 p.m. Just being here puts you in close proximity to one of our nation's most unusual—and important—military and civilian space facilities.

8. **Travis Air Force Base, California** (located between San Francisco and Sacramento)

   Travis Air Force Base's Heritage Center runs a shuttle bus Tuesday through Friday that will pick you up at the gate (the visitor center) and bring you inside. The driver will deliver you to the museum, where there is an outdoor display of 30 or so restored modern jets, old warbirds, and cargo planes.

9. **Fort McCoy, Fort McCoy, Wisconsin**

   Fort McCoy is a major US Army training center with several open houses and plenty to see inside. Watch for them on their website or schedule your own tour of 15 or more during the week.

10. **Edwards Air Force Base, California**

    Edwards Air Force Base's Flight Test Museum runs monthly bus trips into the base on the third Friday of the month, or you can organize a group of your own (minimum of 15 people) and coordinate it through the Edwards Air Force Base public affairs offices. This is a good way to see the flight line of an iconic air base (*The Right Stuff* seems so alive here) on the way to an excellent museum.

THE TOP 100

1. Smithsonian National Air & Space Museum, Washington, D.C.
2. The National Museum of the Marine Corps, Triangle, Virginia
3. National World War I Museum and Liberty Memorial, Kansas City, Missouri
4. National World War II Museum, New Orleans, Louisiana
5. National Museum of the US Air Force, Wright-Patterson Air Force Base, Ohio
6. The National Museum of the Pacific War, Fredericksburg, Texas
7. Airborne & Special Operations Museum, Fayetteville, North Carolina
8. National Naval Aviation Museum, Pensacola, Florida
9. USS *Alabama* Battleship and Memorial Park, Mobile, Alabama
10. National Infantry Museum, Columbus, Georgia
11. *Intrepid* Sea, Air & Space Museum, New York, New York
12. Pima Air & Space, Tucson, Arizona
13. Flying Heritage and Combat Armor Museum, Everett, Washington
14. Museum of Aviation, Robins AFB, Georgia (near Macon, Georgia)
15. Pearl Harbor, Hawaii
16. Air Zoo, Portage, Michigan
17. The Wright Museum of World War II, Wolfeboro, New Hampshire

18. Palm Springs Air Museum, Palm Springs, California
19. The National Navy UDT-SEAL Museum, Fort Pierce, Florida
20. US Army Heritage and Education Center (US Army Heritage Trail), Carlisle, Pennsylvania

And All of the Rest (Listed By State)

21. US Army Aviation Museum, Fort Rucker, Alabama
22. Southern Museum of Flight, Birmingham, Alabama
23. Nike Missile Site, Summit, Alaska
24. Davis-Monthan Air Force Base, Tucson, Arizona
25. Pinal Airpark, Marana, Arizona
26. Titan Missile Museum, Sahuarita, Arizona
27. USS *Midway* Museum, San Diego, California
28. San Diego Air and Space Museum, San Diego, California
29. Castle Air Museum, Sacramento, CAalifornia
30. Air Force Flight Test Center Museum, Edwards Air Force Base, California, Blackbird Air Park, Palmdale, California, and Joe Davies Heritage Air Park, Plant 42, Palmdale, California
31. Pacific Battleship Center, USS *Iowa*, San Pedro, California
32. Pacific Coast Air Museum, Santa Rosa, California
33. USS *Hornet* Sea, Air & Space Museum, Alameda, California
34. US Navy Seabee Museum, Port Hueneme, California
35. Nike Air Defense Missile Site SF-88L, Sausalito, California
36. Suisun Bay Reserve Fleet, Suisan Bay, California
37. Fort Irwin, Fort Irwin, California (near Barstow)
38. Vandenberg Air Force Base, Lompoc, California
39. Travis Air Force Base, Travis AFB, California
40. The March Field Museum, Riverside, California
41. Peterson Air & Space Museum, Colorado Springs, Colorado
42. The Submarine Force Library and Museum, Groton, Connecticut
43. Air Mobility Command Museum, Dover, Delaware
44. Rehoboth Beach, Delaware/Delaware Seashore State Park, Delaware/Cape Henlopen, Delaware
45. Arlington National Cemetery and Memorial, Washington, D.C.
46. Nike Site HM-69, Homestead-Miami, Florida

47. Battery 234, Gulf Islands National Seashore, Fort Pickens, Florida
48. MacDill Air Force Base, Tampa, Florida
49. National Civil War Naval Museum, Columbus, Georgia
50. National Museum of the Mighty Eighth Air Force, Pooler, Georgia (Savannah)
51. Army Aviation Heritage Foundation, Hampton, Georgia
52. First Division Museum at Cantigny Park, Wheaton, Illinois
53. Russell Military Museum, Zion, Illinois
54. PT-305, Lake Pontchartrain, Louisiana
55. Fort Foster, Kittery Point, Maine
56. Patuxent River Naval Air Museum, Patuxent River, Maryland
57. USS *Constitution* Museum, Charlestown, Massachusetts
58. Battleship Cove America's Fleet Museum, Fall River, Massachusetts
59. Nahant Fire Control Towers, Nahant, Massachusetts
60. Minnesota Military Museum, Camp Ripley, Little Falls, Minnesota
61. Mississippi Armed Forces Museum, Camp Shelby, Mississippi
62. Malmstrom Air Force Base Museum and Air Park, Great Falls, Montana
63. Strategic Air Command and Aerospace Museum, Ashland, Nebraska
64. Nevada National Security Site (aka the Nevada Test Site), Las Vegas, Nevada
65. Battleship *New Jersey* Museum and Memorial, Camden, New Jersey
66. Nike Air Defense Missile Battery NY-56, Sandy Hook, New Jersey (Gateway National Recreation Area, New York/New Jersey)
67. Fire Control Tower 23, Cape May Point State Park, New Jersey
68. Bradbury Science Museum, Los Alamos, New Mexico
69. New Mexico Museum of Space History, Alamogordo, New Mexico
70. Trinity Site, Socomo County, New Mexico
71. West Point Museum, US Military Academy, New York
72. Cradle of Aviation Museum, Garden City, New York
73. Brooklyn Army Terminal, Brooklyn, New York
74. Carolinas Aviation Museum, Charlotte, North Carolina
75. Seymour Johnson Air Force Base, Goldsboro, North Carolina
76. Marine Corps Air Station Cherry Point, Cherry Point, North Carolina
77. Ronald Reagan Minuteman Missile State Historic Site, Cooperstown, North Dakota

78. Fort Sill National Historic Landmark and Museum, Fort Sill, Oklahoma; US Army Field Artillery Museum, Fort Sill, Oklahoma
79. Stafford Air & Space Museum, Weatherford, Oklahoma
80. Evergreen Aviation & Space Museum, McMinnville, Oregon
81. Museum of the American Revolution, Philadelphia, Pennsylvania
82. Patriots Point, Mount Pleasant, South Carolina
83. South Dakota Air & Space Museum, Rapid City, South Dakota
84. Minuteman Missile National Historic Site, Philip, South Dakota
85. Ellsworth Air Force Base, Rapid City, South Dakota
86. Lone Star Flight Museum, Houston, Texas
87. USS *Lexington* Museum on the Bay, Corpus Christi, Texas
88. Ox Hunting Ranch/Drivetanks.com, Uvalde, Texas
89. Wings of Freedom/Collings Foundation, Stowe, Massachusetts/Houston, Texas
90. Hill Aerospace Museum, Ogden, Utah
91. Historic Wendover Airfield, Wendover, Utah
92. National Maritime Center Nauticus Featuring Battleship *Wisconsin* and the Hampton Roads Naval Museum, Norfolk, Virginia
93. James River Reserve Fleet, Fort Huger, Virginia
94. Naval Station Norfolk, Norfolk, Virginia
95. US Naval Undersea Museum, Keyport, Washington
96. Museum of Flight, Seattle, Washington
97. Fort Casey's Gun Batteries, Whidbey Island, Washington
98. Naval Inactive Ship Maintenance Facility, Bremerton, Washington
99. Greenbrier Bunker, Hot Springs, West Virginia
100. Fort McCoy, Fort McCoy, Wisconsin

Notes

Introduction

1. National Museum of the Pacific War, plaque on the wall

The Top 100 Military Sites in America

1. Off-ramp per http://www.airplaneboneyards.com/airplane-boneyard-tours.htm
2. https://en.wikipedia.org/wiki/Yuma_Proving_Ground
3. https://en.wikipedia.org/wiki/Seabee#World_War_II
4. https://www.cnic.navy.mil/regions/cnrma/installations/navsubbase_new_london/about/history.html
5. http://www.firecontroltowers.com/fct3.php
6. http://articles.chicagotribune.com/2007-10-03/news/0710020505_1_museum-site-exhibition-space-museum-s-collection
7. Rock Island Arsenal: An Arsenal For Democracy, pdf
8. An engineering feat of impossible size and explosive power, a 16-inch gun turret is a 5-story iron structure that weighs 239,000 pounds and requires a crew of 80 sailors to fire. They fed six 100-pound bags of gunpowder into the breeches behind a 2,700-pound projectile that could be shot 20-plus miles with near-pinpoint accuracy.
9. SAGE oddly stands for Semi-Automatic Ground Environment
10. https://en.wikipedia.org/wiki/16%22/50_caliber_Mark_7_gun
11. See https://www.nps.gov/gate/index.htm for maps
12. https://www.bklynarmyterminal.com/building-information/history/
13. https://www.bklynarmyterminal.com/building-information/history/
14. http://archive.boston.com/news/local/articles/2007/09/09/foundation_maintains_a_rare_collection/
15. http://www.navsea.navy.mil/Portals/103/Documents/TeamShips/SEA21/InactiveShips/InactiveShipInventory-27Sep16(3).pdf

The Top 10 Formerly Secret Military Sites in America

1. https://www.bklynarmyterminal.com/building-information/history/
2. https://en.wikipedia.org/wiki/List_of_Nike_missile_sites

Appendix

General Interest Destinations

Smithsonian National Air & Space Museum, Washington, D.C.

Arlington National Cemetery and Memorial, Washington, D.C.

National Museum of the Pacific War, Fredericksburg, Texas

Intrepid Sea, Air & Space Museum, New York, New York

Pima Air & Space Museum, Tucson, Arizona

Flying Heritage and Combat Armor Museum, Everett, Washington

Museum of Aviation, Robins AFB, Georgia

Air Zoo, Portage, Michigan

Palm Springs Air Museum, Palm Springs, California

Southern Museum of Flight, Birmingham, Alabama

US Space and Rocket Center, Huntsville, Alabama

Alaska Aviation Museum, Anchorage, Alaska

Jacksonville Museum of Military History, Jacksonville, Arkansas

Planes of Fame, Valle, Arizona

San Diego Air and Space Museum, San Diego, California

Pacific Coast Air Museum, Santa Rosa, California

Mare Island Shoreline Heritage Preserve, Vallejo, California

Wings Over The Rockies Air & Space Museum, Denver, Colorado

Military Museum of Southern New England, Danbury, Connecticut

Heritage Park Veterans Museum, McDonough, Georgia

Russell Military Museum, Zion, Illinois

Pritzker Military Museum & Library, Chicago, Illinois

General George Patton Museum and Center of Leadership, Fort Knox, Kentucky

African American Military History Museum, Hattiesburg, Mississippi

Lakehurst Maxfield Field, Joint Base McGuire-Dix-Lakehurst, Lakehurst, New Jersey

Naval Air Station Wildwood Aviation Museum, Cape May, New Jersey

New Mexico Museum of Space History, Alamogordo, New Mexico

White Sands Missile Range Museum, Las Cruces, New Mexico

Cradle of Aviation Museum, Garden City, New York

Empire State Aerosciences Museum, Schenectady, New York

Carolinas Aviation Museum, Charlotte, North Carolina

Fargo Air Museum, Fargo, North Dakota

Stafford Air & Space Museum, Weatherford, Oklahoma

Charles B. Hall Memorial Park, Tinker AFB, Oklahoma

Evergreen Aviation & Space Museum, McMinnville, Oregon

South Dakota Air & Space Museum, Rapid City, South Dakota

The Frontiers of Flight Museum, Love Field, Dallas, Texas

Texas Forts Trail Region

Hill Aerospace Museum, Ogden, Utah

Thiokol Rocket Garden, Brigham City, Utah

Museum of Flight, Seattle, Washington

EAA Aviation Museum, Oshkosh, Wisconsin

Lone Star Flight Museum, Houston, Texas

Virginia War Museum, Newport News, Virginia

Military Branches

US Air Force

National Museum of the US Air Force, Dayton, Ohio

Pima Air & Space Museum, Tucson, Arizona

Museum of Aviation, Robins AFB, Georgia

Historic Wendover Airfield, Wendover, Utah

Davis-Monthan Air Force Base, Tucson, Arizona

Castle Air Museum, Sacramento, California

March Field Air Museum, Riverside, California

Air Force Flight Test Center Museum, Edwards Air Force Base, California

Peterson Air & Space Museum, Colorado Springs, Colorado

Air Mobility Command Museum, Dover, Delaware

Air Force Armament Museum, Eglin Air Force Base, Florida

National Museum of the Mighty Eighth Air Force, Pooler, Georgia

Pacific Aviation Museum, Pearl Harbor, Hawaii

Barksdale Global Power Museum, Barksdale, Louisiana

Selfridge Military Air Museum, Selfridge ANGB, Michigan

Malmstrom Air Force Base Museum and Air Park, Great Falls, Montana

Strategic Air Command and Aerospace Museum, Ashland, Nebraska

Area 51, Las Vegas, Nevada

US Army

National Infantry Museum, Columbus, Georgia

Fort Sill National Historic Landmark and Museum, Fort Sill, Oklahoma

Airborne & Special Operations Museum, Fayetteville, North Carolina

US Army Heritage and Education Center, Carlisle, Pennsylvania

Nike Air Defense Missile Site SF-88L, Sausalito, California

Nike Site HM-69, Homestead-Miami, Florida

Nike Missile Site, Summit, Alaska

Nike Air Defense Missile Battery NY-56, Sandy Hook, New Jersey

US Army Aviation Museum, Ft. Rucker, Alabama

Fort Huachuca Historical Museum and the US Army Intelligence Museum, Cochise, Arizona

Yuma Proving Grounds Heritage Center, Yuma, Arizona

General George Patton Memorial Museum, Chiriaco Summit, California

National Training Center, Fort Irwin, California

Camp Blanding Museum and Memorial Park, Starke, Florida

First Division Museum at Cantigny Park, Wheaton, Illinois

Frontier Army Museum, Leavenworth, Kansas

General George Patton Museum and Center of Leadership, Fort Knox, Kentucky

Minnesota Military Museum, Camp Ripley, Little Falls, Minnesota

Mississippi Armed Forces Museum, Camp Shelby, Mississippi

John B. Mahaffey Museum Complex, Fort Leonard Wood, Missouri

White Sands Missile Range Museum, Las Cruces, New Mexico

West Point Museum, US Military Academy, New York

Museum of American Armor, Old Bethpage, New York

US Army Field Artillery Museum, Fort Sill, Oklahoma

1st Cavalry Museum, Fort Hood, Texas

US Army Transportation Museum, Fort Eustis, Virginia (Newport News)

American Armored Foundation and Tank Museum, Danville, Virginia

US Army Quartermaster Museum, Fort Lee, Virginia

National Armor and Cavalry Museum, Columbus, Georgia

Museum of the American G.I., College Station, Texas

US Marine Corps

National Museum of the Marine Corps, Triangle, Virginia

Flying Leathernecks Aviation Museum, MCAS Miramar, California

US Navy

USS *Constitution* Museum, Charlestown, Massachusetts

Battleship Cove America's Fleet Museum, Fall River, Massachusetts

National Naval Aviation Museum, Pensacola, Florida

USS *Alabama* Battleship and Memorial Park, Mobile, Alabama

National Navy UDT-SEAL Museum, Fort Pierce, Florida

USS *Midway* Museum, San Diego, California

USS *Hornet* Museum, Alameda, California

Pacific Battleship Center, USS *Iowa*, San Pedro, California

Point Mugu Missile Park, Port Hueneme, California

US Navy Seabee Museum, Port Hueneme, California

US Naval Museum of Armament and Technology, China Lake, California

Naval Shipbuilding Museum, Quincy, Massachusetts

Submarine Force Library and Museum, Groton, Connecticut

World War II Valor in the Pacific National Monument, Pearl Harbor, Hawaii

Battleship *Missouri* Memorial, Pearl Harbor, Hawaii

USS *Bowfin* Submarine and Museum & Park, Pearl Harbor, Hawaii

National Museum of the US Navy, Washington, D.C.

USS *Orleck* Naval Museum, Lake Charles, Louisiana

US Naval Academy Museum, Annapolis, Maryland

Patuxent River Naval Air Museum, Patuxent River, Maryland

Albacore Park, Portsmouth, New Hampshire

Naval Air Station Wildwood Aviation Museum, Cape May, New Jersey

Battleship *New Jersey* Museum and Memorial, Camden, New Jersey

USS *North Carolina*, Wilmington, North Carolina

Patriots Point, Mount Pleasant, South Carolina

USS *Lexington* Museum on the Bay, Corpus Christi, California

American Undersea Warfare Center in *Seawolf* Park, Galveston, California

USS *Texas* (Battleship Texas Foundation), LaPorte, Texas

National Maritime Center Nauticus featuring Battleship *Wisconsin* and Hampton Roads Naval Museum, Norfolk, Virginia

US Naval Undersea Museum, Keyport, Washington

Special Operations

Airborne & Special Operations Museum, Fayetteville, North Carolina

National Navy UDT-SEAL Museum, Fort Pierce, Florida

Wars, Alphabetical

Civil War

National Civil War Naval Museum, Columbus, Georgia

National Museum of Civil War Medicine, Frederick, Maryland

American Civil War Museum, Richmond, Virginia

Cold War/Nuclear

Nevada National Security Site, Las Vegas, Nevada

Pinal Air Park, Marana, Arizona

Trinity Site, Socomo County, New Mexico

Minuteman Missile National Historic Site, Philip, South Dakota

Ronald Reagan Minuteman Missile State Historic Site, Cooperstown, North Dakota

Titan Missile Museum, Sahuarita, Arizona

Nike Air Defense Missile Site SF-88L, Sausalito, California

Nike Site HM-69, Homestead-Miami, Florida

Nike Missile Site, Summit, Alaska

Nike Air Defense Missile Battery NY-56, Sandy Hook, New Jersey

Greenbrier Bunker, Hot Springs, West Virginia

Castle Air Museum, Sacramento, California

Strategic Air Command and Aerospace Museum, Ashland, Nebraska

National Atomic Testing Museum, Las Vegas, Nevada

Radar Station Texas Tower #4, Barnegat Inlet, New Jersey

National Museum of Nuclear Science & History, Albuquerque, New Mexico

Bradbury Science Museum, Los Alamos, New Mexico

Nuclear. See Cold War

Revolutionary War

USS *Constitution* Museum, Charlestown, Massachusetts
Museum of the American Revolution, Philadelphia, Pennsylvania

Vietnam

National Vietnam War Museum, Weatherford, Texas
Patriots Point, Mount Pleasant, South Carolina
Heritage Park Veterans Museum, McDonough, Georgia

World War I

National World War I Museum and Liberty Memorial, Kansas City, Missouri
Old Rhinebeck Aerodrome, Red Hook, New York

World War II

National World War II Museum, New Orleans, Louisiana
National Museum of the Pacific War, Fredericksburg, Texas
The Wright Museum of World War II, Wolfeboro, New Hampshire
Brooklyn Army Terminal, Brooklyn, New York
Tuskegee Airmen National Historic Site, Tuskegee, Alabama
Lend-Lease Memorial, Fairbanks, Alaska
Delaware Aviation Museum, Georgetown, Delaware
National Museum of the Mighty Eighth Air Force, Pooler, Georgia
Pacific Aviation Museum, Pearl Harbor, Hawaii
Tillamook Air Museum, Tillamook, Oregon
Historic Wendover Airfield, Wendover, Utah

Index